SEPHARDIC FLAVORS ★

To Harvey

Hope you'll enjoy
cooking or reading!
Best.

Joyce Goldstein

by JOYCE GOLDSTEIN

SEPHARDIC FLAVORS ★

::: JEWISH COOKING OF THE MEDITERRANEAN

photographs by BEATRIZ DA COSTA

CHRONICLE BOOKS

SAN FRANCISCO

: :

TEXT COPYRIGHT © 2000 BY JOYCE GOLDSTEIN.

PHOTOGRAPHS COPYRIGHT © 2000 BY BEATRIZ DA COSTA.

LIBRARY OF CONGRESS CATALOGING-IN-PUBLICATION
DATA AVAILABLE.
ISBN 0-8118-2662-7

PRINTED IN HONG KONG.

PROP STYLING BY JULIE FLYNN
FOOD STYLING BY ALISON ATTENBOROUGH
DESIGNED BY SARA SCHNEIDER

DISTRIBUTED IN CANADA BY RAINCOAST BOOKS
9050 SHAUGHNESSY STREET
VANCOUVER, BRITISH COLUMBIA V6P 6E5

10 9 8 7 6 5 4 3 2 1

CHRONICLE BOOKS LLC
85 SECOND STREET
SAN FRANCISCO, CALIFORNIA 94105

WWW.CHRONICLEBOOKS.COM

contents

:::::: **PREFACE**

While doing the research for *Cucina Ebraica: Flavors of the Italian Jewish Kitchen,* I became immersed in the history of the Sephardic Jews. After their expulsion from Spain and Portugal, many fled east to Italy. While some made Italy their permanent home, many more were passing through on their way to the Ottoman Empire. Naturally my culinary curiosity was aroused. If the Sephardim could adapt their cuisine to harmonize with Italian cooking traditions, even mirroring regional Italian characteristics, what happened to the food of those Spanish and Portuguese Jews after they settled in the Ottoman Empire? Did it retain any distinctly Iberian characteristics? Did it harmonize with and adapt to the food traditions of Turkey, Greece, and the Balkans? Could I still find traces of Moorish flavors layered in the cuisine? Was this culinary marriage a happy one? I had to find out. So began my work on *Sephardic Flavors.*

Since 1957, the year of my first voyage to the Mediterranean, I have been in love with the food and flavors of the region. Over the years I have traveled in Greece and Turkey and dined on dishes that I enjoyed so much I mentally made notes to add them to my repertoire, then cooked them immediately upon my return, so that I would not forget how they tasted. I still continue to cook these dishes for friends and family, and they were much requested by the regular diners at my restaurant, Square One. They even persuaded me to add a Sephardic Passover dinner to our traditional Italian Passover meal.

I knew early on that I was predisposed to love the food of the Sephardim of this region because the flavor combinations have always been some of my favorites. In other words, my palate was already tilted in their direction. I enjoy sweet-and-sour dishes, and I love tart sauces and vinaigrettes, especially those based on the generous use of lemon. (I have always said that if there were no lemons, I would have a hard time cooking.) Thus, it came as no surprise that when I cooked the recipes of the Sephardim at home, they delighted me and my family. They were new, but they tasted familiar, and they are now among the dishes of my everyday table.

: : : : : THE JEWS IN SPAIN AND PORTUGAL

Although the Hebrew place name Sefarad originally may have referred to the city of Sardis, in Asia Minor, it has come to be associated with the Iberian Peninsula. Therefore, Jews of Spanish and Portuguese origins are called Sephardim. While they may have arrived on the peninsula alongside the Phoenicians in the eleventh century B.C.E., we know for sure that Jews were living in Spain at the time of the destruction of the Temple in Jerusalem in 70 C.E., and their numbers increased after the Diaspora. The first written record in which Jews are mentioned is a resolution of the Council of Elvira dated 306. It prohibited Christians from marrying Jews and forbade rabbis to bless fields owned by Christians. Sephardic historians also have discovered that the names of many Spanish towns had Hebrew origins: Maqueda was from Masada, Escalona from Ashekelon, Joppes from Jaffa, Barcelona from Bar-Shelanu, Seville from Shevil-Yah, and Toledo from Toledoth.

Until the late-fifteenth century, Sephardic Jews in Spain and Portugal enjoyed periods of great tolerance under the Visigothic rulers, Muslim caliphs, and Christian kings. From the twelfth to the fourteenth centuries, Jews, Christians, and Muslims lived in relative harmony, a period called *convivencia*. Unlike Ashkenazic Jews (eastern and central European Jews), who did not mingle with non-Jews, the Sephardim were active participants in their community. Yes, there were times when the religious fanaticism and envy of their hosts and neighbors resulted in fear, forced conversions, and sometimes death, but, for the most part, the level of prosperity and culture in Iberia reached heights unknown to Jews anywhere else in Europe. Indeed, the years between the tenth and twelfth centuries of Muslim rule are known as the Golden Age of Sephardic Culture.

The Muslims entered Spain in 711, and by 719, they had conquered most of it. As they made inroads into the peninsula, Jews who had been mistreated under the Visigoths were left in charge of the cities the Muslims occupied, and a close collaboration resulted, both in political administration and culture. Spanish and Portuguese Jews became Arabic speaking and read the great Muslim works of science, philosophy, and literature. Jewish scholars such as Moses Maimonides and Yehuda ha-Levi became luminaries of the time, and distinguished Jews served in the courts of kings, the nobility, and church dignitaries. Jewish merchants played an important role in commerce, handling luxury items such as silk, wool, precious stones, spice, dried fruits, nuts, and coffee. They traded actively with their Jewish brethren in Morocco, Egypt, Syria, and Iraq, as well as with Jews in Christian Spain, France,

Italy, and England. Whenever a noble needed cash, often for waging a war, he turned to Jewish bankers and merchants for loans. Not surprisingly, this prestige and power earned the Jews the envy of the masses. The fact that the Jews had collaborated with the Muslims and continued to prosper in numerous professions, while many Spaniards lived in poverty, contributed greatly to the resentment of the Spanish masses and to their growing anti-Semitism.

Even as these relationships between the Muslims and the Jews were forming, the Catholic reconquest—the *reconquista*—of Spain was under way. Medieval Spain had been a collection of petty kingdoms: Aragon, Asturias, Castile, Galicia, León, and Navarre in the north were Christian strongholds, while Córdoba, Granada, Murcia, Seville, Toledo, Valencia, and Zaragoza in the south were under Moorish rule. Boundaries were constantly shifting, however, and the Christian forces from northern Spain soon rallied and reconquered most of the Muslim-ruled lands. (Portugal was a separate nation with its own language.) Faced with Christian onslaughts, the Muslims called upon fanatic Berber coreligionists in Morocco for help. The Almoravids responded in 1085, and the Almohades in 1148. Unfortunately, these Berber tribes practiced a fundamentalist form of Islam and looked upon their fellow Muslims in Andalusia as pleasure-loving heretics. Although it was counter to the teachings of the Koran, they forced Christians and Jews living in Muslim Spain to convert to Islam. Confronted with this demand, thousands of Jews fled north to the Christian kingdoms of Spain, where they were welcomed by the rulers who valued their knowledge and skills, and they were soon deeply integrated into the Spanish environment. By 1212, the Muslim territories were reduced to the province of Granada.

The cost of warfare during the seven hundred long years of the *reconquista* was enormous. To fund their battles, both Christian and Muslim rulers looked to the Jews to act as tax collectors, and as vulnerable subjects the Jews had no choice but to do so. They collected taxes from peasants, townspeople, and the nobility, attracting the wrath of them all. During those years, the kings and the nobles were engaged in a great power struggle, and in 1350, Pedro I assumed the throne with the intent to quash the civil war. He immediately set about putting down the rebellious nobles and strengthening the position of the king by treating commoners and nobles with equal fairness. But he had inherited a kingdom torn by discord and intrigue, so success evaded him. His closest advisor and treasurer, Samuel Abulafia ha-Levi, the builder of El Transito synagogue in Toledo, had so much influence over the king's decisions that he soon earned the enmity of those nobles who had grievances against the court. They in turn started rumors that Abulafia ha-Levi had enriched himself at the expense of Pedro I. Unfortunately, in 1369, Pedro succumbed to the rumors, confiscated Abulafia ha-Levi's fortune, and had him put to death. Yet, the king continued to employ other Jews in his court, including his personal physician and court astrologer. Then, with the death of Pedro I, the ten-year civil war ended. His half-brother and fiercest enemy, Enrique de Trastamara, assumed the throne and immediately began levying heavy fines against the Jews and gradually seized their possessions.

The troubles facing the Jews were soon compounded by other factors. First, the general populace had suffered severe economic hardships during the ten-year war, a situation that increased their animosity toward the Jews. At the same time, the Black Plague was racing through Europe, and many of these same people believed that the Jews had poisoned the wells and were responsible for the epidemic. Because their religion required stringent standards of cleanliness, the Jews did not suffer as severely from the plague as others did, making them appear to be immune to it. Fanatical priests stirred up the populace, and in March 1391, riots began that eventually led to the massacre of four thousand Jews in Seville, nearly one-eighth of the city's Jewish population. Those who escaped death became *conversos,* that is, converts to Christianity, and allowed themselves to be baptized. Many were sold as slaves to Muslims in Granada. The persecution quickly spread to Toledo and Burgos. Finally, only a few Jews remained in Valencia or Barcelona. The *convivencia* was finished.

The *conversos* assumed that once the hostile situation calmed down, they would be able to return to their faith, just as they had after the forced conversions under the Almohades. This hope faded fast. *Conversos* were required to attend church and observe its teachings. Any contact with Jews had to be kept secret. Their dilemma was that while they were never fully accepted as Christians, they also could never return to Judaism in Spain. Some sought refuge in Italy, in Muslim-ruled Granada, or in North Africa. Others, however, decided to take advantage of the new opportunities available to them as Christians. They gave up what they perceived to be their Jewish role in Spain, as second-class citizens and outcasts, and sincerely and willingly accepted Catholicism as their new faith. One such convert was Salomon Levi, the chief rabbi of Burgos, who, upon conversion, took the name Pablo de Santa Maria and rose within the church to become bishop of Cartagena and later of Burgos.

The situation in which the Jews found themselves continued to deteriorate. Pope Benedict prohibited the study of the Talmud and ordered all copies to be confiscated. Jews were barred from occupying government positions, engaging in handicrafts, or practicing medicine. They were forced to wear the Jewish yellow "badge," to live apart from Christians, and to attend Christian sermons three times a year. In 1412, these anti-Semitic restrictions were reenforced by Queen Catalina of Castile in her *"ordinamiento . . . sobre el encerramiento de los judios y de los moros."* Jews were ordered to live in *juderías,* or ghettos, and to prevent them from hiring Christian household and shop assistants, no Christian women were allowed to enter the neighborhoods. Jews could not change houses at will, bear arms, hold public office, wear expensive clothing, sell food to Christians, or be employed as carpenters, tailors, veterinarians, shoemakers, furriers, butchers, or merchants dealing in such staples as honey, oil, or rice. As in the rest of Europe, Jews were restricted to being moneylenders.

Not everyone observed these strict prohibitions. During the years of civil war between the rival factions battling for the crown of Seville, Don Alvaro de Luna, constable of Castile, in an attempt to restore order and economic well-being, disregarded the anti-Jewish laws and appointed Jews and *conversos* to government positions. He put Jews under the king's protection in the *pragmatica* of April 1445, which he encouraged King Juan II to sign. While many Jewish rights were legally restored, King Juan II was not strong enough to ensure that the *pragmatica* was strictly enforced. But even the church failed to enforce the anti-Semitic laws fully. Church officials still used Jews to collect taxes, and Jewish nobility continued to be found in the courts. Jews dominated the profession of medicine, could take up arms to defend the *judería* if it came under attack, and owned land, vineyards, and cattle.

During this period, the rate of intermarriage between *conversos* and the Spanish nobility rose to a point that, by 1449, a petition was submitted to the Bishop of Cuenca complaining that all of the noblest families of Spain had Jewish blood. Even King Ferdinand of Aragon was descended from Jewish blood on his mother's side. It is logical to assume that *converso* families believed that intermarriage gave them some protection, although their lives were never truly secure. Anti-Semitism was already established among the populace, and it didn't take much to set them off. During the reign of Henry IV of Castile, Jews were accused of ritual murder of Christian children in order to use their blood to make the Passover matzoh. Massacres and riots were directed against Jews and *conversos* in Sepulveda, Valladolid, and Córdoba. When King Henry died, his sister, Queen Isabella, had to compete with his illegitimate daughter Juana for succession to the throne. Many nobles supported Juana, while *conversos* and Jews wanted Isabella because of her marriage to Ferdinand, who was of Jewish descent.

Isabella and Ferdinand had two primary goals: to strengthen their position as rulers and to replenish their empty treasury. They knew they would need funds for the last major war, to take Granada from the Muslims, and they already were heavily in debt to the *converso* families who had advanced them the money that financed their battle against the Portuguese, whom they had fought to remain in power. Ferdinand unified the nobles and enlisted them—and their bank accounts—in the battle for Granada. At the same time, to avoid repayment to the *conversos,* he decided to support the establishment of the Inquisition. Through that move he hoped to fill the treasury by taking all the possessions of those brought before the authorities. Meanwhile, Isabella was being advised by Alonso de Hojeda, a Dominican prior; Pedro Gonzales de Mendoza, the archbishop of Seville; and Tomás de Torquemada, her personal confessor. All three of them insisted that the *conversos* were insincere and deceitful and were still secretly practicing Judaism. Thus, in 1478, with both monarchs in accord, the Inquisition was established to stamp out heresy among the *conversos*.

By 1480, the Inquisition in Seville was at full force and many *converso* families had already fled. Some stayed on and secretly plotted to arm and defend themselves but were betrayed by spies. *Conversos* were routinely thrown into jail, tortured, condemned as relapsed heretics, deprived of their possessions and property, and some were even executed. In Seville, over seven hundred *conversos* were burned at the stake in a public auto-da-fé, and five thousand others were sentenced to various forms of punishment. Interestingly, the Inquisition had no authority over Jews, because, as they had not converted, they could not be accused of heresy. But Jews were called to testify against *conversos*. Just a word that the accused bathed on Friday or made a stew on Friday but saved it to eat the next day was enough to bring someone to trial. Ironically at this time, two of the monarchs' most trusted advisors were Jews; both Isaac Abravanel and Abraham ben Senior helped raise funds for the war against the Muslims in Granada and for Columbus's voyage.

In 1492, when Granada fell, the fate of the Jews was sealed. With the wealth of Granada at their disposal, Ferdinand and Isabella no longer needed the Jews. Torquemada convinced the Catholic monarchs that the presence of Jews in Spain would weaken their control by tempting the *conversos* away from adherence to Catholicism. The Edict of Expulsion was signed into law in March 1492. It offered the Jews of Spain three choices, all of them bad: they could convert, they could go into exile, or they could be put to death. They had ninety days to decide. Spain was not the first nation in Europe to expel the Jews. England had done so in 1290, and France had followed in 1394. Many areas of eastern Europe, Russia, and Germany had already expelled most of their Jews. What made this expulsion particularly overwhelming and disheartening was that more than half of European Jewry was living in Spain at the time, and nowhere else had the Jews enjoyed such freedom and been able to achieve so much. As for strange symmetry and bad timing, the last day for departure was July 31, 1492 (August 3 on the modern calendar), the ninth day of the Jewish month of Av. It is the holiday of Tisha B'Av, which marks the anniversary of the destruction of the First and Second Temples of Jerusalem.

∷∷∷ THE DIASPORA FROM SEFARAD

After seeing what had happened to *conversos* during the Inquisition, very few Jews chose Catholicism as an option, and the Edict of Expulsion led to their massive exodus from Spain. During those terrible times, Jews realized their futures would be bleak if they were to remain in Spain. Indeed, they had seen the writing on the wall even before the edict, and had begun to leave. Some Jews and *conversos* slipped into Portugal, their closest neighbor and home to a sizable Jewish population, while others fled to Italy. Some crossed the Straits of Gibraltar to Morocco, where there was already a large Jewish community. Some traveled through Navarre to the border with France, from which they headed for Bayonne and Bordeaux (France had rescinded its expulsion order). Many more, including Jews who had lived in Sicily and Sardinia, which had been under Spanish rule, went to the Ottoman Empire.

Historians disagree on the actual number of exiles. We can guesstimate from the figures reported that it totaled about 250,000. About 50,000 went to Portugal, where they were still free to practice Judaism, although not for long. The 40,000 Jews of Granada, fluent in Arabic and comfortable among Muslims, went to North Africa. Several Italian states, including Rome, the seat of the Papacy, gave shelter to about 50,000 Jews. Some settled in Venice and others in Naples, while Ferrara became a center for the printing of Jewish books in Spanish and Portuguese. For many of the Sephardim, however, Italy was just a resting place on the way to the Ottoman Empire. It is estimated that about 120,000 went to the empire, where Sultan Beyazit II welcomed them and issued a decree announcing that they were not to be persecuted.

To the Jews, the prospect of exile was traumatic. It meant giving up their livelihood until, or if, they could reestablish themselves, and it meant separation from all that was familiar to them. Spain had been their home for over a thousand years, and as Heinrich Graetz writes in his *History of the Jews*, they left with very little: "The Jews who owned land were forced to part with it at absurd prices, because no buyers applied . . . magnificent houses . . . beautiful estates . . . were sold for a trifle. . . . A house was bartered for an ass, and a vineyard for a piece of cloth or linen. Thus the riches of the Spanish Jews melted away, and could not help them in their time of need." Ferdinand ordered all debts owed to Jews in the Kingdom of Aragon to be canceled. King John II of Portugal demanded that Jews who entered his country pay a substantial fee in gold, even if they were only passing through, en route to another place.

The plight of the Jews in Portugal is particularly poignant. Jews had lived in relative peace and harmony in Portugal for centuries, and had experienced financial success and prestige similar to that they had enjoyed in Spain. King Manuel, who succeeded John II, was not unfavorably inclined toward the Jews, but, in the hope of someday being able to unite Spain and Portugal, he arranged to marry the daughter of Ferdinand and Isabella. Alas, she was as anti-Semitic as her mother and refused to set foot in Portugal as long as there were Jews in the country, so Manuel ordered all Jews to become Christians. Those who refused to convert had to leave. They mobbed the ports and shelters. While waiting for passage, they were denied bread and water, in hopes that they would break down and convert. Some were dragged to churches and forcibly baptized. In this turmoil, many were killed and many committed suicide to avoid conversion. In 1497, all Jews had to leave Portugal, too, and what had seemed like a haven proved to be only a temporary respite.

Life was not any easier for the Sephardic Jews who went south. Those who sailed to North Africa were often denied permission to land because of the fear that they might carry disease. Ship captains practiced extortion, raped women, or left Jews off in uninhabited parts of the coast. While Jews were welcomed in Naples and Genoa, as soon as an epidemic occurred, they were forced into exile again. Only those Jews who reached the Ottoman Empire found a safe haven and a genuine welcome. Sultan Beyazit II, who issued a decree that the exiles from Spain were to be well treated, realized that the Jews would enrich his empire with their learning, energy, and expertise and would show great loyalty to those who treated them fairly. He is reported to have said, "You call Ferdinand a wise ruler when he impoverished his country to enrich mine?"

Jews who stayed in Portugal, now "New Christians," were given the pejorative name Marranos, which means "swine." In 1499, a decree was issued that forbade the New Christians to leave the country without special license. (Over the years freedom to travel was alternately permitted and forbidden many times. It was not until 1629 that it was finally restored.) Some New Christians found ways to escape, however. One common excuse for travel was trade and another was the feigned desire to go on a pilgrimage to Rome. Once they arrived there, they reverted to Judaism. Spain and Portugal were united from 1580 to 1640, and during that time many Marranos returned to their homeland after years in exile. They felt enough time had passed to be able to live in relative safety, out of the reach of the Inquisition. Other New Christians intermarried with Portuguese nobility, as they had in Spain, and there was hardly a noble house that did not have Jewish blood. They rose to positions of wealth and power and even secretly practiced Judaism. Those who left settled in Bordeaux and Bayonne, in Antwerp and Amsterdam. They also established small communities in England, Germany, Denmark, Sweden, Poland, and all over Italy, especially in

Ferrara, Ancona, Pisa, Naples, and Venice. They formed a separate congregation in Salonika and in other cities of the Ottoman Empire, and they traveled to remote outposts of the Portuguese empire, such as Brazil, Africa, and India. The Portuguese Inquisition was abolished in 1821, and although anti-Semitism didn't disappear, it no longer had official sanction.

In Spain the Inquisition was ended in 1812 by the liberal constitution ratified by the Cortés of Cádiz during the Napoleonic invasion, but this was nullified in 1817 by Ferdinand VII, after the reestablishment of the monarchy. The Edict of Expulsion remained in force until 1869. Professor Victor Perera, in his book *The Cross and the Pear Tree*, describes the years from 1817 to 1910 and after: "Jews were not permitted to practice their religion openly until the twentieth century when the Spanish Constitution's Article II declaring Catholicism the official state religion was finally rescinded. In 1910 the first Sephardic community in more than four centuries was established in Barcelona. Its founder, Ignacio Bauer, an Alsatian Ashkenazi, was the first Jew to become a member of the Spanish Parliament. In 1924 . . . the Spanish Cortés restore(d) citizenship to Sephardic Jews all over the world. The order was implemented by the socialist Spanish Republic after it overthrew the Bourbon regime in 1931. Encouraged by these developments, a small number of Sephardim took up the offer and settled in Spain. By 1935 there were about six thousand Jews in Spain, several hundred of whom found themselves fighting on opposite sides of the Spanish Civil War. . . . Not until 1938, in the final decade of Franco's thirty-five-year rule, did the government grant a license authorizing a Jewish community in Madrid."

In 1943, Generalissimo Francisco Franco, a Galician of *converso* descent and Hitler's ally in the war, realized that the Axis was losing the war and, in a change of heart, granted free transit to some thirty thousand Jews in flight from France and the Balkans. He also restored two ancient synagogues in Toledo. On December 16, 1968, Minister of Justice Antonio Oriol presented Samuel Toledano, the president of the Federation of Spanish Jewish Communities, with a government proclamation officially revoking the Edict of Expulsion. In 1978, Israel's most important Sephardic rabbi, Ovadia Yossef, was welcomed to Madrid with state honors by King Juan Carlos and Queen Sofia.

: : : : : THE SEPHARDIM OF THE EAST

While there were Sephardim who stayed in the west, settling in London, Antwerp, Amsterdam, and in cities in France, or went south to North Africa, the majority went east, to Italy and the Ottoman Empire. In this book I have chosen to limit my scope of study to the majority of Sephardic Jews, those who left Spain and Portugal and traveled from west to east, to the countries along the northern borders of the Mediterranean. Their story is rather different from that of the Jews who traveled to, or were already settled in, the southern Mediterranean, that is, North Africa and the Arab countries. Their history is a rich one that deserves its own book.

I have written about the Jews in Italy in *Cucina Ebraica: Flavors of the Italian Jewish Kitchen,* and some of the Sephardim joined the Italkim (native Italian Jews), Ashkenazim (Germanic Jews), and the Levantine Jews in such centers as Rome, Ferrara, and Venice. Once they did, their fates were inextricably linked. In 1555, Jews were forced to live in ghettos until liberated by Napoleon's armies in 1796. After his defeat they suffered some setbacks to their freedom, but they finally were emancipated in 1848 during the Risorgimento, the unification of Italy. Jews quickly assimilated into the mainstream of Italian life and culture. Compared to much of Europe, relatively few perished in the Holocaust, a few emigrated, and today most Italian Jews live in major cities such as Rome, Turin, Milan, and Florence.

The largest number of Sephardim went farther east, to the Ottoman Empire, because of the spirit of tolerance and the freedom it afforded them. Much of the sixteenth-century Ottoman Empire had formerly been part of the Byzantine Empire, and Jews had been living in the region since the third century B.C.E. There were Jews in Macedonia from the time of Alexander the Great, and Crete, Halkis, Salonika, and Thrace were among the ancient Jewish communities, as was Constantinople. Benjamin of Tudela, a gem merchant from Spain, traveled to Greece and Constantinople in the twelfth century. In his visit to Byzantine Constantinople in 1170, he wrote of the less-than-wonderful conditions of the Jews at that time. But when Rabbi Isaac Sarfati visited the Ottoman Empire in 1430, just after the Turks had conquered Salonika, conditions had changed for the better. He wrote that Turkey was a land where nothing was lacking and where all should be well for the Jews. He queried, "Is it not better to live under Muslims than under Christians? Every man may dwell in peace and have his own vine and fig tree."

By 1453, when Mehmet conquered Constantinople, now renamed Istanbul, the city's population had been decimated by years of war. He needed to build a constituency. Therefore, when the Jews were expelled from Spain, Sultan Beyazit II continued Mehmet's policy of welcome. It is reported that he even sent ships to Cádiz to transport the exiles. Free to worship and live unmolested, the Sephardim prospered, and the Spanish Jews soon came to dominate the existing Jewish communities of the empire. The number of Sephardic refugees from Spain and Portugal, and later Italy, was continually augmented, as conditions for Jews worsened elsewhere in Europe.

As the Ottoman Empire expanded, it took control of all of Greece, including the Greek-speaking Jews of the old Byzantine Empire, the Romaniotes (although not Crete, which remained under Venetian control), as well as the mostly Arabic-speaking Jews of the Middle East. The arrival of the Sephardim caused a great deal of tension in many older Jewish communities, for the Romaniote Jews, pejoratively called *gregos*, were faced with a much more sophisticated culture. In Salonika, Edirne, Bursa, Izmir, Belgrade, Thrace, Macedonia, and Rhodes and other Aegean islands, the Romaniote communities were eventually obliged to accept Sephardic cultural dominance and language. (In Epirus, the Ionian Islands, and in the Peloponnesos, Romaniote language and culture continued, while Crete remained under the influence of the Venetian Jews.)

A particularly striking feature of Ottoman Jewry was the continued dominance of Castilian Spanish in the Jewish community. In Spain, Jews had spoken the same dialects, interspersed with Hebrew expressions, as their neighbors. In the Ottoman Empire, many languages were spoken: Greek, Armenian, Turkish, Arabic, Italian, Spanish, and Portuguese. Since the whole populace lived in relative harmony, no one language dominated, so the Jews continued to speak Spanish in their own settlements. Over time the Spanish of the Ottoman Empire developed a character all its own—essentially Spanish that included many Turkish and Greek words. This language came to be called Ladino or Judezmo. It is still spoken by an ever-dwindling number of elderly Sephardim.

Salonika was, along with Istanbul, the main metropolis of Sephardic life and culture, and its greatest period was the sixteenth century. As in many Ottoman cities, the Jewish community of Salonika was divided into many smaller communities. The original Romaniotes, who were proud of their previous association with the Roman Empire, had been joined by some Bavarian Ashkenazim. Then came the flood of Jews from Spain, Portugal, Italy, France, and North Africa. Each small neighborhood community, or *kehal*, had its own synagogue named after its place of origin: Sicily, Calabria, Apulia, Lisbon, Catalonia, Toledo, Castille, Aragon, and so on. At first, every group kept its identity separate, but gradually all of them became more and more Spanish in language, customs, and dress. The Jews of Salonika were active in international trade, jewelry manufacturing, weaving, and dyeing of wool and silk, while Jewish merchants in Turkey and Macedonia started tobacco commerce. The cultural and intellectual lives of the Sephardim flourished in Ottoman times as well, just as it had in Islamic Spain, and Jews created schools for medicine, science, astronomy, and music.

Wealthy, cosmopolitan Sephardim kept in contact with their brethren in Spain, Portugal, Italy, and the Netherlands. Many of them rose to positions of power and influence as doctors, financiers, diplomats, and statesmen and were actively involved in community life. The close contacts between the Ottomans and Jews became apparent in the Jews' adoption of Turkish dress. As this was an era during which most Turkish women were confined to the home or harem, Jewish women became go-betweens, helping to spread local news. In *The Cookbook of the Jews of Greece*, Nicholas Stavroulakis writes, "Jewish women and Muslim lady friends . . . shared recipes, stories, songs and gossip. Through these contacts much Turkish cuisine, especially sweets, was adopted by Jews. The Greek Christian versions of Turkish dishes are less accurate than the Jewish because Greek Christian contacts were much less intimate . . . what is most important in reference to the cooking of the Jews of Greece is that both Romaniote and Sephardic cooking reflect traditions, either medieval Greek or Spanish, which are older than Ottoman traditions."

The Ottoman Empire reached its greatest heights under the rule of Suleiman the Magnificent, in the years between 1520 and 1566. Suleiman conquered Belgrade in 1521 and Rhodes in 1522. Both cities soon became Sephardic centers, along with Istanbul, Salonika, Izmir (Smyrna), and Edirne. Egypt, Syria, and the Holy Land also came under his rule. His greatest rival for power was Charles I of Spain, who took Tunis from the Turks and prevented their conquest of Vienna. To keep Charles I in check, the French and the Pope formed an alliance with Suleiman. Don Joseph Nasi, a Jew and close adviser to Suleiman, used his position to take vengeance upon the Spanish. He encouraged Suleiman's expansion plans and supported the Dutch in their revolt against Spain. He also took his revenge on the Venetians, who had detained him and his aunt, the powerful Doña Gracia Mendes, under the orders of the Inquisition. Nasi brought about a declaration of war between the Ottomans and the Venetians, which resulted in Cyprus coming under Turkish rule. In 1566, when he acceded to the throne, Selim II, Suleiman's son, made Nasi Duke of Naxos and Count of Andros. He received a grant from Selim to rebuild the city of Tiberius in the Holy Land, possibly to serve as a home for Marrano refugees. He also secured the safety of and helped to revive the city of Safed in the upper Galilee, which became a center of cabalistic literature and home to the most religious of the Jews and to mystics.

From the mid-sixteenth into the seventeenth century, a wave of messianic agitation swept through Europe. Some say it was in part a delayed intellectual reaction to the exile of the Jews from Spain, while many others believed it presaged the coming of the Messiah, an arrival some predicted would occur in 1648. It was during this period of messianic fervor and mysticism that Shabbatai Zevi emerged. Zevi, a young rabbi and cabalist, was born in Izmir in 1626, and he attracted numerous followers as he traveled to Istanbul, Salonika, Cairo, and Jerusalem. He truly believed himself to be the Messiah and pronounced himself as such in 1666. This prompted his excommunication, but he continued to gain power and a large following. He went back to Istanbul to open the messianic age by dethroning the sultan. The sultan, fearing any threat to his influence over the Jews, arrested Shabbatai Zevi and put him to a test of his so-called divinity. If the sultan's archers shot him full of arrows and Zevi lived, he would be considered divine. If Zevi refused this test, he would have to convert to Islam. Zevi chose life and became a Muslim, as did thousands of his followers. Zevi died in 1676, but his followers, led by Nathan of Gaza, claimed that their leader would still vanquish the force of evil and that he had not died but had gone to a higher sphere. Rather than follow the strict tenets of the Talmud and other paths to asceticism, Zevi's followers relied on ecstasy as a way of freeing the spirit to find God. Feasts instead of fasts were their form of worship. The movement resembled that of the Muslim dervishes and the Hungarian Hasidim, in that religious rites are accompanied by frenzied dancing. This sect of Muslimized Jews of Sephardic origin was called Dönme (which can be translated as "converts" or "turncoats," depending upon which text you read), and it still exists in Turkey. Followers who later moved to Salonika call themselves Ma'min, or "faithful." It is believed that the Dönme continue to practice many Jewish rituals in secret.

The Shabbatai Zevi movement had serious consequences for the Jews of the Ottoman Empire. Merchants neglected their businesses and put much of their life on hold waiting for the messianic era to begin. Jewish dominance in international trade was lost. The Ottoman Empire also entered into a period of economic and cultural decline. The central government's control over the provinces had already begun to weaken, and the economy turned stagnant. With the reign of Murad III, in 1574, discriminatory regulations began to be enforced against the Jews. Local authorities preyed upon minorities. The empire's failure to conquer Vienna, followed by the loss of Hungary and much of the Balkans, led to greater demoralization. Islamic society withdrew and became more religiously conservative. Jews lost the protection of the law, and construction of new synagogues was forbidden. Jewish prosperity also suffered because of a decrease in the flow of Iberian refugees to the empire, who were now heading to Holland and Italy. This reduced the Ottoman Jews' contact with Western Europe, which was undergoing rapid expansion and modernization. The sultan gave French merchants a monopoly on trade, causing Ottoman Jews to lose their advantage, and banking gradually was dominated by the Armenians. The center of Sephardic Jewry shifted from the Mediterranean to the Atlantic Coast of northern Europe, to England, France, and Holland. The Jews were forced to turn to crafts and manual work for their livelihood, weaving and dyeing wool, carpentry, printing, sailing, stevedoring, and fishing. By the end of the eighteenth century, most Ottoman Jews were living in poverty and degradation.

Napoleon's invasion of Egypt in 1798 marked the beginning of the intensified intervention of Europe in the affairs of the Ottoman Empire. Fear that the empire would collapse and upset the balance of power led European powers to pressure the Ottomans to institute reforms. By 1839, the government extended civil equality to non-Muslims. In 1856, it decreed that non-Muslims could no longer be referred to abusively in official documents, and by 1876, it granted full citizenship to all Ottoman subjects. This was a major break from the past. Previously in Islamic lands, an individual's status had always been determined by religion and by membership in a religious community. Now, the state would define a person's status. Although this new Western concept of citizenship could not immediately be instituted throughout the empire, especially in its Arab provinces, it had its effect: the power of the Jewish communities declined.

During the nineteenth century, the Jews of the Middle East become progressively more Westernized and urbanized. A generation gap developed as the young adopted European dress and culture and women began to take part in the cultural life outside their homes. The modernization of the Middle Eastern Jews was aided and abetted by the Alliance Israelite Universelle, founded in Paris in 1860, to work for the emancipation and improved welfare of all Jews. The Jews' legal status, economic situation, and educational level slowly improved, but their relations with the Muslim majority did not follow apace. Whereas the Jews embraced Westernization as an avenue of escape from poverty and backwardness, the Muslims saw it as colonialism and exploitation. They resented the success of the Jews and Christians, so while the situation of the Jews improved legally and economically, their safety was threatened.

Considerable ethnic strife ensued during the struggles for freedom of the various Christian populations of the Ottoman Empire, first in the Balkans, then in the Greek battle for independence in 1821. Successive uprisings of Greeks, Romanians, Serbs, and Bulgarians each involved killings of Jews. Once independence was achieved, however, no amount of pressure from the West succeeded in gaining protection for the Jews.

The Balkan wars of 1912–13 brought extensive territory, including Salonika, within the borders of modern Greece. The Romaniote Jews of Epirus agreed to a pattern of Hellenization. The Greeks also wanted to hellenize Salonika, a city whose life was not only

Jewish, but also Spanish in tradition. To quote Nicholas Stavroulakis, "Salonika was a Sephardic island in the midst of a troubled sea of nationalism." In 1900, the total population of Salonika was 173,000, of whom 80,000 were Jews, 60,000 were Muslims, and 30,000 were Christians, the majority of whom were Greek Orthodox. The Ma'min or Dönme made up about 10 percent of the total Muslim population. When the Jewish quarter of Salonika burned down in 1917, the Greek government refused to allow the Jews to resettle in their ancient district and instituted other discriminatory edicts against them.

Once again the Jews had three choices: flight, Hellenization, or retreat into conservatism and relative silence. Some emigrated to Athens or went abroad. The Ma'min who tried to stay in Greece and reassert their Jewish roots were forced to leave along with the other Muslims. Many resettled in Turkey. At this same time vast numbers of Christian refugees from Turkey settled in Salonika. What is amazing is that during this period of turmoil and decline, Sephardic culture remained strong. Jewish newspapers appeared in all the major cities of the Balkans and the Ottoman Empire, in French, Turkish, and Ladino, and Ladino fiction, poetry, and music flourished. Salonika emerged from this chaotic period a prosperous, modern, cosmopolitan, and Westernized city.

The Ottoman Empire continued to shrink. France conquered Algeria and Morocco in 1830, and Egypt gained Palestine in 1831. World War I spelled the end of what was left of the Ottoman Empire, which in 1923 became Turkey and consisted of little more than Anatolia. Turkey gave all its citizens, including the Jews, equal rights and religious freedom. Jews of other Middle Eastern countries were not so fortunate. To survive, many embraced assimilation and Westernization, while others emigrated to Palestine.

The German invasion of the Balkans finally put an end to Jewish life there. Between 1938 and 1945, the Holocaust, a cataclysm of murder and suffering, changed the shape of world Jewry forever. In Serbia, Croatia, and Greece, the destruction of the Jews, the majority of whom were Sephardic, was almost total. When Mussolini's troops attacked Greece, Jews showed their loyalty by sending six thousand troops to help defend the border. When Hitler's troops invaded in 1941, however, they were successful, and German troops occupied Athens. The Germans put an end to the Jewish communities of Salonika, Rhodes, and Crete. By 1945, seventy thousand Jews had been deported to extermination camps in Poland. Only ten thousand remained after the war, many emigrated, and today there are only about five thousand Jews in Greece.

World War II convinced most Jews of the Middle East that it was fruitless to continue to hope for normal relations with the local populations. They became disillusioned with the European powers from whom they had previously sought support. Modern Zionism increased in appeal, and Greek, Turkish, Bulgarian, and Yugoslavian Jews left for

the new state of Israel. Others emigrated to other parts of Europe and the United States. In a census taken in 1908 by the Alliance Israelite Universelle, the Jews in the Ottoman Empire numbered about 440,000. By 1948, the figure in the modern state of Turkey had been reduced to about 80,000, which has subsequently dwindled to about 20,000 today. By the mid 1950s, the once powerful Jewish communities of the Middle East had been reduced to near insignificance.

: : : : : THE SEPHARDIM IN THE UNITED STATES

While most Jews in the United States are Ashkenazic, that is, of eastern and central European origins, some small Sephardic communities exist. One of the earliest settlements was in Newport, Rhode Island. The first Sephardim arrived there in 1658, and by 1776, the community numbered about twelve hundred persons. When the English occupied Newport during the Revolutionary War, the Jewish community abandoned the city. The British occupation of New York also caused many Jewish families to flee, primarily to Philadelphia where they joined Congregation Mikveh Israel, established in 1743. It counted both Sephardim and Ashkenazim as members. Charleston, South Carolina, was home to many Jews as well, again with combined Sephardic and Ashkenazic congregations, and in 1733, Sephardic Jews arrived in Savannah, Georgia. While most of the early Sephardic settlers were from Holland or England, the Jewish community of New Haven was founded by Italian Jews. After World War II, the majority of Sephardic Jews in the Balkans and Near East emigrated to Israel, but some came to the United States. Their language was Judeo-Spanish mingled with Greek, Turkish, and Italian.

While the Sephardim are a minority among American Jews, many large cities have active Sephardic communities. Some of them, such as Temple Bikur Holim in Seattle and Temple Or Ve Shalom in Atlanta, have assembled cookbooks with recipes collected from members of their congregation. It has been interesting for me to see that many of the traditional dishes are still being prepared, although with modern touches and the latest cooking equipment. So the cuisine is still alive and well here, as it is in Greece and Turkey with the Sephardim who remain to light the Sabbath candles.

ABOUT THE RECIPES

: *the* SOURCES

Sephardic cuisine is incredibly rich and varied. Because its scope is so large, I have chosen to limit my focus to Sephardic food of the northern Mediterranean, the scene of the greatest migration from Spain after the Inquisition.

Although it would be wonderful to discover a cookbook of classic Spanish and Portuguese Sephardic recipes, to the best of my knowledge one does not exist. Yes, there are Jewish recipes documented from the late medieval period in Spain, primarily recipes from Arab cookbooks that cover the years before Columbus and the introduction of the foods from the New World. They are, like many recipes of the time, excessively sweetened or sea-soned with too many spices used in what today are considered unconventional or unpleasing combinations. Some of these recipes are loosely described in three medieval texts, the thirteenth-century *Cocina Hispano-Magrebi al-Andaluz*, the fourteenth-century *Libre de Sent Sovi*, and Roberto de Nola's *Libro de cocina*, published in 1520. Other Sephardic recipes are referred to obliquely in the transcripts of Inquisition trials, during which people testified as to what was cooked in the *converso* household. An interesting recent book that attempts to re-create and guesstimate some of these early Sephardic recipes is *Drizzle of Honey: the Lives and Recipes of Spain's Secret Jews*, prodigiously researched by David Gitlitz and Linda Kay Davidson. Although both fine scholars, they are not accomplished culinary professionals, which they readily admit. The stories are fascinating, but the food is mostly unappealing.

Different cooking styles existed in northern and southern Iberia. The north pre-served the cooking styles of the Roman Empire, while the south was more heavily Islamized. The Romans put in vineyards, olive trees, and wheat. The Arabs sowed rice in Valencia, planted sugarcane in Levante, and cultivated almonds, citrus fruits, eggplants, spinach, and artichokes in Algarve and Andalusia. They also introduced the use of cumin, nutmeg, saffron, and black pepper and the custom of double cooking, that is, frying and then stewing. Their mark is everywhere, from the bread-based soups to the egg-based sweets to the nut- or bread-thickened sauces that are now a signature of Portugal and Spain and continue to manifest themselves in the Sephardic kitchen.

The overwrought use of spices and herbs and the excessive use of sweeteners (except in desserts) were abandoned in the Sephardic kitchen. Once the Sephardim emigrated to Italy and the Ottoman Empire, learned local styles of cuisine, and became familiar with

New World foods, they dropped much of the old style, adopting in its place these new ingredients and local Turkish and Greek recipes. Some older terms, such as *almodrote* (refers to sauces with garlic and cheese) and *albóndiga* (meatball), and certain Arab ingredients, such as *alcachofas* (artichokes), *arroz* (rice), *almendras* (almonds), *azafrán* (saffron), and *naranjas* (oranges), as well as eggplants and beans, remain in the repertoire, of course, along with the occasional nut-thickened sauce or sprinkle of cinnamon or sugar on fried eggplant. But that is nearly the extent of the medieval Arab-inspired cuisine. Gone are the various *almori,* thick pastes made from fermented grains, salt, spices tempered with water, and cilantro juice (cilantro is used now primarily in Portuguese and North African cooking but not in Spain or Greece, and only seldom in Turkey). Saffron, cinnamon, and cumin remain, but they are joined on the spice shelf by allspice, paprika, and chile. Two Arabic egg-based sauces are still popular, too: *agristada,* an egg-and-lemon mixture; and *alioli,* a garlic mayonnaise. Other common culinary practices underwent dramatic changes, however. For example, in *Eat and Be Satisfied,* John Cooper observes that although Sephardic Jews were used to cooking with lots of onions and garlic in Spain, they cut back on garlic when they moved to Turkey, as they sensed that Muslim Turks had an aversion to the pungent bulb.

The recipes of the Sephardim in Turkey bear the greatest resemblance to the cuisines of Andalusia, Valencia, and the Balearic Islands. Most of the Spanish-inspired recipes from Méri Badi's *250 recettes de cuisine juive espagnol* appear almost totally Turkish in style. One of my primary resources has been, along with Badi's book, a book titled *Sefarad Yemekleri,* a collection of recipes edited by Viki Kornoyo and Sima Ovadyo, published by Subat, the Society for Assistance to Old People, in Istanbul. Many of these recipes are derived from the oral tradition, and cooking instructions are vague or nonexistent.

For Greece I am indebted to *The Cookbook of the Jews of Greece* by Nicholas Stavroulakis, a thorough compilation of recipes by a multitalented historian, artist, and scholar. He lives in Crete and was previously the director of the Jewish Museum in Salonika. I had the pleasure of meeting him in Greece some time ago, and I have enjoyed cooking from his book over the years. He also helped to put together the interesting *Salonika, A Family Cookbook,* a collection of recipes from the family of Esin Eden. She and her family were Ma'min, or Dönme, Muslimized Jews who emigrated to Salonika from Turkey. While over the years the recipes of the Ma'min had drifted away from the kosher laws, using dairy with meat, I have brought them back to their Jewish roots. Esin Eden's family recipes are outstanding in flavor, and they have become some of my favorites.

Both volumes of *La table juive,* by Martine Chiche-Yana, have revealed traditions and holiday specialties from Greece and Turkey. I have included a few Italian recipes that didn't fit into *Cucina Ebraica* (see the bibliography for those sources), and, of course, my friend Claudia Roden's masterpiece, *The Book of Jewish Food,* has been most helpful and inspiring. We have used many of the same original sources for recipes and share a certain predilection for similar flavors. But Claudia has an extraordinary family history to tell, and she generously shares many of her family's recipes and traditions.

In doing my research I have looked at classic Greek, Turkish, Spanish, and Portuguese cookbooks to search for ancestors of, and variations on, the recipes. I needed to see what remains from the Spanish and Portuguese repertoire, or was derived from it, and how the recipes have changed and evolved as the Sephardim changed locale. These points of comparison often reveal minor variations or surprising historic origins. In addition to studying the roots of the cuisine, I wanted to see what happened to it years later, as the Sephardim emigrated to the New World. Sephardic cookbooks put out by Temple Bikur Holim in Seattle and Temple Or Ve Shalom in Atlanta reveal that not much has changed, except for a few contemporary cooking shortcuts or name variations. The titles of the recipes may vary from Ladino to Turkish to French to Greek to Italian. I have tried to keep them in the language of my original sources. It follows that many of the same recipes appear under different names and, because of no fixed transliteration system and a wealth of dialects, spellings for the same words differ from source to source and in these pages as well.

Finally, I have given preference to recipes that have a long history and that mesh with my Mediterranean-accented palate. They appealed to me because of flavor combinations, techniques, and their sense of history. I seem to have been born with the Sephardic penchant for tartness: to me, acidity is often the key to flavor balance. Also, the recipes chosen for *Sephardic Flavors* are family food, not fancy restaurant cuisine. They are the kinds of dishes you can eat over and over again. They represent the comfort of home and hearth, simple celebrations, the value of tradition, and a sense of cultural and culinary continuity with our ancestors. It is thrilling for me to see my grandchildren eat these dishes with delight, because it gives me hope that perhaps they will continue to cook them long after I have given up my place at the stove.

: *in the* MODERN KITCHEN

In the traditional Sephardic kitchens of Spain, Portugal, Italy, Greece, and Turkey, basic cooking ingredients were locally grown, organic, and unadulterated. They naturally tasted clean, pure, and vibrant. Seasoning was kept to a minimum, as there was no need to heighten flavors. Salt, sometimes pepper, a pinch of spice such as cinnamon or cloves, and a good squeeze of lemon juice might be all that were used. Common herbs were parsley and bay and occasionally mint or dill.

Today, with industrial food production, agribusiness, long-distance transport, and warehousing, most basic ingredients are not the match of those found in early Sephardic pantries. To compensate for this lack of flavor, manufacturers have laced their foods liberally with spices and herbs and have relied heavily on salt, sweeteners, and artificial flavorings. With our palates now accustomed to this flavor manipulation, it is not surprising that many of the original Sephardic recipes seem flat, stripped down, barebones.

After many years of cooking Mediterranean food, I believe I have acquired a natural affinity for the seasonings of the region. I love cinnamon, nutmeg, allspice, cumin, and a bit of heat. Mint and dill grow in my garden, along with flat-leaf parsley and lemons. I am fortunate to live in San Francisco, where abundant fresh organic produce is available, long growing seasons prevail, and there are farmers who raise poultry, lamb, and beef in a responsible manner. I have tested all of the recipes with the best ingredients possible. Still, in some instances, I have increased the amounts of spices, herbs, and garlic to brighten the flavors—not because the dish was not good, but because it could be better. Authenticity is important to me, but not at the expense of maximum flavor appeal. After a number of years in the restaurant business, I am still obsessed with selling flavor. I also realize that not everyone has access to ideal ingredients. So after you have cooked these recipes you will, as I have, adjust your seasoning according to the intensity of flavor and quality of your raw materials and to suit your personal palate preferences. I recommend using kosher or sea salt, as they are not chemically enhanced. Herbs, except for oregano, which is traditionally used in its dried form, are preferably fresh. For greater pungency, whenever possible grind pepper and spices when you need them.

The Sephardim typically used olive oil and unsalted butter (in dairy meals) for cooking. Today, sunflower oil is prevalent in recipes of Turkish Sephardic origin and olive oil in recipes from Greece and Spain. While olive oil was traditional in Turkey, it has been seen by some to be old-fashioned and too heavy. The sunflower oil seems lighter and therefore more fashionable. According to Claudia Roden, another contributory factor is that European market subsidies have made sunflower oil cheaper than olive oil. When I was last in Istanbul, cooking at a food conference, I was shocked when I went into the kitchen and saw giant tubs of margarine. This was not a kosher kitchen. In Turkey, to use margarine is considered "modern."

I have shortened cooking times in many recipes. Recommended times were so lengthy that I knew the food would fall apart or be unpleasantly mushy. I also reorganized some methods to make them more time-efficient in the kitchen. I have not advised culinary shortcuts at the expense of quality, but rather revised the sequence of procedures. Having worked in busy restaurant kitchens for many years, I understand how to set up a recipe for maximum efficiency of effort, as well as for flavor.

The recipes in this book are primarily those of home cooks working in kitchens that were far from the modern, mechanically enhanced marvels that we have today: no food processors, blenders, or electric mixers; few refrigerators; burners but sometimes no oven. While personal recipe journals existed, cookbook collections were not the norm, and most dishes were prepared from memory, having originally been learned by watching others make them. Technique was not challenged and speed was not a criterion. There was time for cooking. Most women worked at home, feeding the immediate family or entertaining guests and extended family in a hospitable and generous manner. Marketing was a daily affair, and both lunch and dinner were prepared. Women put up food for future meals when ingredients might not be available. They cooked special feasts for weddings, holidays, and the Sabbath. Most didn't work outside the home, so they did not have to rush to get a meal together for the family, as so many of us do today.

It would be wonderful to return to the traditions of the Sephardic dinner table, to the joy of the family meal and the pleasure of extended conversation. I hope that these recipes will tempt you into the kitchen, and that your family and friends will gather around the table to enjoy the delicious food of the Sephardic kitchen and the sense of community, continuity, and conviviality it represents.

:::::: THE KOSHER LAWS

You may wonder what makes these recipes Jewish because, at first glance, they don't appear any different from similar Greek, Turkish, Italian, Portuguese, or Spanish recipes. What sets them apart is that although they are the dishes of these countries, they are made in accordance with kashrut, the dietary laws that govern the kosher kitchen. The story persists that these dietary laws came about as a health measure, that they were to prevent the Jews from eating foods that were unclean. This was not the primary basis for them, however. The rabbis of the Talmudic period were content to cite the Bible when explaining the dietary laws, making holiness the only reason for adherence to them. The twelfth-century philosopher Maimonides, in seeking a rationale for the dietary laws, surmised that they "train us to master our appetites, to accustom us to restrain our desires; and to avoid considering the pleasure of eating and drinking as the goal of man's existence." Those of us enamored of the world of food and wine might find it hard to accept this point of view. Others of us, who believe in total permissiveness in the kitchen, see kosher laws as a kind of culinary straitjacket. But this is a very contemporary point of view. In fact, subscribing to kosher laws brought about great creativity in observant Jewish cooks. Indeed, they joyfully embraced the opportunity to prepare traditional recipes with local ingredients and at the same time stay within kosher boundaries.

The primary kosher laws are set forth in the Book of Leviticus, which lists kosher and nonkosher animals. Foods that are not kosher are labeled *terayfa* or *treyfe*. Only animals with split hooves and who chew their cud are kosher. They also must be slaughtered in a ritual manner by a *shochet,* a specially trained butcher. If the animal has died of natural causes or has been killed by a hunter, it is forbidden to eat it. The *shochet* must sever the jugular vein in one clean cut and drain off all of the blood, as blood symbolizes life. To remove further all signs of blood, the meat must be salted and soaked. The only exception is meat that will be broiled, or flame-cooked.

Before eating the hind quarter of an animal, the sciatic nerve and blood vessels attached to it must be removed. This law derives from the biblical event in Genesis when Jacob wrestled with the angel and became lame. Expert butchers can remove the nerve, but it is a time-consuming process and many kosher butchers choose not to handle the hind quarter of an animal, instead selling it to nonkosher butchers. This restriction explains why there are so few recipes for steak or leg of lamb in the Jewish repertoire. In Israel today, more butchers are learning how to remove this vein, thus broadening the kosher table.

A kosher fowl is a domesticated bird such as a chicken, turkey, game hen, duck, or goose, and, like the split-hooved animals, it must be slaughtered in a ritual manner. Only eggs from kosher birds may be eaten. Only fish with scales and fins are permitted. All shellfish are nonkosher. Some fish start out with fins and scales but lose them at some point in their development, so fish such as swordfish and sturgeon are controversial and not all authorities permit their use.

Glatt kosher is a more restrictive category used by the very observant. But the original concept has become distorted. At one time, the term *glatt* referred only to animal foods and meant smooth, that is, the lungs of the animal had to be smooth and not broken or perforated in any way. Today, a whole set of rules has been created under its aegis, probably to foster the notion of separatism.

Foods are categorized as meat *(fleishig)* or dairy *(milchig)*. The term *pareve,* or "neutral," is reserved for foods that can be served at both meat and dairy meals. Fish is pareve, as are spices, grains, fruits, and vegetables. Jews are not permitted to eat meat and milk at the same meal, due to a passage in Deuteronomy that says one must not cook a kid in its mother's milk. In fact, cheeses made from animal rennet are not considered kosher by the most Orthodox. Conservative Jews, however, will eat those cheeses. (In *Eat and Be Satisfied,* John Cooper points out that the Greek cheese called *kasseri* or *casheri* means "kosher.")

The length of waiting time between eating meat and dairy can range from one to six hours, depending upon the orthodoxy of the community and local rabbinical views. Two sets of dishes and of pots and pans are kept for meat meals and dairy meals. In the old days, the dishes could not even be washed in the same dishwasher. Nowadays, water temperatures are high enough that the dishes are essentially sterilized in the process, so the same machine can be used, although dairy dishes and meat dishes must be washed separately. Glass plates, because they are not absorbent, can be used for both meat and dairy meals.

Passover presents a whole other set of dietary laws. Any product considered hametz, that is, fermented or something that could cause fermentation, may not be eaten during the holiday. Only unleavened products are served, so matzoh replaces bread. Ashkenazic Jews will not eat any grains, such as wheat, spelt, oats, rye, or barley. Post-Talmudic authorities added rice and legumes to this list of forbidden foods. The Sephardic Jews did not accept this ruling, however, as rice and legumes formed the basis of their diet. So at Passover, the Sephardim eat rice and legumes, as well as some seeds or spices (allspice, fennel, cumin, nutmeg, sesame) and seasonings such as rose water or orange-flower water, all of which the most observant avoid during the period. The repertoire of foods labeled kosher for Passover is growing all the time, however. Years ago, one could not use confectioners' sugar during Passover because it contained cornstarch. Now it comes cornstarch-free for the holidays.

: : : : : **THE JEWISH HOLIDAYS**

: *the* SABBATH

This is the Jewish day of rest and spiritual rejuvenation. It is a holy day, and according to Orthodox law, no work or business of any kind is permitted. It begins on Friday before sundown and ends at nightfall on Saturday evening. The Sabbath is ushered into the home by the lighting of the candles, and then the wine and the bread are blessed. The Sabbath dinner is a festive meal. But since no cooking, which is, of course, work, is permitted until sundown on Saturday, the Saturday midday meal has to be prepared before sunset on Friday.

In the days before refrigeration and microwave ovens, these religious rules inspired great ingenuity. Dishes were cooked slowly over very low heat, or buried in the *hamin*, or "oven," for many hours, even overnight. A versatile assortment of plates was created that tasted good while warm but also were delicious served at room temperature. Today, many of them would be called meze.

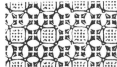

SABBATH MENU I

PIYAZ (SALATA *de* GARBANZOS), : : : BEAN SALAD *with* EGGS *and* ONIONS,
SALATA *de* BERENJENA ASADA   ROASTED EGGPLANT SALAD

PESHKADO PLAKI *or* : : : FISH, PLAKI STYLE *or with* RED PEPPER SAUCE
AHILADO *kon* SALSA COLORADO

GAYNA *kon* MANZANA *or* GAYNA *al* ORNO : : : CHICKEN *with* APPLES *and* APRICOTS
or with APPLES *and* POMEGRANATE

KOMIDA *de* SEFANORYA : : : RICE *with* CARROTS *and* LEMON

FRESH OR DRIED FRUITS

SUTLATCH : : : CREAM *of* RICE PUDDING

SABBATH MENU II

BIBER TARATORU : : : PEPPER SALAD

CEVIZLI ISPANAK SAPI : : : SPINACH STEMS *with* WALNUT SAUCE

PESHKADO FRITO *in* AGRISTADA : : : FRIED FISH *with* EGG-*and*-LEMON SAUCE

SOPA *de* AVIKAS : : : WHITE BEAN SOUP

FLAN *d'*ARANCIA : : : ORANGE CUSTARD

SABBATH DAIRY MENU

PESHKADO PLAKI : : : FISH, PLAKI STYLE

TAPADA *de* ESPINAKA Y QUESO : : : SPINACH *and* CHEESE PIE

ALMODROTE *de* BERENJENA : : : EGGPLANT GRATIN

FRESH FRUITS

ZERDE *or* INCHUSA *de* LECHE : : : SAFFRON RICE PUDDING *or*
DOUBLE-CRUSTED CUSTARD TART

: ROSH HASHANAH (THE JEWISH NEW YEAR)

The first day of the month of Tishri, usually in late September or early October, is Rosh Hashanah, the start of the New Year. The celebration, which lasts for two days, is a joyful holiday for the most part, a time for wishing people good luck for the coming year. It culminates with the blowing of the *shofar,* or ram's horn, on Yom Kippur, the day of atonement and a fast day. Yom Kippur is the most solemn day of the year, a time when everyone seeks forgiveness from people they may have hurt or offended during the past twelve months, so that the new year is begun with a clean slate. At Rosh Hashanah a whole fish is often served, the head of it representing the head of the new year, and many sweets are traditional, to ensure sweet months ahead.

ROSH HASHANAH MENU I

TAHINI SALATA : : : PARSLEY SALAD *with* TAHINI DRESSING

BOREKAS *de* SPINAKA : : : SMALL PASTRIES *with* SPINACH FILLING

SAZAN *en* SALTSA *or* CEVIZLI BALIK : : : CARP *with* SWEET-*and*-SOUR SAUCE *or*
FISH *with* WALNUT SAUCE

GAYNA *kon* MANZANA : : : ROAST CHICKEN *with* APPLES *and* APRICOTS

LEGUMBRES YENOS *de* KARNE : : : MEAT-STUFFED VEGETABLES

BALKABAK TATLISI *or* DULSE *de* IGO : : : PUMPKIN SPOON SWEET *or* FIG PRESERVE

ROSH HASHANAH MENU II

SALATA *de* SPINAKA : : : SPINACH SALAD *from* THRACE

RODANCHES *de* KALAVASA : : : PUMPKIN-FILLED FILO ROSES

KEFTES *de* PRASA *or* KEFTIKES *de* LENTIJA : : : LEEK FRITTERS *or* LENTIL *and*
BULGUR CROQUETTES

PESHKADO AVRAMILA : : : FISH *with* ABRAHAM'S FRUIT

FRUITS SUCH AS DATES, APPLES, GRAPES

TISPISHTI : : : WALNUT CAKE

: SUKKOT (THE FEAST OF THE TABERNACLES)

Beginning on the evening of the fifteenth day of the month of Tishri, usually in October, Sukkot, a harvest festival, lasts for seven days. Tabernacles is derived from the Latin word *tabernaculum,* meaning a hut or temporary shelter, and temporary branch- or straw-covered booths *(sukkahs)* are constructed outdoors, in memory of the ancestors who were forced to dwell outside during their wanderings in the wilderness. Four plants are carried during this holiday: *etrog,* or citron; *lulav,* or palm branch; *hadas,* or myrtle branch; and *aravah,* or willow branch. All of them symbolize the moral and ethical values of eternal faith. Simchat Torah is the last day of Sukkot. Its name means "joy of the Torah," and it marks the day when the annual cycle of Torah reading, the five Books of Moses, is completed.

SUKKOT MENU

SALATA DJOBAN : : : SHEPHERD'S SALAD

SALATA *de* BERENJENA ASADA : : : ROASTED EGGPLANT SALAD

BOREKAS *de* KARNE : : : MEAT-FILLED PASTRIES *from* RHODES

OJAS *de* PARRA *kon* AVAS : : : STUFFED GRAPE LEAVES *with* WHITE BEANS

FRESH FRUITS

TRAVADOS, BAKLAVA, *or* RODANCHES *de* : : : NUT-FILLED PASTRIES, LAYERED FILO
KALAVASA   PASTRY *or* PUMPKIN-FILLED FILO ROSES

: HANUKKAH (THE FESTIVAL OF LIGHTS)

This festive holiday begins on the twenty-fifth day of Kislev, which usually falls in December, and it lasts for eight days. It commemorates the recapturing of Jerusalem by the Macabees. When they arrived at the old temple in the city, there appeared to be enough lamp oil for only one night, but the oil burned for eight days. To celebrate this miracle, the candles of the menorah are lit for eight consecutive evenings. In addition, fried foods are prepared as a symbol of the miracle of the oil. While you wouldn't serve all fried foods, here are some dishes that can be served during the eight days.

DISHES FOR HANUKKAH

KEFTES *de* PRASA : : : LEEK FRITTERS

SKALTSOUNIA : : : FRIED TURNOVERS

PIPIRIZAS *con* QUESO : : : CHEESE-STUFFED PEPPERS

PESCADO FRITO : : : FRIED FISH *with* GARLIC MAYONNAISE *or* EGG-*and*-LEMON SAUCE

CROCHETTE *de* PATATE ALLA SICILIANA : : : SICILIAN POTATO CROQUETTES

FRITTELLE *de* HANUKKAH : : : HANUKKAH FRITTERS

: TU B'SHEVAT (THE NEW YEAR OF THE TREES)

Also called *Las Frutas* by the Sephardim, this holiday occurs in late January or early February, the time of year in the Mediterranean when the trees are just starting to bloom. It is celebrated with the planting of trees. At the table, an abundance of fresh winter fruits and of dried summer fruits, such as dates and figs, are served.

TU B'SHEVAT MENU

MIJAVYANI : : : VEGETABLE SOUP *with* PLUMS

DOLMAYANI : : : MEAT-STUFFED CABBAGE LEAVES *with* FRUIT

DRIED *and* FRESH FRUITS

TRAVADOS : : : NUT-FILLED PASTRIES

: PURIM (THE FESTIVAL OF LOTS)

This joyful holiday is celebrated on the fourteenth day of the month of Adar, usually in March, and commemorates the triumph of Queen Esther, who was aided by her cousin Mordecai. Together they outwitted the evil minister Haman, who had advised King Ahasueros to kill all the Jews. Many dishes are sweet and sour, to recall how sweet it was to conquer adversity.

PURIM MENU

BOREKAS *de* KARNE : : : MEAT-FILLED PASTRIES *from* RHODES

ROLLO *me* HAMINADOS *or* BOBOTKALI KOFTE : : : MEATLOAF *with* SWEET-*and*-SOUR TOMATO SAUCE *or* MEATBALLS *with* FRUIT SAUCE

GAYNA *al* ORNO : : : ROAST CHICKEN *with* APPLES *and* POMEGRANATE

FIDELLOS TOSTADOS : : : FRIED NOODLES

TRAVADOS : : : NUT-FILLED PASTRIES

: PESACH (PASSOVER)

This holiday begins on the fourteenth day of Nissan, usually in April, and lasts for eight days. It celebrates the exodus of the Jews from Egypt, which occurred in such haste that their bread dough did not have time to rise. To commemorate the event, no leavened foods (hametz) may be eaten on the holiday. The main bread product served is matzoh, which is made with a special wheat flour ground just before baking, so that it will not have time to ferment. In earlier days, matzohs were round, but in 1875, a square press was invented in England, and it has been in use ever since. Orthodox Jews eat handmade "guarded" matzoh called *shemura* matzoh, baked quickly under rabbinical supervision to make sure that no fermentation takes place.

Special china and silverware are used for this holiday, and a major spring cleaning is usually undertaken to rid the house of any traces of hametz. Ritual dinners called Seders (the word means "order") are held on the first and second nights. At these dinners, Jews recite passages from the Haggadah, the prayer book of the Seder ritual. Four glasses of wine are drunk in memory of God's four promises of freedom in Israel. The centerpiece of the table is the Seder plate, which is divided into sections to hold the ritual foods: the *karpas,* a mild green herb such as parsley or romaine lettuce representing new growth, is dipped in salt water that represents the tears of the slaves; the *maror,* or bitter herb, usually horseradish or chicory, recalls the bitter times of slavery; the *betza,* or roasted egg, symbolizes the sacrificial offering to God in the temple and is required as an expression of Thanksgiving; the *zeroah,* or roasted lamb bone, represents the sacrifice of a lamb by the slaves on the eve of the exodus and symbolizes religious freedom; and finally, the *haroset,* a fruit-and-nut paste, represents the mortar used by the Jews to construct the pyramids.

PASSOVER MENU I

MATZOH

HAROSET : : : SWEET FRUIT CONDIMENT *for* PASSOVER

BADEMLI BALIK, SAZAN *en* SALTSA, *or* : : : POACHED FISH *with* ALMOND SAUCE, CARP
KEFTES *de* PESCADO   *with* SWEET-*and*-SOUR SAUCE, *or* FISH CAKES

MANGIR CORBASI / SODRA : : : PENNY SOUP

KODRERO *con* AJO FRESCO : : : LAMB STEW *with* GREEN GARLIC

ANGINARAS *or* APYO : : : SWEET-*and*-SOUR ARTICHOKES *or*
BRAISED CELERY ROOT

FRESH FRUITS

PANDESPANYA *or* TISPISHTI : : : SPONGE CAKE *or* WALNUT CAKE

PASSOVER MENU II

MATZOH

SOPA *de* PRASA : : : LEEK SOUP

PESHKADO *kon* RUIBARBARO : : : FISH *with* RHUBARB SAUCE

KOTOPOULO PSITO : : : STUFFED ROAST CHICKEN *for* PASSOVER

MEGINA : : : MEAT *and* MATZOH PIE *from* RHODES

FRESH FRUITS

MANZAPADES : : : LEMON MARZIPAN

: SHAVUOT (THE FESTIVAL OF WEEKS)

A culmination of the seven weeks following Passover, Shavuot celebrates the anniversary of the Revelation on Mount Sinai and the giving of the Torah, or Five Books of Moses. It falls on the sixth day of Sivan, usually in late May or early June, and it is traditional to decorate the synagogue with flowers, leaves, and tree branches. Another name for Shavuot is the Festival of First Fruits, or Yom Ha-Bikkurim, because it was at this time that the first wheat crop was harvested. This is usually a dairy meal, and cheese-filled pastries are featured.

SHAVUOT MENU I

ASSORTED SALADS

TAPADA : : : PIE *with* SPINACH, CHEESE, *or* EGGPLANT FILLING

KACHKARIKAS *de* KALAVASA *kon* AYO *i* PIMYENTA : : : ZUCCHINI PEEL *with* GARLIC *and* PEPPER

MOUSSAKA *di* PESCE : : : BAKED FISH *with* RICE *and* EGGPLANT

FRESH FRUITS

INCHUSA *de* LECHE : : : CUSTARD TART

SHAVUOT MENU II

TAPADA *de* PATATAS *kon* KEZO : : : POTATO *and* CHEESE PIE

ALMODROTE *de* BERENJENA : : : EGGPLANT GRATIN

PESCADO FRITO *kon* AGRISTADA *or* KEFTES *de* PESCADO : : : FRIED FISH *with* EGG-*and*-LEMON SAUCE *or* FISH CAKES

ARROZ *or* MAKARONIA *kon* LECHE : : : RICE PILAF *or* MACARONI *and* CHEESE *from* THRACE

BOUGATSA *or* REVANI : : : CHEESE-FILLED FILO PASTRY *or* SEMOLINA CAKE *with* SYRUP

: TISHA B'AV

Tisha B'Av falls on the ninth day of Av (mid-July to early August) and commemorates the fall in Jerusalem of the First Temple in 586 B.C.E. and of the Second Temple in 70 C.E. From the seventeenth day of Tammuz, observant Jews enter a three-week period of mourning until Tisha B'Av commences. During this time, weddings are not performed, music is not played, and no new clothing may be worn. Beginning with the first day of Av, only vegetarian and dairy menus are prepared. Tisha B'Av is a fast day among Orthodox Jews. Symbolic foods of mourning such as lentil soup are served. The soup is often accompanied by *borekas* or *boyikos de kaser,* small cheese pastries.

APPETIZERS AND SALADS

chapter 1

✡

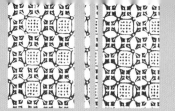

APPETIZERS AND SALADS

Sephardic cooks call many dishes salads that are simply cooked vegetables served at room temperature and treated to a tart dressing—dishes that are more commonly thought of as antipasti, meze, and tapas. Some of the other so-called salads would be described in contemporary terms as dips or spreads. A few are leafy salads, and a few others are prepared with uncooked vegetables.

What I have found to be the most unusual aspects of these dishes are the vinaigrettes. In Spain, Portugal, Italy, and France, the ratio of oil to vinegar for a vinaigrette is generally three to one. In many of the Sephardic Turkish and Greek recipes, however, the ratio is often the reverse. In other words, the Sephardic palate is a tart one.

Vinegar is not the only acid used, however. There is a passion for lemon, too, and hardly a dish hits the table without a plate of lemon wedges on the side. I have a natural affinity for acidic foods, but you may need to play with these recipes until you arrive at a tartness that suits your palate.

SALATA *de* SPINAKA ✦ **SPINACH SALAD FROM THRACE**

SALATA *de* SPINAKA

SPINACH SALAD FROM THRACE

Most Mediterranean spinach salads call for cooking the spinach before dressing it with oil and vinegar or lemon. Sometimes garlic is added to the dressing, and sometimes chopped nuts or pomegranate seeds are used as a garnish. This Greek Sephardic salad from Thrace is unusual in that it is made with uncooked spinach. The recipe comes from my friend Nicholas Stavroulakis, author of *The Cookbook of the Jews of Greece* and former director of the Jewish Museum in Salonika. The egg yolks in the dressing make it rich and creamy, but if you are worried about the danger of consuming raw eggs, you may leave them out and whisk in a tablespoon or two of commercial mayonnaise instead. The mixture of two acids, lemon juice and vinegar, perfectly balances the bitter walnuts, earthy mushrooms, and sweet spinach.

Serves 4

1 POUND BABY SPINACH (2 MEDIUM BUNCHES),
   LARGE STEMS REMOVED

$1/2$ CUP WALNUT HALVES, TOASTED

$1/4$ CUP OLIVE OIL

1 TABLESPOON WINE VINEGAR

1 TABLESPOON FRESH LEMON JUICE

2 EGG YOLKS

$1/2$ TEASPOON DRY MUSTARD

SALT AND FRESHLY GROUND BLACK PEPPER

$1/3$ POUND FRESH WHITE MUSHROOMS, BRUSHED
   CLEAN AND THINLY SLICED

If the spinach leaves are large, tear them into smaller pieces. Chop the walnuts coarsely, leaving large pieces. They need to be large enough for you to be able to pick them up with a fork. In a small bowl, whisk together the olive oil, vinegar, lemon juice, egg yolks, and mustard. Season with salt and pepper. You may want a bit more vinegar or lemon juice.

In a large salad bowl, combine the spinach, mushrooms, and walnuts. Drizzle the dressing over the top, toss well, and serve.

: : : : : :

CEVIZLI ISPANAK SAPI

SPINACH STEMS WITH WALNUT SAUCE

When thrifty Italian, Greek, and Turkish cooks clean spinach, they rarely discard the stems, as they can be served as a room-temperature salad dressed simply with olive oil and lemon juice. This recipe, which comes from *Salonika, a Family Cookbook,* has a Turkish name, but the nut sauce is Hispano-Arabic. (If it had a few minced cloves of garlic, the sauce would be a Greek skordalia.) In Moorish Spain, nut sauces were widely used, and almonds were the predominant thickener. Walnuts are more common to the Sephardic cooking of Greece, Turkey, and the Balkans, however. You could prepare this dish with Swiss chard stems as well, and the sauce also would be good on cooked zucchini, green beans, beets, or cauliflower.

Serves 4

STEMS FROM 3 POUNDS SPINACH

1 SMALL ONION

2 TABLESPOONS OLIVE OIL

For the walnut sauce:

1 CUP GROUND TOASTED WALNUTS

1 SLICE RUSTIC BREAD, CRUSTS REMOVED,
   SOAKED IN WATER, AND SQUEEZED DRY

1/4 CUP WHITE WINE VINEGAR

2 TABLESPOONS EXTRA-VIRGIN OLIVE OIL

3 TO 4 TABLESPOONS WATER, OR AS NEEDED

SALT AND FRESHLY GROUND BLACK PEPPER

Put the spinach stems, onion, and olive oil in a saucepan and add water to cover. Bring to a boil over high heat, reduce the heat to low, and simmer until stems are tender, 8 to 10 minutes. Lift out and discard the onion. Pour the contents of the pan into a sieve or colander and let drain for 15 minutes.

To make the walnut sauce, combine the ground nuts, soaked bread, vinegar, olive oil, and 3 tablespoons water in a small bowl. Stir to mix well and season with salt and pepper. Salt is the key ingredient for balance here. The sauce should be thick but spreadable. If it is too thick, add the remaining 1 tablespoon water and taste again for seasoning.

Place the well-drained spinach stems in a serving bowl and pour the sauce over them. Allow to marinate for a few hours or as long as overnight. Serve at room temperature.

: : : : : :

HUEVOS HAMINADOS

ONION SKIN EGGS

An integral part of Sephardic cuisine, huevos haminados are often served at the Sabbath meal and for Passover. Cooks save brown onion skins during the week and then gently simmer the eggs under them, adding coffee grounds or tea leaves to give the eggs a rich color. Occasionally a dash of wine vinegar is added to the cooking water along with the olive oil.

The word *hamin* means "oven," as the eggs were traditionally cooked in a baker's oven, although today they are more easily prepared on top of the stove. During the long cooking process, the eggs pick up a slight onion perfume and a creamy texture. Italian Jews from Trieste call the same eggs Turkish eggs, while Greek Jews call them *Selanlik yamurta* (Salonika eggs) or *Yahudi yamurta* (Jewish eggs).

Serves 8

8 EGGS

3 TO 4 CUPS BROWN OR RED ONION SKINS

1/4 CUP TEA LEAVES, OR 1 1/2 CUPS COFFEE GROUNDS

1/4 CUP OLIVE OIL

1 TABLESPOON RED WINE VINEGAR

Put the eggs in a large saucepan. Cover them with the onion skins and the tea leaves or coffee grounds, then add the olive oil, vinegar, and water to cover. Bring to a boil over high heat, reduce the heat to very low, cover the pan tightly, and simmer gently for 6 hours. Check the water level from time to time and add more water as needed to maintain the original level.

When the eggs are ready, plunge them into a bowl of cold water placed under a tap of running cold water.

: : : : : :

YAPRAKES *de* PARRA

RICE-STUFFED GRAPE LEAVES

Stuffed grape leaves are a culinary classic through-out Greece, Turkey, and most of the Middle East. They have long been favored by Sephardic Jews, as they can be prepared ahead of time and served on the Sabbath. Rice-stuffed *yaprakes* are generally offered cold, while most meat-filled leaves are served warm (see page 164). Méri Badi's version is somewhat original in that it uses fennel leaves along with the usual mint and parsley. If you like, line the pan with a layer of tomato slices before you add the filled grape leaves.

Makes about 3 dozen pieces

For the filling:

3 TABLESPOONS OLIVE OIL

2 ONIONS, CHOPPED

3 CLOVES GARLIC, MINCED

1 CUP LONG-GRAIN WHITE RICE, SOAKED IN WATER
    FOR 30 MINUTES AND DRAINED

$2/3$ CUP PEELED, SEEDED, AND DICED TOMATO

$1/4$ CUP FINELY CHOPPED FRESH FENNEL LEAVES

6 TABLESPOONS CHOPPED FRESH MINT

$1/4$ CUP CHOPPED FRESH FLAT-LEAF PARSLEY

2 TEASPOONS SALT

1 TEASPOON FRESHLY GROUND BLACK PEPPER

$1/4$ CUP PINE NUTS, TOASTED (OPTIONAL)

$1/4$ CUP DRIED CURRANTS, PLUMPED IN HOT
    WATER UNTIL SOFTENED AND DRAINED (OPTIONAL)

36 TO 40 BRINE-PACKED GRAPE LEAVES,
    WELL RINSED AND PATTED DRY

1 CUP OLIVE OIL

JUICE OF 2 LEMONS

LEMON WEDGES

PLAIN YOGURT

To make the filling, warm the olive oil in a sauté pan over medium heat. Add the onions and sauté until tender and translucent, about 10 minutes. Add the garlic and sauté for a few minutes longer. Add the drained rice to the sauté pan along with all of the remaining ingredients. Stir well and remove from the heat.

Lay out some of the grape leaves on a work surface, shiny side down. Snip off the stems with scissors. Place a teaspoon or so of the mixture near the stem end of a leaf. Fold the stem end over the filling, fold in the sides, and then roll up the leaf into a cylinder. Do not roll too tightly, as the rice expands during cooking. Repeat until all the filling is used.

Place the filled leaves, close to each other and seam side down, in a single layer in a wide saucepan. Pour the olive oil, lemon juice, and hot water to cover over them. Place 1 or 2 heavy plates only slightly smaller than the diameter of the pan on top of the leaves to weight them down. Make sure that the leaves are just covered with liquid, adding more hot water, if necessary. Bring the liquids to a boil over medium heat, cover, reduce the heat to low, and simmer gently until the filling is cooked, 35 to 40 minutes. Remove from the heat, uncover, and remove the plate(s) so that the stuffed leaves can cool quickly. Using a spatula, transfer the filled leaves to a platter. Cool to room temperature before serving. (They can be transferred to a container, covered, and refrigerated for up to 1 week; bring to room temperature before serving.) Accompany with lemon wedges and a bowl of yogurt.

Note: This same filling can be used for stuffing various vegetables. See Meat-Stuffed Vegetables (page 169) for directions.

: : : : : :

SALATA *de* BERENJENA ASADA

ROASTED EGGPLANT SALAD

You may recognize this Mediterranean classic as eggplant caviar. Some recipes combine the pureed eggplant with part yogurt and part olive oil for a creamier result, and a few add a bit of tahini. A baroque version calls for the addition of chopped roasted peppers, walnuts, yogurt, and farmer or feta cheese (see variation). But this recipe is the simplest and most widely served Sephardic eggplant salad. Once the eggplants are roasted, discard any large seed pockets. This will reduce your yield, but the seeds are bitter and add an unpleasant texture to the smooth salad. To keep the eggplant white, a point of pride in Turkey, soak the hot cooked pulp in acidulated water until it cools. In *La table juive,* Martine Chiche-Yana recommends serving this dish as part of the Sukkot table.

Serves 6 to 8 as part of a meze assortment

3 OR 4 LARGE GLOBE EGGPLANTS
    (ABOUT 3 POUNDS TOTAL)
2 OR 3 LEMONS, OR MORE TO TASTE
4 TO 6 TABLESPOONS EXTRA-VIRGIN OLIVE OIL
SALT AND FRESHLY GROUND BLACK PEPPER
2 TEASPOONS GROUND CUMIN (OPTIONAL)
4 CLOVES GARLIC, GREEN SPROUTS
    REMOVED AND MINCED (OPTIONAL)
$1/4$ CUP FINELY CHOPPED FRESH FLAT-LEAF PARSLEY
CUCUMBER OR TOMATO SLICES (OPTIONAL)
CRUMBLED FETA CHEESE (OPTIONAL)
PITA BREAD, CUT INTO QUARTERS IF LARGE,
    HALVES IF SMALL, AND WARMED

For a smoky taste, preheat the broiler and broil the eggplants, turning often, until they are very soft and have collapsed, about 20 minutes. Alternatively, cook them slowly on a stove-top cast-iron griddle, turning them often. You also can bake them in a 400 degree F oven until they are soft throughout, about 45 minutes. Transfer the eggplants to a colander. Halve the lemons and squeeze the juice. Set the juice aside and put the peels into a small bowl of cold water along with a few extra drops of lemon juice. When the eggplants are cool enough to handle, strip away the skin and discard large seed pockets. Place the eggplant pulp in acidulated water. This helps the eggplant stay white. After a few minutes, drain the eggplant pulp and squeeze dry, then place in a bowl.

Mash with a fork, then mix in the olive oil, reserved lemon juice, salt, pepper, and the cumin and garlic, if using. Cover and chill well.

To serve, garnish with the parsley and with the cucumber or tomato slices and/or feta cheese, if you like. Set out pita with the salad

Variation: Dokuz turlu patlican taratoru, or nine-ingredient eggplant salad, is a most interesting and delicious variation on the basic eggplant salad. Prepare the eggplant as directed, then fold the following into the basic threesome of eggplant, oil, and lemon: 2 green bell peppers, roasted, seeded, and chopped; $1/2$ cup ground or finely chopped walnuts; $1/4$ pound farmer or feta cheese, crumbled; $1/2$ cup plain yogurt, drained in a sieve for 4 hours; 4 or 5 cloves garlic, green sprouts removed and mashed or minced; and 1 fresh hot chile, seeded and finely minced (optional). Season well with salt.

: : : : : :

TAHINI SALATA

PARSLEY SALAD WITH TAHINI DRESSING

Although called a salad, this is really a Greek dip
for serving with pita bread. I sometimes add toasted
pine nuts to the mixture, but they are not part of
Nicholas Stavroulakis's version of this recipe from
the town of Edirne.

If you don't have green onions, you may
use 1/4 cup chopped fresh chives instead. The tahini
dressing also is excellent slathered on sliced cucumbers and tomatoes.

Serves 4 TO 6

1 1/2 TO 2 CUPS CHOPPED FRESH FLAT-LEAF PARSLEY

3 GREEN ONIONS, INCLUDING GREEN TOPS,
    FINELY CHOPPED

2 TABLESPOONS PINE NUTS, TOASTED AND
    COARSELY CHOPPED (OPTIONAL)

PITA BREAD, CUT INTO QUARTERS IF LARGE,
    HALVES IF SMALL AND WARMED

For the tahini dressing:
1/4 CUP TAHINI

6 TABLESPOONS WATER

JUICE OF 2 LEMONS (ABOUT 1/2 CUP)

SALT AND FRESHLY GROUND BLACK PEPPER

Put the parsley, green onions, and pine nuts in a
serving bowl.

To make the dressing, combine tahini, water, lemon
juice, and salt and pepper to taste in a blender or mini
food processor. Process to make a dressing thin enough
to coat the parsley mixture. Salt is crucial for the proper
balance of flavor. Pour the dressing over the parsley
mixture and toss well. Diners scoop up the "salad"
with pita bread.

: : : : :

TARATOR

YOGURT AND CUCUMBER SALAD

Recipe names can be confusing. Cooks acquainted with
the Arabic table know *tarator* as a tahini-thickened nut
sauce. Cooks familiar with Greek and Turkish cuisines
see this salad as a cousin to *tzatziki* and *cacik,* with the
addition of chopped walnuts.

Serves 4 TO 6

2 CUPS PLAIN YOGURT

1 LARGE OR 2 SMALL CUCUMBERS

SALT FOR SPRINKLING, PLUS 1 TEASPOON

5 OR 6 CLOVES GARLIC, GREEN SPROUTS
    REMOVED AND FINELY MINCED

2 TO 3 TABLESPOONS WHITE WINE VINEGAR

1/3 CUP CHOPPED TOASTED WALNUTS

3 TABLESPOONS EXTRA-VIRGIN OLIVE OIL

1 TABLESPOON CHOPPED FRESH DILL OR MINT,
    OR A MIXTURE

PITA BREAD, CUT INTO QUARTERS IF LARGE,
    HALVES IF SMALL, AND WARMED

Spoon the yogurt into a sieve placed over a bowl and
place in the refrigerator to drain for 4 hours.

Peel and seed the cucumber(s). If using the large
cucumber, grate it; if using the small cucumbers, cut
into tiny dice. Place the grated or diced cucumber in
a colander and sprinkle with salt. Allow to drain for
30 minutes, then squeeze dry in a kitchen towel.
Refrigerate until needed.

In a bowl, stir together the garlic, 1 teaspoon salt, and
vinegar. Add the nuts and olive oil, and fold in the
drained yogurt and cucumber(s). Stir in the herbs.
Spoon into a shallow bowl and surround with warmed
pita. Serve at once.

: : : : :

ARMIKO *de* TOMAT

CHOPPED TOMATO SALAD

This recipe for *armiko de tomat,* a cooked tomato puree, is based on a recipe from *Sefarad Yemekleri*, a book put together by Subat, the Society for Assistance to Old People, in Istanbul. It also appears in *250 recettes de cuisine juive espagnol* by Méri Badi, but she drops the diminutive and calls it *armi.* The salad resembles a Spanish *salmorejo,* a tomato-based spread that recalls gazpacho but without the water. Unlike *salmorejo* or gazpacho, however, *armiko* is thickened with rice instead of bread, and Badi serves it warm. Esin Eden considers the same dish a salad and serves it chilled, garnished with mint, basil, or parsley. She calls it *domatasi pilaki* and adds quite a bit chopped garlic and lots of lemon juice to the mixture. I share her palate and have added these ingredients to the list. The puree can be served with assorted crudités in place of the pita. It also makes a delicious sauce for fish, or you can serve it as a side dish.

Serves 6 TO 8

4 TO 5 TABLESPOONS EXTRA-VIRGIN OLIVE OIL

2 ONIONS, CHOPPED

3 TO 4 POUNDS RIPE TOMATOES, PEELED,
   SEEDED, AND COARSELY CHOPPED

2 GREEN BELL PEPPERS, SEEDED AND FINELY CHOPPED

3 TABLESPOONS RICE, SOAKED IN WATER FOR
   1 HOUR AND DRAINED

1 TABLESPOON SUGAR

$1/4$ CUP CHOPPED FRESH FLAT-LEAF PARSLEY

3 TO 5 CLOVES GARLIC, MINCED (OPTIONAL)

$1/4$ CUP FRESH LEMON JUICE (OPTIONAL)

SALT AND FRESHLY GROUND BLACK PEPPER

CHOPPED FRESH MINT, FLAT-LEAF PARSLEY, OR BASIL

PITA BREAD, CUT INTO QUARTERS IF LARGE,

Warm the olive oil in a large sauté pan over medium heat. Add the onions and sauté until tender and translucent, about 10 minutes. Add the tomatoes, peppers, rice, sugar, parsley, and the garlic and lemon juice, if using, and simmer, uncovered, until the juices released by the tomatoes have been absorbed and the rice is tender, about 20 minutes. Season to taste with salt and pepper. Transfer to a bowl, let cool, cover, and chill well.

Garnish the salad with herb of choice and serve chilled. Accompany with pita bread.

: : : : : :

PIYAZ

BEAN SALAD WITH EGGS AND ONIONS

Bean salads are ever present on the Sephardic table. This particular Turkish recipe from Esin Eden uses *huevos haminados* and thin onion slices tossed with parsley as garnishes. The latter garnish is an interesting variation on the usual bean salad. Typically chopped raw onion is tossed with the cooked beans, making it a component rather than a garnish. In summer, sliced tomatoes can join the sliced onions. Sumac, the ground dried berries of a bush that flourishes in the Middle East, heightens the tartness of the dressing.

Serves 6

2 CUPS DRIED WHITE BEANS

1 TEASPOON SALT

5 TABLESPOONS EXTRA-VIRGIN OLIVE OIL

$^1/_2$ CUP WHITE WINE VINEGAR

FRESHLY GROUND BLACK PEPPER

2 ONIONS, CUT IN HALF AND SLICED PAPER-THIN

5 TABLESPOONS CHOPPED FRESH FLAT-LEAF PARSLEY

2 ONION SKIN EGGS (PAGE 44) OR HARD-COOKED EGGS

GROUND SUMAC (OPTIONAL)

Pick over the beans for stones and other impurities and rinse well. Place in a bowl with water to cover generously and let soak overnight. The next day, drain the beans and place in saucepan with water to cover. Bring to a boil over high heat, cover, reduce the heat to low, and simmer until tender, 45 to 60 minutes, adding $^1/_2$ teaspoon of the salt midway through the cooking.

When the beans are ready, drain them and transfer to a bowl or deep platter. In a small bowl, whisk together the olive oil, vinegar, the remaining $^1/_2$ teaspoon salt, and freshly ground black pepper to taste. Pour most of the dressing over the beans while they are still hot and toss well. Place the onions and parsley in a bowl and pour the remaining dressing over them. Let stand for 15 to 20 minutes until the onions soften and lose their bite.

Surround the bean salad with the onions. Peel the eggs, thinly slice them, and arrange the slices over and around the beans. Sprinkle the beans and onions with a little dusting of sumac, if desired. Serve at room temperature.

Variation: In Suzy David's *The Sephardic Kosher Kitchen,* chopped tomatoes and green peppers are added to the cooked white beans and the salad is garnished simply with chopped fresh mint.

: : : : : :

BIBER TARATORU

PEPPER SALAD

Despite its Turkish title, this salad, which is in the tradition of Middle Eastern and North African chopped salads, is Hispano-Arabic in its use of bread to thicken the dressing. A garnish of dried oregano or fresh marjoram would not be out of place. As with the parsley salad on page 48, this pepper mixture is meant to be scooped up with pita bread. If you prefer more of an antipasto-type salad, cut the peppers into strips, dress them with lemon, oil, and herbs, and then sprinkle them with bread crumbs, or omit the bread altogether.

Serves 4

1 POUND GREEN BELL PEPPERS (2 LARGE)

1 SLICE RUSTIC BREAD, CRUSTS REMOVED, SOAKED IN
    WATER, AND SQUEEZED DRY

$1/4$ CUP FRESH LEMON JUICE

2 TABLESPOONS EXTRA-VIRGIN OLIVE OIL, OR TO TASTE

2 TABLESPOONS CHOPPED FRESH FLAT-LEAF PARSLEY

$1/2$ TEASPOON DRIED OREGANO, OR 2 TEASPOONS
    CHOPPED FRESH MARJORAM (OPTIONAL)

SALT AND FRESHLY GROUND BLACK PEPPER

PITA BREAD, CUT INTO QUARTERS IF LARGE,
    HALVES IF SMALL, AND WARMED

Place the peppers over an open flame on a gas stove or in a broiler until they are charred almost black on all sides and are softened. Slip the peppers into a plastic bag or covered container and let steam for 15 minutes, then scrape off the charred peel with a knife. Do not peel under running water, or you will lose much of the roasted flavor. Slice each pepper open and remove the seeds and thick ribs.

Mash or finely chop the roasted peppers and place in a bowl. Stir in the soaked bread, lemon juice, and 2 tablespoons olive oil. Toss in the parsley and the oregano or marjoram if you like. Season with salt and pepper, then taste and adjust with more olive oil if the mixture is too tart. Serve at room temperature with the pita bread for scooping.

: : : : : :

SALATA DJOBAN

SHEPHERD'S SALAD

Salata djoban is a cross between the Spanish chopped salad called *pipirrana* from Jaén and a classic Turkish chopped salad. In *250 recettes de cuisine juive espagnol*, Méri Badi does not use any garlic, although it certainly adds a bit of liveliness. I also like to add mint to this salad along with the parsley.

Serves 6 TO 8

3 LARGE, RIPE TOMATOES, PEELED, SEEDED,
    AND CHOPPED

1 LARGE OR 2 SMALL CUCUMBERS, PEELED,
    SEEDED, AND CHOPPED

1 RED ONION, FINELY MINCED

2 CLOVES GARLIC, GREEN SPROUTS REMOVED
    AND MINCED (OPTIONAL)

$1/2$ CUP CHOPPED FRESH FLAT-LEAF PARSLEY

$1/4$ CUP CHOPPED FRESH MINT

1 SMALL BELL PEPPER, ANY COLOR, SEEDED
    AND CHOPPED

4 TO 6 TABLESPOONS EXTRA-VIRGIN OLIVE OIL

$1/2$ CUP RED WINE VINEGAR, OR MORE TO TASTE

SALT AND FRESHLY GROUND BLACK PEPPER

OIL-CURED BLACK OLIVES

4 TO 8 ANCHOVY FILLETS (OPTIONAL)

In a bowl, combine the tomatoes, cucumber(s), red onion, garlic, parsley, mint, and bell pepper. Drizzle with the oil and vinegar and toss well. Season with salt and pepper and toss again. Place in a serving bowl and garnish with olives and with the anchovy fillets, if desired. Serve at room temperature.

Note: This is a last-minute salad. If you should want to assemble it a few hours ahead of time, be aware that the tomatoes will continue to give off water, so either add them just before serving or drain the excess liquids from the assembled salad and reseason with oil, vinegar, salt, and pepper.

: : : : : :

KEFTIKES *de* LENTIJA
LENTIL AND BULGUR CROQUETTES

These croquettes, a specialty of Salonika, are usually served with lemon wedges. They also taste great with a dollop of yogurt, however, and because they are rather filling, they can be a complete meal when served with soup.

Makes about 15 *croquettes; serves* 4 TO 6

$1/4$ CUP GREEN OR BLACK LENTILS

$3/4$ CUP LIGHTLY SALTED WATER

$1/2$ CUP BULGUR OR CRACKED WHEAT

3 TABLESPOONS OLIVE OIL, PLUS MORE FOR FRYING

1 LARGE ONION, CHOPPED

2 TEASPOONS GROUND CUMIN

2 ONION SKIN EGGS (PAGE 44) OR HARD-COOKED EGGS, PEELED AND CHOPPED

1 TEASPOON SALT

$1/2$ TEASPOON FRESHLY GROUND BLACK PEPPER

3 TABLESPOONS CHOPPED FRESH MINT

3 TABLESPOONS CHOPPED FRESH FLAT-LEAF PARSLEY

1 EGG, BEATEN

ABOUT $1/4$ CUP TOASTED BREAD CRUMBS OR MATZOH MEAL, OR AS NEEDED

LEMON WEDGES OR PLAIN YOGURT

Pick over the lentils and rinse well. Place in a small saucepan and add the lightly salted water. Bring to a boil over high heat, reduce the heat to low, cover, and simmer until tender, 20 to 25 minutes.

When the lentils are ready, uncover, add just enough water (about 1 scant cup) to cover them, and stir in the bulgur or cracked wheat. Remove from the heat, re-cover, and let stand until the grain has absorbed the liquid, about $1 1/2$ hours.

Warm the 3 tablespoons olive oil in a small sauté pan over medium heat. Add the onion and sauté until golden, about 10 minutes. Add the cumin, chopped eggs, salt, and pepper; stir well and remove from the heat. Stir in the onion mixture to the lentils, then the mint, parsley, and beaten egg. Form the mixture into flat cakes each about $2 1/2$ inches in diameter and $1/2$ inch thick. If mixture seems too wet, add bread crumbs or matzoh meal to bind it. You also can lightly coat the croquettes with bread crumbs as they are formed.

Pour olive oil to a depth of $1/4$ inch into a large sauté pan and place over medium heat. Add the croquettes, in batches, and fry, turning once, until well browned on both sides, 8 to 10 minutes total. Using a slotted spatula, transfer to paper towels to drain briefly, then sprinkle lightly with salt.

Serve the croquettes hot with lemon wedges, or if this is a dairy meal, with yogurt.

: : : : : :

SARDALYE SALATASI

SARDINE SALAD

Esin Eden's sardine salad is reminiscent of a Spanish salad from Murcia called *mojete,* which means "to soak," because bread is used to soak up the tart vinaigrette. The sardines are cleaned, boned, and marinated in vinegar and then served atop a green salad garnished with thinly sliced green onions and hard-cooked eggs. As in Spain, Eden's salad is dressed in a casual manner, with just a drizzle of olive oil and a more generous drizzle of lemon juice. That is too haphazard for me, however. To make sure the greens are evenly dressed, I whisk together the oil and lemon juice and toss the greens with most of the mixture, then drizzle the rest on top of the eggs and sardines. If you cannot find fresh sardines or anchovies, use salt-packed anchovies. Fillet them under running cold water to rinse away the salt at the same time you remove the bones, and then marinate them in the vinegar with a bit of oil for a few hours.

Serves 4 OR 5

10 FRESH SARDINES OR ANCHOVIES

KOSHER SALT

2 TABLESPOONS WHITE WINE VINEGAR

$1/3$ CUP FRESH LEMON JUICE

$1/4$ CUP EXTRA-VIRGIN OLIVE OIL

SALT AND FRESHLY GROUND BLACK PEPPER

8 CUPS ASSORTED TORN GREENS SUCH AS
    ARUGULA, CRESS, AND ROMAINE

2 TABLESPOONS CHOPPED FRESH MINT

2 TABLESPOONS CHOPPED FRESH FLAT-LEAF PARSLEY

2 TABLESPOONS CHOPPED FRESH DILL

5 GREEN ONIONS, INCLUDING GREEN TOPS,
    CHOPPED OR THINLY SLICED

2 HARD-COOKED EGGS, PEELED AND SLICED

Sprinkle the fresh sardines or anchovies with kosher salt, place on a plate, cover, and refrigerate overnight.

Slit each fish along the belly and remove the bones and heads. Place the fish in a shallow, nonaluminum dish and pour the wine vinegar evenly over them. Cover and marinate in the refrigerator for a few hours.

In a small bowl, combine the lemon juice and olive oil and season with salt and pepper. In a large bowl, combine the greens, mint, parsley, and dill and toss with most of the dressing, leaving a few tablespoons in reserve.

Arrange the greens on a large platter. Top with the fish and the sliced onions and eggs, then drizzle with the remaining dressing. Serve at once.

: : : : : :

SAVORY PASTRIES

chapter 2

✡

SAVORY PASTRIES

Savory pastries form a large and important category in Sephardic cooking. They may take a bit of work to prepare, but given contemporary conveniences such as refrigerators and freezers, the pastries are easy to have on hand. The name game is challenging. Depending upon where people lived, or family traditions, the identical recipe may go under a variety of titles. A *tapada* is a double-crusted pie. Its name comes from the Spanish verb *tapar*, "to cover," which also is the origin of the term *tapas*. Occasionally a double-crusted pie is called an *inchusa*.

Borekas are small pastries traditionally served on holidays and the Sabbath. They may have a savory or a sweet filling. In concept they resemble Spanish empanadas, but their name comes from the Turkish *boerek*, meaning "pie," and in Italy they are called *burriche*. Some Sephardic families call these smaller pastries *boyos* and make them with a strudel-type dough. *Boyos* are related to *bolo*, Spanish for "cake." Although some families call these pastries *borekas, boyos*, or the diminutive *boyikos*, they are usually cheese pastries, with cheese incorporated into the dough and the filling.

Bulemas are Sephardic filo pastries long enjoyed in Greece and Turkey, especially on the Sabbath and holidays. When coiled or rolled, they also were called *tsaizika,* in Greece, and are a variation on the Greek *rodanches* (roses), or the Turkish *kol boregi*. As if all of these terms were not confusing enough, when the filo pastries are not rolled but are formed into triangles, they are called *holjadres, rojaldes,* or *filas*. Same filo, same filling but a different shape means a different name. These filo pastries can be baked or deep-fried.

Savory fillings called *gomos* might be potato and cheese, leeks and cheese, spinach and cheese, eggplant and cheese, or only cheese. Sometimes meat or fish is used, too. These fillings are similar to the various gratins—*sfongo, quajado, fritada, almodrote*—found in the chapter on vegetables, but they lack the bread binders because now they are enclosed in a dough or filo crust. Keep in mind that *gomos* should be quite intense in flavor, as the bland pastry crust dulls the impact of the filling. My advice is to season with a heavy hand and to add more herbs than you would if you were eating the filling as a dish in itself.

During Passover, of course, pastries must be made with matzohs or matzoh meal. *Minas* are matzoh pies layered with vegetables or cheese. A meat-filled pie may be called a *mina* or *megina*, while in Italy these pies are called *scacchi*.

TAPADA *de* PATATAS *kon* KEZO

POTATO AND CHEESE PIE

A *tapada* is a double-crusted pie, much like a classic Greek pita. It can be filled with various vegetables and cheese, and chopped walnuts are sometimes added for an interesting contrast in texture. According to *La table juive,* this pie is served at Shavuot in Turkey. This same dough and filling can be used to make smaller pastries called *borekas* (page 60).

Serves 6 TO 8

For the filling:

3 LARGE BOILING POTATOES, PEELED

2 TABLESPOONS OLIVE OR VEGETABLE OIL

1 BUNCH GREEN ONIONS, CHOPPED, OR
    1 MEDIUM YELLOW ONION, CHOPPED

2 EGGS, LIGHTLY BEATEN

$1/2$ POUND FETA, FARMER, OR RICOTTA CHEESE,
    CRUMBLED (ABOUT $1^{1}/4$ CUPS)

1 CUP GRATED KASHKAVAL OR GRUYÈRE CHEESE

$1/4$ CUP CHOPPED FRESH DILL (OPTIONAL)

$1^{1}/2$ TEASPOONS SALT

1 TEASPOON FRESHLY GROUND BLACK PEPPER

$1/2$ TEASPOON FRESHLY GRATED NUTMEG (OPTIONAL)

For the pastry:

$3^{1}/2$ CUPS ALL-PURPOSE FLOUR, OR AS NEEDED

1 TEASPOON SALT

$1/2$ CUP SUNFLOWER OIL

$1/2$ CUP MARGARINE, MELTED AND COOLED

$1/2$ CUP WATER

$1/2$ CUP FINE DRIED BREAD CRUMBS

1 EGG, LIGHTLY BEATEN, FOR GLAZE

To make the filling, place the potatoes in a saucepan with salted water to cover generously. Bring to a boil and cook until tender, about 30 minutes. Drain well and pass through a ricer or food mill placed over a bowl, or simply mash. Warm the oil in a sauté pan over medium heat. Add the onions and sauté for 2 to 3 minutes to remove the sharpness. Add them to the mashed potatoes, then fold in the eggs, cheeses, and the dill, if using. Add the salt, pepper, and the nutmeg, if using, and mix well. You should have 4 to $4^{1}/2$ cups. Set aside.

Preheat the oven to 400 degrees F.

To make the pastry, stir together the flour and salt in a bowl. Gradually add the sunflower oil, margarine, and water, stirring and tossing with a fork until the dough comes together. Alternatively, combine the flour and salt in a food processor and pulse to combine, then add the oil, margarine, and water and process until a dough forms. Turn out the dough onto a lightly floured work surface and knead it until it is cohesive.

Divide the dough into 2 pieces, one slightly larger than the other. Roll out the larger portion into a 13-inch round about $1/8$ inch thick. Carefully transfer to an 11-inch pie dish. Sprinkle with the bread crumbs.

Roll out the remaining dough portion in the same way into a 12-inch round $1/8$ inch thick. Spoon the filling into the pastry-lined pan and carefully place the second pastry round over the filling. Trim any excessive overhang, then turn under the pastry edges and pinch to seal. Brush the top crust with the beaten egg. Cut a few steam vents in the top.

Bake until the crust is golden, 25 to 30 minutes. Serve hot or warm.

Eggplant Filling Variation: Select 3 or 4 eggplants (about 4 pounds total) and broil, turning often, until they are very soft and have collapsed, about 20 minutes. (Alternatively, bake them in a 400 degree F oven, turning occasionally, until soft, about 45 minutes.) Transfer the eggplants to a colander. When cool enough to handle, peel away the skins and remove any large seed pockets. Leave the pulp in the colander for 30 minutes to release the bitter juices. Transfer to a bowl, mash well, and mix with 2 eggs and 1 cup each crumbled feta cheese and grated kashkaval, Monterey Jack, or Gruyère cheese. Add $1/2$ cup chopped walnuts, if desired. Fold in some fine dried bread crumbs if the mixture seems too wet; you may need as much as $1/2$ cup. Season generously with salt and pepper. You should have $3 1/2$ to 4 cups. Bake as directed for potato filling.

Spinach Filling Variation: Remove the stems from 2 pounds spinach, cook until wilted in the rinsing water clinging to the leaves, squeeze dry, and chop finely. Or use 3 packages (10 ounces each) frozen chopped spinach, thawed and squeezed dry. Place in a bowl and add 4 eggs; 1 pound feta cheese, crumbled; and 1 cup grated kashkaval, Monterey Jack, or Gruyère cheese. Season with salt and pepper and with freshly grated nutmeg, if you like. You should have $3 1/2$ to 4 cups filling. Bake as directed for potato filling.

Cheese Filling Variation: Combine 1 pound feta cheese, crumbled, and 1 pound ricotta or cottage cheese or part ricotta and part grated Monterey Jack or Gruyère cheese in a bowl. Add 4 eggs, $1/2$ cup chopped fresh flat-leaf parsley, $1/4$ cup chopped fresh dill, $1/2$ teaspoon freshly grated nutmeg, and salt and pepper to taste. You should have about 4 cups filling. Bake as directed for potato filling.

: : : : : :

BOREKAS

SMALL STUFFED PASTRIES

The same fillings used for *tapadas* (page 59) can be used for *borekas*. Cut the filling recipes in half, or you will have too much. Half a batch of each filling will yield about thirty 3- to 4-inch pastries. You can use the dough from the *tapada* recipe or the dough for *handrajos* (page 65).

Prepare a dough and filling of choice. Preheat the oven to 375 degrees F. Line baking sheets with parchment paper.

On a lightly floured work surface, roll out the dough $1/2$ inch thick. Cut out rounds 3 to 4 inches in diameter. Place a scant tablespoon of filling on the center of each round, fold in half, and seal by pinching the edges together with your fingers, or moisten first with a bit of water. Place the pastries on the parchment-lined sheets. Brush with egg wash and sprinkle with a bit of cheese or sesame seeds. Bake until golden, 25 to 30 minutes. Serve hot or warm.

: : : : : :

BOYIKOS *de* KESO

PEPPERY CHEESE BISCUITS

The word *boyo* is derived from the Spanish *bolo,* or "cake." There the resemblance ends, however. For some Sephardic families, *boyos* are small pies like empanadas or *borekas,* made with a strudel-type dough and filled with spinach, potatoes, or eggplant. In Turkey, they seem to be cheese pastries. Sometimes *boyos* are rolled into balls, flattened with a fork, sprinkled with cheese, and baked. Other times they are cut into biscuitlike shapes, and still other times they are formed into pinwheels. But no matter how they are shaped, *boyos,* or their diminutive, *boyikos,* are typically cheese pastries, often with cheese in the dough. The more full flavored the cheese, the tastier the *boyiko.* This recipe from *Sefarad Yemekleri* is particularly interesting because the biscuits are spicy and rich with cheese. These festive pastries are served at Shavuot and Tisha B'Av.

Makes about 20 *biscuits*

2 $^1/_2$ CUPS ALL-PURPOSE FLOUR, OR AS NEEDED

2 $^1/_4$ TEASPOONS SALT

$^1/_2$ TO $^3/_4$ TEASPOON RED PEPPER FLAKES

1 CUP GRATED KASSERI OR FULL-FLAVORED
   CHEDDAR CHEESE, PLUS MORE FOR SPRINKLING
   ON THE TOPS (OPTIONAL)

$^3/_4$ CUP SUNFLOWER OR CANOLA OIL

$^1/_4$ CUP WATER

1 EGG YOLK, LIGHTLY BEATEN

Preheat the oven to 350 degrees F. Line a baking sheet with parchment paper or oil lightly.

In a bowl, stir together the flour, salt, red pepper flakes, and 1 cup cheese. Add the oil and water and stir until the dough comes together. Alternatively, combine the flour, salt, red pepper flakes, and 1 cup cheese in a food processor and pulse to combine. Add the oil and water and process until the dough comes together.

Shape the dough into a ball and place on a floured work surface. Flatten the dough and roll out or pat out into a round $^1/_4$ inch thick. Using a 2-inch biscuit cutter, cut out rounds. Place the rounds on the prepared baking sheets about $^1/_2$ inch apart. They do not spread. Gather up the scraps, roll out or pat out again, and cut out more rounds. Brush the tops with the egg yolk and, if desired, sprinkle them lightly with grated cheese.

Bake the biscuits until golden, about 25 minutes. Remove from the oven and serve warm. They also can be allowed to cool on a rack, stored in an airtight container for several days, and then reheated in a low oven.

: : : : : :

RODANCHES *de* KALAVASA

PUMPKIN-FILLED FILO ROSES

Rodanches are called "roses" because some Greeks think they resemble the flowers. (If one is less poetically inclined, the image of snails or coiled snakes may come to mind.) Sephardic Turkish pastries made in this shape are called *bulemas* or *kol boregi* and can be filled with spinach or just cheese. The pumpkin filling is traditionally served for Rosh Hashanah and Sukkot. In *The House by the Sea,* authors Elia Aeolian and Rebecca Camhi Fromer refer to a *pastel de calavasa,* a squash pie served the day after Yom Kippur, the culmination of the Jewish New Year holiday.

These pumpkin *rodanches* walk a fine line between being a savory pastry and a dessert. (The sweet versions in Turkey are called *bulemas dulces de balkabak.*) You can reduce the amount of sugar and add some salty cheese to make the filling more savory or, conversely, you can increase the sugar to make it a dessert pastry. In Greece, this filling is also put into a large filo pie called *kolokithopita.*

Mediterranean pumpkin-type squash is much redder than the pumpkin in the United States. It is quite large, is often sold by the piece, and is closest in texture and taste to butternut squash or to Japanese kabocha squash, which is a bit looser in texture. If you cannot find butternut squash, you can use canned pumpkin. In fact, some versions of this recipe call for zucchini instead of pumpkin, but the mixture is still sweetened.

Makes 10 TO 12 *pastries*

1 BUTTERNUT SQUASH, ABOUT 2 POUNDS,
   OR 1 CAN (16 OUNCES) UNSWEETENED
   SOLID-PACK PUMPKIN PUREE, DRAINED

$^1/_2$ TO 1 CUP SUGAR

1 TEASPOON GROUND CINNAMON

2 TABLESPOONS OLIVE OR VEGETABLE OIL

1 CUP CHOPPED TOASTED WALNUTS (OPTIONAL)

PINCH OF SALT

$^1/_2$ CUP CRUMBLED FETA OR OTHER
   SALTY CHEESE (OPTIONAL)

$^1/_4$ CUP CHOPPED FRESH MINT OR
   FLAT-LEAF PARSLEY (OPTIONAL)

8 FILO SHEETS, THAWED IN THE REFRIGERATOR
   IF FROZEN

$^1/_2$ CUP UNSALTED BUTTER, MELTED AND COOLED,
   OR OLIVE OR VEGETABLE OIL

If using the butternut squash, halve it lengthwise and scoop out and discard the seeds. Peel and cut into 1-inch cubes. Place in a saucepan with water to cover, bring to a boil over high heat, reduce the heat to low, cover, and cook until the squash is very soft, 25 to 35 minutes. Drain well, return to the saucepan, and mash with a fork. Alternatively, bake the whole squash in a 350 degree F oven until tender, about $1^1/_2$ hours. Cut it in half, scoop out and discard the seeds, and scoop out and mash the pulp. You should have 2 cups puree. Place in a saucepan.

Add the sugar (use the smaller amount—or even less—if you wish to make a more savory filling and the entire cup for a sweet version), cinnamon, and oil to the puree (or to the canned pumpkin) and place over low heat. Cook, stirring occasionally, until thick. If you have baked the squash, this will take only moments. If you have boiled the squash, there will be more moisture to cook away. At this point, if you have time, I recommend that you drain the puree in a colander for a few hours to make sure the filling is not too wet, especially if you plan to assemble the pastries ahead of time. When the puree is thick, fold in the walnuts, if using, and season with a pinch of salt, especially if you are accenting the savory rather than the sweet aspects of the filling. You also can add the cheese and chopped mint or parsley for a savory version.

Preheat the oven to 350 degrees F. Oil 2 baking sheets.

Cut each filo sheet into thirds so that you end up with rectangles measuring about 6 by 12 inches. When you are not working with the filo sheets, keep them covered with a sheet of plastic wrap to prevent them from drying out.

Brush 1 filo rectangle with melted butter or oil. Layer another rectangle on top and brush with butter or oil. Place a narrow line of squash filling just inside a long edge. Fold over the edge to cover the filling and continue to roll, brushing with butter or oil as you roll, until you have a long snake. Do not roll too tightly or the cylinder may crack when you try to coil it. Coil the snake into a spiral. Again, do not form the spiral too tightly, as you do not want it to break. Repeat until all the filling and filo is used. Place the spirals on the prepared baking sheets.

Bake the pastries until golden brown, 30 to 45 minutes. Serve hot or warm.

Notes: You may assemble the spirals completely and refrigerate them for up to 2 days. Tent them loosely with aluminum foil, making sure the foil does not touch them. Just before baking, remove the pastries from the refrigerator and brush with melted butter or oil. Increase the baking time by 10 minutes.

The savory version of this filling can be stuffed into *boreka* dough (page 60). The pastries can be sprinkled lightly with grated cheese, or for contrast, cinnamon sugar.

: : : : : :

HANDRAJOS

EGGPLANT AND SQUASH PASTRIES, IZMIR STYLE

These Turkish pastries from *Sefarad Yemekleri* are also known as *borekas,* although the dough is slightly richer and more tender due to the addition of yogurt than the usual dough for *borekas.* The same filling could also be used in a *tapada* (page 59) or in filo pastries. *Handrajos* were typically served at a festive *desayuno* (breakfast).

Makes about 30 *pastries*

For the filling:

1 LARGE ZUCCHINI

SALT

1 GLOBE EGGPLANT, ABOUT 1 POUND

3 TABLESPOONS OLIVE OR VEGETABLE OIL

1 ONION, FINELY CHOPPED

1 LARGE, RIPE TOMATO, PEELED, SEEDED,
    AND FINELY CHOPPED (ABOUT 1 CUP)

1 CUP GRATED KASHKAVAL OR GRUYÈRE CHEESE
    OR A MIXTURE OF KASHKAVAL AND FETA CHEESE

FRESHLY GROUND BLACK PEPPER

FINE DRIED BREAD CRUMBS OR MATZOH MEAL,
    IF NEEDED

For the pastry:

3 $1/2$ CUPS ALL-PURPOSE FLOUR, OR AS NEEDED

1 TEASPOON SALT

$1/2$ CUP SUNFLOWER OR VEGETABLE OIL

$1/2$ CUP MARGARINE, MELTED

$1/2$ CUP PLAIN YOGURT

1 EGG, LIGHTLY BEATEN

SESAME SEEDS OR EXTRA GRATED CHEESE (OPTIONAL)

To make the filling, trim the ends of the zucchini and grate on the large holes of a cheese grater. You should have about 1 $1/2$ cups. Place in a colander, sprinkling the layers with salt. Let drain for about 20 minutes. Peel the eggplant, quarter lengthwise, and grate on the large holes of the cheese grater. You should have about 3 cups. Place in a colander, sprinkling the layers with salt, and let drain for about 20 minutes.

Warm the oil in a sauté pan over medium heat. Add the onion and sauté until translucent, about 5 minutes. Add the tomato and cook, stirring occasionally, until thickened, about 10 minutes. Rinse the zucchini and eggplant, squeeze dry, and add them to the sauté pan. Continue to sauté, stirring occasionally, until tender, about 5 minutes. Add the cheese and season with salt and pepper. Remove from the heat and let cool. If the mixture seems too wet, add the bread crumbs or matzoh meal until the ingredients bind together nicely.

Preheat the oven to 350 degrees F. Line 2 baking sheets with parchment paper.

To make the pastry, stir together the flour and salt in a bowl. Gradually add the oil, margarine, and yogurt, stirring and tossing with a fork until the dough comes together. Alternatively, combine the flour and salt in a food processor and pulse to combine, then add the oil, margarine, and yogurt and process until a dough forms. Turn out the dough onto a lightly floured work surface and knead briefly until it is cohesive.

On the floured surface, roll out the dough about $1/4$ inch thick. Cut out rounds 3 to 4 inches in diameter. Place a scant tablespoon of filling on the center of each round, brush the edge of the round

with a little of the beaten egg or some water, fold
in half, and seal securely. Place the pastries on the
parchment-lined sheets. Brush the pastries with
the beaten egg and sprinkle with sesame seeds or
grated cheese, if using.

Bake until golden, about 30 minutes. Serve hot or
warm.

: : : : : :

BOREKAS *de* KARTOF
MEAT-STUFFED POTATO PASTRIES

There are two ways to make this dish from the
Balkans. The simplest is to make mashed potatoes,
roll them into a ball, poke a hole with your finger,
tuck in the meat filling, and pinch the potato over
the filling to close. This technique is messy, however, and the potato coating can fall apart. The version presented here, which adds flour, will give you
more consistent results. The pastry is similar to one
in *Cucina Ebraica,* for a *pitta di ricotta,* a ricotta-
topped open-faced pizza made with a potato crust.
Here the dough is rolled or patted out, circles are
cut, and a meat filling is added. Then the dough is
folded over and the pastries are deep-fried. Yes,
they may be baked, but they are infinitely more
tender and the filling more juicy when fried.
Although the recipe calls for boiling the potatoes
for the dough, I prefer baking them, as the dough
will be less moist, making shaping easier.

Makes about 20 *pastries*

For the dough:
2 POUNDS POTATOES, RUSSETS IF BAKING OR YUKON
    GOLDS IF BOILING
2 EGGS, LIGHTLY BEATEN
1 TABLESPOON SALT
$1/2$ TEASPOON FRESHLY GROUND BLACK PEPPER
$1 1/2$ CUPS ALL-PURPOSE FLOUR, PLUS MORE
    FOR KNEADING

For the filling:
2 TABLESPOONS OLIVE OIL
1 ONION, MINCED
2 CLOVES GARLIC, MINCED
$1/2$ POUND GROUND BEEF
1 TEASPOON SALT
$1/2$ TEASPOON FRESHLY GROUND BLACK PEPPER

2 TABLESPOONS CHOPPED FRESH FLAT-LEAF PARSLEY

1 SLICE RUSTIC BREAD, CRUSTS REMOVED, SOAKED IN
    WATER TO COVER, AND SQUEEZED DRY (OPTIONAL)

1 EGG, LIGHTLY BEATEN

1 EGG WHITE, LIGHTLY BEATEN

VEGETABLE OIL FOR DEEP-FRYING

1 EGG YOLK, LIGHTLY BEATEN, IF BAKING PASTRIES

First, make the dough: If baking the potatoes, pre-heat the oven to 400 degrees F. Pierce the potatoes with a fork, place on the oven rack, and bake until very soft, about 1 hour. Remove from the oven and, when just cool enough to handle, cut in half, scoop out the potato flesh, and pass it through a ricer or food mill placed over a bowl. Add the eggs, salt, pepper, and enough of the flour to make a smooth dough that holds together like a gnocchi dough. Start with $1 \frac{1}{2}$ cups and knead in more flour if it is too wet. If boiling the potatoes, peel them and place in a saucepan with salted water to cover generously. Bring to a boil and cook until tender, about 30 minutes. Drain well and pass through a ricer or food mill placed over a bowl, or simply mash. Add the eggs, salt, pepper, and flour as directed above. Knead the dough on a lightly floured surface for a few minutes until it holds together and feels a bit elastic but not wet.

While the potatoes cook, make the filling: Warm the olive oil in a sauté pan over medium heat. Add the onion and sauté until tender and translucent, about 10 minutes. Add the garlic and beef and cook, breaking up the meat, until the meat is no longer pink, about 5 minutes. Add the salt, pepper, and parsley and stir well. Cook until meat is browned, about

10 minutes. Remove from the heat and stir in the soaked bread, if using, and the egg. Let the mixture cool.

On a lightly floured surface, roll out the dough $\frac{1}{3}$ to $\frac{1}{2}$ inch thick. Using a 3-inch biscuit cutter or glass, cut out rounds. Place a heaping teaspoonful of the meat mixture in the center of each circle. Run a stripe of egg white around the edge, fold in half, and press the edges together, sealing securely.

Pour vegetable oil to a depth of 2 inches into a sauté pan and heat to 350 degrees F on a deep-frying thermometer. When the oil is hot, add the pastries, in batches, and fry, turning once, until golden, about 6 minutes. Using a slotted spoon or tongs, transfer to paper towels to drain. Alternatively, arrange the pastries on an oiled baking sheet, brush the top of each pastry with egg yolk or olive oil, and bake in a 400 degree F oven until golden, about 30 minutes. Serve the pastries hot.

: : : : : :

PESAH BIRMUELOS

PASSOVER FRITTERS

Sometimes Passover *birmuelos* are made with only matzohs and eggs. But here is a mashed potato variation from *Sefarad Yemekleri.* I think these have a nicer texture than the plain matzoh ones. Chopped parsley, chives, or dill is a nice addition.

Makes about 30 *fritters*

4 MATZOHS

2 CUPS MASHED POTATOES

1 CUP GRATED PARMESAN CHEESE

4 EGGS

2 TEASPOONS SALT

$1/2$ TEASPOON FRESHLY GROUND BLACK PEPPER

$1/4$ CUP CHOPPED FRESH FLAT-LEAF PARSLEY,
    CHIVES, OR DILL (OPTIONAL)

VEGETABLE OIL FOR DEEP-FRYING

In a bowl, soak the matzohs in water to cover until soft, about 3 minutes. Drain well, squeeze dry, and transfer to a dry bowl. Add the potatoes, cheese, eggs, salt, pepper, and the herb, if using, and mix well with your hands. Dampen your hands and shape the mixture into 2-inch balls.

Pour the vegetable oil to a depth of 3 inches into a large, deep sauté pan and heat to 375 degrees F on a deep-frying thermometer. Add the fritters, in batches, and fry until golden, 3 to 4 minutes. Using tongs or a slotted spoon, transfer to paper towels to drain. Serve hot.

: : : : : :

BOREKAS *de* KARNE

MEAT-FILLED PASTRIES FROM RHODES

These borekas, also known as *pastilicos de carne,* are a Hanukkah treat from Rhodes. Gilda Angel uses a meat filling similar to the one used for *borekas de kartof* (page 66), but note that the dough is folded in a different way. This dough is crispier than that used for a *tapada* (page 59). Fish fillings are sometimes used as well, and one is included here.

Makes 20 TO 24 *pastries*

For the meat filling:

2 TABLESPOONS OLIVE OIL

1 ONION, MINCED

2 CLOVES GARLIC, MINCED

$1/2$ POUND GROUND BEEF

1 TEASPOON SALT

$1/2$ TEASPOON FRESHLY GROUND BLACK PEPPER

2 TABLESPOONS CHOPPED FRESH FLAT-LEAF PARSLEY

For the fish filling:

2 TABLESPOONS OLIVE OIL

1 LARGE ONION, CHOPPED

2 CUPS FLAKED COOKED FISH SUCH AS SALMON,
    MACKEREL, OR TUNA

$1/2$ CUP COOKED WHITE RICE OR MASHED POTATO

$1/4$ CUP CHOPPED FRESH FLAT-LEAF PARSLEY

$1/4$ CUP CHOPPED FRESH DILL (OPTIONAL)

$1/4$ CUP CHOPPED WALNUTS (OPTIONAL)

1 EGG, LIGHTLY BEATEN

SALT AND FRESHLY GROUND BLACK PEPPER

For the pastry:
1 CUP WARM WATER
$^1/_2$ CUP VEGETABLE OIL
1 TEASPOON SALT
3 $^1/_2$ CUPS ALL-PURPOSE FLOUR, OR AS NEEDED

1 EGG, LIGHTLY BEATEN
SESAME SEEDS

Make either the meat filling or the fish filling. To make the meat filling, warm the olive oil in a sauté pan over medium heat. Add the onion and sauté until tender and translucent, about 10 minutes. Add the garlic and beef and cook, breaking up the meat, until the meat is no longer pink, about 5 minutes. Add the salt, pepper, and parsley and continue to cook, stirring occasionally, until the meat is browned, about 10 minutes longer. Remove from the heat and let cool.

If making the fish filling, warm the olive oil in a sauté pan over medium heat. Add the onion and sauté until tender and golden, about 12 minutes. Remove from the heat and let cool, then place in a bowl. Add the fish, rice or potato, parsley, and the dill and walnuts, if using. Mix well, add the egg, and season with salt and pepper. Set aside.

To make the pastry, combine the warm water and oil in a bowl. Add the salt, then gradually work in 3 $^1/_2$ cups flour with a fork to form a dough, adding more flour if it seems too wet. Turn out the dough onto a lightly floured work surface and knead it until it is elastic and holds together.

Preheat the oven to 400 degrees F. Line 2 baking sheets with parchment paper.

On the floured work surface, roll out the dough about $^1/_4$ inch thick. Cut out rounds 3 to 4 inches in diameter, reserving the trimmings. Place a tablespoon of filling on the center of each round and fold up three sides into a triangular shape, similar to shaping hamantaschen. Using the dough scraps, top each pastry with a piece of dough, forming a cap and pressing to seal. Alternatively, do not roll out the dough. Instead, pull off pieces of the dough and shape into walnut-sized balls. Make a hollow with your fingers, forming a cuplike shape, and tuck a little of the filling into the hollow. Then top the hollow with a small, flat piece of dough. Pinch the edges to seal. (The fish-filled pastries also may be made into simple half-moons, using the same-sized rounds as for the triangular pastries and folding them in half.) Arrange the pastries on the prepared baking sheets. Brush with the beaten egg and sprinkle with the sesame seeds.

Bake the pastries until golden, about 25 minutes. Serve hot or warm.

: : : : : :

MANTIKOS

STUFFED BREAD DOUGH PASTRIES

Traditional Turkish *manti* are made with a kind of pasta dough and are usually dressed with paprika and melted butter or yogurt and garlic sauce. The Sephardic *mantikos* pastry from Cannakale is a yeast-raised dough. The meat-filled pastries might accompany a bowl of soup for supper.

Makes 18 TO 24 *pastries*

For the starter:

1 ENVELOPE (2 $^1/_4$ TEASPOONS) ACTIVE DRY YEAST

$^1/_2$ TEASPOON SUGAR

1 CUP LUKEWARM WATER

2 TABLESPOONS ALL-PURPOSE FLOUR

For the dough:

2 $^3/_4$ CUPS ALL-PURPOSE FLOUR

1 TEASPOON SALT

1 TEASPOON PLUS $^1/_3$ CUP VEGETABLE OIL

For the meat filling:

2 TO 3 TABLESPOONS OLIVE OR VEGETABLE OIL

2 ONIONS, CHOPPED

2 CLOVES GARLIC, MINCED

1 POUND GROUND BEEF

2 TEASPOONS SALT

1 TEASPOON FRESHLY GROUND BLACK PEPPER

$^1/_4$ CUP CHOPPED FRESH FLAT-LEAF PARSLEY

For the spinach filling:

1 POUND SPINACH, STEMS REMOVED

2 EGGS, LIGHTLY BEATEN

$^1/_4$ POUND FETA CHEESE, CRUMBLED

$^1/_2$ CUP RICOTTA CHEESE, OR $^1/_4$ POUND KASHKAVAL
    OR GRUYÈRE CHEESE, GRATED

FRESHLY GRATED NUTMEG

SALT AND FRESHLY GROUND BLACK PEPPER

For the onion and cheese filling:

3 TABLESPOONS OLIVE OR VEGETABLE OIL
    OR MARGARINE

4 LARGE ONIONS, THINLY SLICED

$^1/_2$ POUND FETA CHEESE, CRUMBLED

$^1/_2$ POUND RICOTTA CHEESE, FROMAGE BLANC,
    OR COTTAGE CHEESE

2 EGGS, LIGHTLY BEATEN

$^1/_4$ CUP CHOPPED FRESH DILL

FRESHLY GRATED BLACK PEPPER

FRESHLY GRATED NUTMEG (OPTIONAL)

1 EGG, BEATEN WITH A LITTLE WATER

To make the starter, in a small bowl, dissolve the yeast and sugar in the lukewarm water, then stir in the flour. Set aside for 10 minutes until frothy.

To make the dough, in a bowl, stir together the flour, salt, and the 1 teaspoon oil. Add the starter and using a stand mixer fitted with a dough hook, beat on medium speed until a soft dough forms, about 10 minutes. Turn out the dough onto a lightly floured work surface and divide into 18 to 24 balls. Place the balls in a bowl, add the $^1/_3$ cup oil, and toss to coat the balls with the oil. Cover with a kitchen towel and let rise until almost doubled in size, about 30 minutes.

Meanwhile, select one of the fillings and prepare it. If making the meat filling, warm the olive oil in a sauté pan over medium heat. Add the onions and sauté until tender and translucent, about 10 minutes. Add the garlic and beef and cook, breaking up the meat, until the meat is no longer pink, about

5 minutes. Add the salt, pepper, and parsley and continue to cook, stirring occasionally, until the meat is browned, about 10 minutes. Remove from the heat and let cool.

To make the spinach filling, cook until wilted in the rinsing water clinging to the leaves, squeeze the spinach dry, and chop finely. Place in a bowl and add the eggs and cheeses. Mix well and season with the nutmeg, salt, and pepper.

To make the onion and cheese filling, warm the oil or margarine in a sauté pan over medium heat. Add the onions and sauté until soft and golden, about 15 minutes. Remove from the heat, place in a bowl, and let cool. Fold in the cheeses, eggs, and dill and season with pepper and with nutmeg, if using.

Preheat the oven to 350 degrees F. Line 2 baking sheets with parchment paper.

On a lightly floured work surface, roll out a ball of dough into a rectangle or square about 1/3 inch thick. Place a generous tablespoon of filling on the center of the dough. Fold in the sides, fold up the bottom, then fold the top over the bottom to seal. Pinch the seams together securely and place seam side down on a prepared baking sheet. Repeat until all the pastries are filled. Brush the tops with the egg wash.

Bake the pastries until golden, 25 to 30 minutes. Serve hot or warm.

: : : : : :

REVANADAS de PARIDA PASQUALES
FRIED MATZOH SQUARES FOR PASSOVER

The name translates as "Passover toast for the new mother," but if this recipe from *Sefarad Yemekleri* reminds you of *matzoh brei* (omelet), you would be almost right. In this Turkish Sephardic dish, however, each matzoh is broken into four squares, soaked in lightly salted water, and then dipped in pairs in beaten egg and fried. The hot squares are topped with either grated cheese or, for a sweet *desayuno* version, with syrup or honey.

Serves 4

2 MATZOHS
1 EGG
SUNFLOWER OIL FOR FRYING
GRATED KASSERI OR OTHER SHEEP'S MILK CHEESE
    OR WARMED SYRUP OR FRAGRANT HONEY

I think it is difficult to break each matzoh into 4 even squares. Your chances are much improved if you soak them for about 3 minutes in salted cold water to cover and then cut them with a sharp knife. Drain well and layer them in pairs. Lightly beat the egg in a shallow bowl.

Film a large sauté pan with vegetable oil and place over medium heat. When the oil is hot, dip the layered matzoh squares in the beaten egg and slip them into the pan. Fry, turning once, until golden, about 5 minutes. Using a slotted spatula or pancake turner, transfer to paper towels to drain.

Place the squares on a platter and, while still warm, sprinkle with grated cheese or drizzle or spoon on the warmed syrup or honey. Serve warm.

: : : : : :

SKALTSOUNIA

FRIED TURNOVERS

The dough used in these fried turnovers, also known as *kalsones,* is almost identical to an Italian egg pasta. The pastries can be filled with cheese or meat, and in Crete are traditionally spicy with red chile. Both fillings would work in *mantikos* (page 71) as well. As these are fried, they would be ideal for Hanukkah.

Makes about 24 pastries

For the dough:

3 CUPS ALL-PURPOSE FLOUR, OR AS NEEDED

1 TEASPOON SALT

2 EGGS BEATEN WITH $^1/_4$ CUP COLD WATER, OR 4 EGGS

For the meat filling:

1 TABLESPOON OLIVE OIL

1 ONION, FINELY CHOPPED

$^1/_2$ POUND GROUND BEEF

1 TO 2 TEASPOONS RED PEPPER FLAKES

1 TEASPOON GROUND CUMIN

2 TABLESPOONS CHOPPED FRESH MINT

SALT AND FRESHLY GROUND BLACK PEPPER

For the cheese filling:

2 OR 3 EGGS, LIGHTLY BEATEN

$^3/_4$ CUP GRATED PARMESAN CHEESE

$^3/_4$ CUP FARMER OR RICOTTA CHEESE

2 TO 3 TABLESPOONS PLAIN YOGURT

1 TO 2 TEASPOONS RED PEPPER FLAKES

$^1/_4$ CUP CHOPPED FRESH MINT

VEGETABLE OIL FOR DEEP-FRYING

To make the dough, stir together the 3 cups flour and salt in a bowl. Make a well in the center and add egg-water mixture or the eggs. Using a fork, gradually pull the flour into the egg mixture and stir until a dough forms. Turn out onto a lightly floured work surface and knead until smooth and elastic, about 10 minutes, adding more flour if the dough seems too wet. Let the dough rest for 30 minutes.

To make the meat filling, warm the oil in a sauté pan over medium heat. Add the onion and sauté until tender and translucent, about 10 minutes. Add the beef and cook, breaking it up, until well browned, about 10 minutes longer. Remove from the heat and stir in the red pepper flakes, cumin, and mint and season with salt and pepper.

To make the cheese filling, in a bowl, combine the eggs and cheeses. Add only enough yogurt to hold mixture together and make it creamy. Mix in the red pepper flakes and mint.

On the floured work surface, roll out the dough as thinly as possible—$^1/_8$ inch thick or less. (You can roll the dough through a pasta machine.) Cut out rounds 4 inches in diameter. Then roll out the rounds even thinner, until they are 5 inches in diameter. Place a heaping tablespoon of filling in the center of each round, moisten the edges with water, fold in half, and pinch the edges together.

Pour vegetable oil to a depth of 2 inches into a deep sauté pan or saucepan and heat to 350 degrees F on a deep-frying thermometer. Add the pastries, in batches, and fry until golden, 4 to 5 minutes. Using a slotted spoon or wire skimmer, transfer to paper towels to drain. Serve hot.

: : : : : :

PESAH TYROPITA

PASSOVER CHEESE PIE FROM HANIA

Although this pie is called *tyropita* by Nicholas
Stavroulakis, it is not the familiar triangle-shaped
filo pastry that most people recognize by that
name. It is a *mina* or *pastel de kwezo,* that is, a cheese
pie. Using just mezithra and/or feta and Parmesan
makes for a dryish but tasty filling, despite the 6
eggs. I suggest adding some ricotta to the mix,
using perhaps 1 cup in place of an equal amount of
the mezithra. Or serve with something a bit soupy
on the same plate. Or, better yet, serve with soup.

Serves 8 as a main dish, or 12 for a side dish

1 POUND MEZITHRA CHEESE, GRATED; $^1/_2$ POUND
    EACH FETA CHEESE, CRUMBLED, AND PARMESAN
    CHEESE, GRATED; OR $^1/_4$ POUND EACH FETA CHEESE,
    CRUMBLED, AND MONTEREY JACK OR GRUYÈRE
    CHEESE, GRATED
$^1/_4$ CUP OLIVE OIL, PLUS MORE FOR DRIZZLING
$^1/_2$ CUP CHOPPED FRESH DILL
$^1/_4$ CUP CHOPPED FRESH MINT
6 EGGS, SEPARATED
SALT, IF NEEDED
6 TO 8 MATZOHS, OR ENOUGH TO LINE
    THE PAN IN 2 FULL LAYERS

Preheat the oven to 375 degrees F. Oil a 10-by-14-
by-2-inch baking pan.

In a bowl, combine the cheeses, $^1/_4$ cup olive oil, dill,
and mint. In a separate bowl, whisk together the egg
yolks until creamy and fold into the cheeses. In yet
another bowl, beat the egg whites until stiff peaks
form. Fold the whites into the cheese mixture. You
probably will not need any salt, as the cheeses are
rather salty.

Select a shallow bowl large enough to hold about
half of the matzohs and fill with cold water. Dip 3
matzohs in the water for about 3 minutes to soften,
then drain well and place in the prepared pan. Drizzle
with olive oil. Top with the cheese filling and drizzle
more oil over the top. Soften as many more matzohs
as are needed to cover the filling. Drizzle the top
with olive oil.

Bake the pie until the top is browned, 30 to 45
minutes. Remove from the oven and let rest for
10 minutes, then cut into squares and serve.

Note: You can make half the recipe and bake
the pie in an 8-inch square baking pan.

: : : : : :

MEGINA

MEAT AND MATZOH PIE FROM RHODES

The meat-filled version of a *mina,* a layered matzoh pie, is called a *megina,* and it is a specialty of Rhodes. This recipe is a composite of those from Gilda Angel, Nicholas Stavroulakis, and the authors of *Sefarad Yemekleri.* Occasionally, mashed potato is added to the ground meat filling, but the primary variables are the amounts of eggs and matzohs. I find the seasoning rather bland, so some cinnamon added to the meat would not be out of place. Serving the *megina* with tomato sauce or sautéed mushrooms would liven it up as well. Otherwise you may find it rather dry.

Serves 8

2 TABLESPOONS OLIVE OR VEGETABLE OIL

2 ONIONS, CHOPPED

2 POUNDS GROUND BEEF

2 TEASPOONS SALT

$1/2$ TEASPOON FRESHLY GROUND BLACK PEPPER

1 TEASPOON GROUND CINNAMON (OPTIONAL)

8 OR 9 EGGS

$1/2$ CUP CHOPPED FRESH FLAT-LEAF PARSLEY

$1/2$ CUP CHOPPED FRESH DILL

8 TO 10 MATZOHS, OR ENOUGH TO LINE
    THE PAN IN 2 FULL LAYERS

Warm the oil in a large sauté pan over medium heat. Add the onions and sauté until tender and translucent, about 10 minutes. Add the meat and cook, breaking it up, until well browned, about 15 minutes. Season with the salt and pepper and the cinnamon, if using, then remove from the heat. In a bowl, lightly whisk 4 or 5 of the eggs and fold into the meat mixture along with the parsley and dill.

Preheat the oven to 375 degrees F. Oil a 10-by-13-by-2-inch baking dish.

Select a shallow bowl large enough to hold about half the matzohs and fill with cold water. In a second shallow bowl of the same size, whisk 2 of the eggs until blended. Dip 4 or 5 matzohs in the water for about 3 minutes to soften, then drain well and dip them in the beaten eggs until the eggs are absorbed. Lay the matzohs on the bottom of the prepared baking dish, covering it completely. Top with the meat mixture. Whisk the remaining 2 or 3 eggs until blended, then soften the remaining 4 or 5 matzohs in the same way and dip them in the eggs until they absorb the eggs. Place the matzohs on top of the filling. Pour any remaining beaten egg over the top.

Bake the pie until golden, about 45 minutes. Remove from the oven and let rest for 10 minutes, then cut into squares and serve.

: : : : : :

MINA *di* PRASA *con* QUESO

LEEK-AND-CHEESE MATZOH PIE

Minas are Passover pies, lasagnelike pastries using soaked matzoh in place of pasta. They can be filled with vegetables, cheeses, or meat. Early recipes advise a soaking time that would be too long for our crackerlike matzohs. The handmade matzohs of Greece and Italy were often round and were much thicker and harder than our delicate and crisp factory-made ones. The time it takes for our matzohs to soften without disintegrating is about 3 minutes. Often they are soaked in water and then dipped in egg, which is impossible to do if they have fallen apart. Some recipes call for soaking the matzohs in water, beating the eggs, and then pouring the eggs over the top.

Serves 4 as a main course, or 6 TO 8 *as a side dish*

5 MEDIUM LEEKS

3 TABLESPOONS UNSALTED BUTTER, VEGETABLE OIL,
   OR MARGARINE

1 ONION, CHOPPED

1 CUP ($^1/_2$ POUND) RICOTTA OR FARMER CHEESE

3 EGGS

1 $^1/_2$ TEASPOONS SALT, OR TO TASTE

$^1/_2$ TEASPOON FRESHLY GROUND BLACK PEPPER

FRESHLY GRATED NUTMEG

$^1/_4$ CUP CHOPPED FRESH DILL

4 MATZOHS

1 $^1/_3$ CUPS GRATED KASHKAVAL OR GRUYÈRE CHEESE
   (ABOUT 5 OUNCES)

Cut away the root ends from the leeks and most of the green part and discard. Peel away any loose layers, cut the leeks in half lengthwise, and then cut crosswise into thin slices. If the leeks are very fat, coarsely-chop them. Soak the leeks in a sink full of cold water, swish them around to loosen any dirt, remove with a slotted spoon, and drain well in a colander. You will have about 3 $^1/_2$ cups chopped leeks.

Warm the butter, oil, or margarine in a large sauté pan over medium heat. Add the leeks and onion and cook, stirring often, until the leeks are very tender, 15 to 20 minutes, adding water as needed to help soften them. Make sure that all of the water has evaporated by the time the leeks are ready. If it has not, drain them well. Remove from the heat, cool, and mix in the ricotta or farmer cheese, 2 of the eggs, salt, pepper, nutmeg to taste, and dill.

Preheat the oven to 375 degrees F. Oil an 8-inch square baking pan.

Beat the remaining egg in a shallow bowl large enough to hold a matzoh. Put cold water in another bowl. Soak the matzoh in the water for about 3 minutes, then drain. Dip the matzoh in the egg, then place in the prepared baking pan. Repeat, using enough additional matzoh to fill in any spaces in the pan. Sprinkle with $^2/_3$ cup of the grated cheese, and top with the leek mixture. Dip the remaining matzohs in water for about 3 minutes, drain, and then dip in the egg and place on the leek mixture. Top with the rest of the grated cheese. Bake the pie until browned, 30 to 40 minutes. Remove from the oven and let rest for 10 minutes, then cut into squares and serve.

Variation: Use 1 to 2 pounds spinach, cooked and chopped, in place of the leeks or in addition to them. This will make the filling wetter, however, so you may need to add 1 cup mashed potatoes and increase the grated cheese to $^1/_2$ pound.

: : : : : :

SOUPS

chapter 3

✶

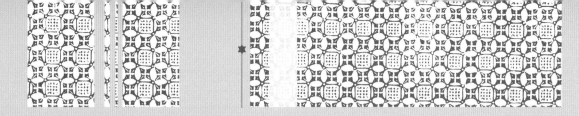

SOUPS

Soup was an everyday affair in the traditional Sephardic kitchen. But because cooks usually relied on leftovers to fill the soup pot, recipes were rarely recorded. Therefore, I have been unable to put together a large repertoire of recipes for this chapter. Most Sephardic soups are simple stocks enriched with rice or matzoh, embellished with small balls of beef or chicken, or thickened with cheese or with egg and lemon. Stocks are often based on vegetables or a vegetable puree, and lentils and chickpeas are sometimes added. *Skordozoumi,* a garlic broth garnished with croutons and thickened with yogurt and cheese, is a good example of a typical soup.

The Sephardic community in every country has a signature long-simmered one-pot meal of meats and vegetables eaten in a single big bowl, or in courses, with the soup followed by the meats and vegetables. For the Ashkenazic Jews, it is *cholent,* probably from the Spanish *escallento,* which means "to keep warm." In Morocco, it is *adafina,* meaning "buried," as the pot was traditionally buried in the ashes of the oven. The *cocido* in Spain and the *cozido* in Portugal are believed to have originated with the *adafina,* arriving with the Moors in the eighth century.

In keeping with the kosher laws that forbade cooking on the Sabbath, ingredients for these hearty dishes would be assembled in a single pot and cooked over very low heat overnight, to be served for lunch the next day. Thus, many Sephardic "soups" became these hearty meals-in-a-bowl on the Sabbath. *Sopa de avikas*—white beans with beef—is the classic. The importance of *cocido* and beans in the Sephardic kitchen is revealed in the fact that the Spanish word both for bean and for Jewess is *judía.* In Spain, the *cocido* eventually was used by the leaders of the Inquisition as a litmus test of faith for *conversos.* Confronted with a *cocido* prepared with lard or pork, true *conversos* would eat it. Anyone who refused revealed his or her continued adherence to Judaism.

MIJAVYANI ★ VEGETABLE SOUP WITH PLUMS

MIJAVYANI

VEGETABLE SOUP WITH PLUMS

From *Sefarad Yemekleri* comes this deliciously lively "Georgian-style" soup served in Turkey. Greengage plums add both sweetness and tartness to the combination of herb-scented beef, onion, and rice. Keeping with Turkish Sephardic tradition, lemon juice is added for additional tartness. If you don't have leftover stewing beef, you can braise some cubed beef chuck or brisket in water or stock for about an hour and add it and the cooking liquid to the soup. And if you cannot find Greengage plums, any tart plum will do.

Serves 6

3 TABLESPOONS VEGETABLE OIL

2 YELLOW ONIONS, CHOPPED, OR 2 BUNCHES GREEN
   ONIONS, INCLUDING GREEN TOPS, CHOPPED

1/2 POUND GREENGAGE OR OTHER TART PLUMS (3 OR 4),
   PITTED AND CHOPPED

1 BUNCH FRESH DILL, CHOPPED (4 TO 6 TABLESPOONS)

3 TABLESPOONS CHOPPED FRESH MINT

1/2 CUP CHOPPED FRESH FLAT-LEAF PARSLEY

1/4 CUP LONG-GRAIN WHITE RICE

4 TO 6 TABLESPOONS FRESH LEMON JUICE

1 TEASPOON SUGAR

2 TEASPOONS TOMATO PASTE

1 POUND COOKED BEEF BRISKET, CUT INTO
   BITE-SIZE PIECES

MEAT STOCK OR WATER, TO COVER

SALT AND FRESHLY GROUND BLACK PEPPER

Warm the vegetable oil in a large saucepan over medium heat. Add the onions and sauté until tender and translucent, about 10 minutes. Add the plums, half of the dill, the mint, half of the parsley, the rice, lemon juice to taste, sugar, tomato paste, and beef. Stir well and add meat stock or water to cover. Bring to a boil, reduce the heat to low, cover, and simmer until the rice is cooked, about 20 minutes.

Season with salt and pepper and sprinkle with the remaining dill and parsley. Ladle into bowls and serve.

: : : : : :

SOPA *de* LENTEJAS COLORADA

LENTIL SOUP

When served during the Nine Days of Tisha B'Av, lentil soup is traditionally accompanied with cheese *borekas* for a complete meal, although you can serve this soup any time you like. Méri Badi's recipe is fairly austere, but some optional spicing would be a pinch or two of ground cumin, a small pinch of cayenne, and a spritz of lemon juice to brighten the flavors. Sometimes cooked wheat or rice is added. Greek Jews commonly pass olive oil and vinegar at the table.

Serves 4 TO 6

1 1/2 CUPS RED LENTILS

1/4 CUP VEGETABLE OR OLIVE OIL

2 OR 3 ONIONS, CHOPPED

3 CELERY STALKS, CHOPPED

4 CARROTS, PEELED AND CHOPPED

1 OR 2 RIPE TOMATOES, PEELED, SEEDED,
   AND FINELY CHOPPED, OR 2 TABLESPOONS
   TOMATO PASTE (OPTIONAL)

1/2 CUP CHOPPED FRESH FLAT-LEAF PARSLEY

1 BAY LEAF

8 CUPS WATER

2 TEASPOONS SALT

FRESHLY GROUND BLACK PEPPER

1 TO 2 TEASPOONS GROUND CUMIN (OPTIONAL)

PINCH OF CAYENNE (OPTIONAL)

LEMON JUICE OR VINEGAR (OPTIONAL)

Pick over the lentils for any stones or other impurities and rinse well. Place in a bowl with water to cover and let stand for a few hours. Drain.

Warm the oil in a large saucepan over medium heat. Add the onions and sauté until tender and translucent, about 10 minutes. Add the lentils, celery, carrots, tomatoes or tomato paste (if using), parsley, bay leaf, and water and bring to a boil. Reduce the heat to low, cover, and simmer until the lentils are tender, about 1 hour.

Remove the bay leaf and add the salt, pepper to taste, the cumin, and the cayenne and lemon juice or vinegar to taste, if using. Taste and adjust the seasonings. Ladle into bowls and serve.

: : : : : :

SOPA *de* ALBÓNDIGAS

MEATBALL SOUP

While I found this recipe in *Sefarad Yemekleri,* a cookbook compiled by the Jewish community in Istanbul, the word *albóndiga,* which comes from the Arabic word for "round," is actually Spanish for "meatball." In this version of the soup, the meatballs are cooked directly in the stock rather than being browned first. The optional onion and cinnamon give the meatballs a nice flavor boost.

Serves 4 TO 6

1 POUND GROUND BEEF OR LAMB

1 LARGE SLICE RUSTIC BREAD, CRUSTS REMOVED,
    SOAKED IN WATER, AND SQUEEZED DRY

SALT AND FRESHLY GROUND BLACK PEPPER

$^{1}/_{4}$ CUP GRATED ONION (OPTIONAL)

PINCH OF GROUND CINNAMON (OPTIONAL)

6 TO 7 CUPS WATER OR MEAT STOCK

VEGETABLE OIL

4 BOILING POTATOES, PEELED AND CUT INTO
    BATONS EACH ABOUT $^{1}/_{4}$ INCH WIDE AND
    THICK AND 1$^{1}/_{2}$ INCHES LONG

3 CARROTS, PEELED AND CUT INTO BATONS EACH ABOUT
    $^{1}/_{4}$ INCH WIDE AND THICK AND 1$^{1}/_{2}$ INCHES LONG

$^{1}/_{2}$ CUP FINELY CHOPPED CELERY LEAVES

In a bowl, combine the meat, bread, salt and pepper to taste, and the onion and/or cinnamon, if using. Knead the meat mixture until it holds together. Form into tiny meatballs about $^{3}/_{4}$ inch in diameter. Set aside.

In a large saucepan, combine the water or meat stock and a few tablespoons of vegetable oil and bring to a boil. Add the potatoes and carrots and simmer for 10 minutes. Add the meatballs and simmer until the vegetables are tender and the meatballs are cooked through, about 10 minutes longer. Ladle into bowls and sprinkle with celery leaves.

Variation: You can thicken this soup with egg and lemon. Whisk 2 egg yolks with $^{1}/_{4}$ cup fresh lemon juice until quite frothy. Whisk in a little of the hot soup to temper the eggs, then gradually stir the eggs into the soup over very low heat. Cook very gently for about 1 minute, but do not boil. Remove from the heat. Once the egg-and-lemon mixture is added, you may not reheat the soup or it will curdle.

: : : : : :

MANGIR CORBASI

PENNY SOUP

A *mangir* was an Ottoman coin of very low value. In Turkey, the pasta used in this soup was *farfur,* a tiny, flat pelletlike homemade pasta in the shape of a coin, thus the name Penny Soup. This Ma'min recipe is from Esin Eden. For ease, use broken vermicelli, orzo, or *pastina* in place of the homemade egg pasta. This same soup made with rice instead of noodles is called *sopa de huevo y limon* and was eaten to break the Yom Kippur fast in Salonika. During Passover in Greece and Turkey, broken matzohs replace the noodles, and the soup is called *sodra,* which means "deaf." In *La table juive,* the recipe for *sodra* calls for simmering 3 broken matzoh in 6 cups chicken stock for 5 minutes, and then adding a mixture of 4 eggs and the juice of 2 lemons. Although the addition of the egg-and-lemon mixture in all these versions guarantees a nicely tart soup, lemon wedges are still passed at the table.

Serves 4 TO 6

2 TABLESPOONS MARGARINE

1$^{1}/_{2}$ CUPS ORZO, *PASTINA,* OR OTHER SMALL PASTA

4 CUPS MEAT OR CHICKEN STOCK, OR AS NEEDED

2 EGGS

JUICE OF 2 LEMONS

SALT AND FRESHLY GROUND BLACK PEPPER

2 TO 3 TABLESPOONS CHOPPED FRESH MINT OR
   FLAT-LEAF PARSLEY

LEMON WEDGES

Melt the margarine in a saucepan over medium heat. Add half of the pasta and cook, stirring often, until pale gold, about 5 minutes.

Meanwhile, bring the 4 cups stock to a simmer in a separate saucepan. When the pasta is golden, add the hot stock and the remaining uncooked pasta to the pan and simmer gently, uncovered, until the pasta is tender. The timing will depend upon the type of pasta used. If the soup is too thick, thin with more stock.

In a bowl, beat together the eggs and lemon juice until quite frothy. Whisk in a little of the hot soup to temper the eggs, then gradually stir the eggs into the soup over low heat. Cook very gently for about 1 minute, but do not boil. Season to taste with salt and pepper. Ladle into bowls and garnish with the mint or parsley. Pass the lemon wedges at the table.

: : : : : :

SKORDOZOUMI

GARLIC SOUP

Skordo is Greek for "garlic." Unlike the Spanish and Portuguese garlic soups, which add only eggs for thickening, this Greek version, adapted from a recipe by Nicholas Stavroulakis, adds yogurt and feta cheese, along with the eggs, to thicken and enrich the basic soup. *Skordozoumi* may be related to the famous *sopa maimonides,* which is described as a specialty of the Andalusian Jews in Pepita Aris's *A Flavor of Andalusia.* The latter lacks the Middle Eastern additions of yogurt and feta, however. In the Sephardic cookbook published by Temple Or Ve Shalom in Atlanta, a similar garlic soup is called *pappa,* a term that probably relates more to bread than to garlic. In the Atlanta version much less garlic is used, milk replaces the yogurt, and lots of toasted croutons are added.

Serves 4

SKORDOZOUMI ★ GARLIC SOUP

3 CUPS WATER

2 TABLESPOONS OLIVE OIL

1 HEAD GARLIC, SEPARATED INTO CLOVES, PEELED,
     AND VERY THINLY SLICED

SALT AND FRESHLY GROUND BLACK PEPPER

$1/4$ POUND FETA CHEESE, FINELY CRUMBLED

1 CUP PLAIN YOGURT, BEATEN UNTIL CREAMY

2 EGGS, BEATEN UNTIL FROTHY

2 TO 4 SLICES RUSTIC BREAD, TOASTED, CRUSTS
     REMOVED, AND CUT INTO CROUTONS

In a saucepan, combine the water and olive oil and bring to a boil over high heat. Add the garlic and salt and pepper to taste, reduce the heat to medium, and simmer, uncovered, for 10 minutes. Add the cheese and yogurt and stir over very low heat for 2 to 3 minutes until well combined. Do not allow the soup to boil.

Remove the soup from the heat, let stand for a minute or two, and then gradually beat in the eggs. Taste and adjust the seasonings, then ladle into bowls. Garnish each serving with a generous helping of croutons.

: : : : : :

DOMATESLI PIRINC CORBASI

TOMATO AND RICE SOUP

In her book on the food of the Ma'min Jews of Salonika, Esin Eden offers this tomato soup recipe, but she uses butter with chicken stock. Members of the Ma'min sect, followers of Shabbatai Zevi, eventually became Muslims. Although their recipes carry a Jewish heritage, they have a casual disregard for the no-dairy-with-meat rule. I have adjusted this recipe and others to stay within the kosher laws. If you prefer butter over margarine or oil, use vegetable stock in place of the chicken stock.

Serves 4 TO 6

2 TABLESPOONS OLIVE OIL OR MARGARINE

3 POUNDS VERY RIPE TOMATOES, PEELED, SEEDED,
     AND COARSELY CHOPPED

3 OR 4 CUPS CHICKEN STOCK

$1/4$ CUP LONG-GRAIN WHITE RICE

SALT AND FRESHLY GROUND BLACK PEPPER

3 TABLESPOONS CHOPPED FRESH FLAT-LEAF PARSLEY

LEMON WEDGES

Warm the olive oil or margarine in a large saucepan over medium heat. Add the tomatoes and cook, stirring often and smashing them down with a wooden spoon, until they break down completely into a puree, about 10 minutes.

Meanwhile, heat the chicken stock in a separate saucepan to a simmer. Add 3 cups of the hot stock and the rice to the tomatoes and bring the mixture to a boil over high heat. Reduce the heat to low and simmer uncovered, stirring occasionally, until the rice is tender, 15 to 20 minutes. If the soup is too thick, thin as needed with the remaining 1 cup stock.

Season with salt and pepper and stir in the parsley. Ladle into bowls and pass the lemon wedges at the table.

: : : : : :

SOPA *de* AVIKAS

WHITE BEAN SOUP

This Greek soup closely resembles a *cocido,* the classic Spanish Sabbath dish. The beans and meat are simmered over very low heat for hours, and sometimes eggs are cooked in their shells along with them. In Christian Spain, pork was added to this Sabbath stew, as a test to prove a Jew had converted. This version from Salonika can be served quite thick and stewlike, or it can be thinned and served as a filling soup. Nicholas Stavroulakis suggests accompanying it with lemon wedges, as the acidity cuts the richness.

Serves 6

1 CUP DRIED WHITE BEANS

1 POUND BONELESS BEEF STEW MEAT SUCH AS CHUCK,
    SHANK, OR BRISKET, CUT INTO 1$^{1}/_{2}$-INCH CUBES

3 TABLESPOONS OLIVE OIL

2 ONIONS, CHOPPED

2 CLOVES GARLIC, MINCED

3 LARGE, RIPE TOMATOES, PEELED, SEEDED, AND
    CHOPPED

SALT AND FRESHLY GROUND BLACK PEPPER

$^{1}/_{4}$ CUP CHOPPED FRESH FLAT-LEAF PARSLEY

LEMON WEDGES

Pick over the beans for stones or other impurities and rinse well. Place in a bowl with water to cover generously and let soak overnight.

The next day, put the beef in a saucepan and add water to cover. Bring to a boil over high heat and cook for 10 minutes, skimming off any foam from the surface. Cover, reduce the heat to low, and simmer, for 30 to 40 minutes.

Meanwhile, drain the beans, place them in a saucepan, and add fresh water to cover. Bring to a boil over high heat and cook, uncovered, for 15 minutes. Drain the beans and add them to the meat.

Warm the olive oil in a sauté pan over medium heat. Add the onions and sauté until tender and translucent, about 10 minutes. Add the garlic and tomatoes and cook until the tomatoes break down and form a sauce, about 10 minutes. Add the contents of the sauté pan to the beans and meat, stir well, cover, and simmer until the meat and beans are tender, about 1 hour longer. If the soup is too thick, thin with a little water. Season to taste with salt and pepper and add the parsley. Ladle into bowls and pass the lemon wedges at the table.

Variation: In his book *The Cross and the Pear Tree,* Victor Perera lovingly talks of the Sabbath dinner cooked by his mother. "Mother had made her traditional hamin . . . eggs and a shank of beef, all cooked with white beans. The pleasant cooking smells would waft all over the house . . . after the meal we would all sing the lovely and unusual Sabbath melodies in Spanish." He may have been talking about a variation on *sopa de avikas* called *fijones con seboya moraderba con toutano* (beef and bean soup with marrow) in which 6 eggs are cooked in their shells along with the beans. Marrow bones are cooked separately, then the beans, bones, and eggs are simmered together. To serve, the very soft beans and stock are ladled into soup bowls. The eggs are shelled under cold water, coarsely chopped, and added to the soup. Finally, the marrow is scooped out of the bones and added to the bowls.

: : : : : :

SOPA *de* PRASA

LEEK SOUP

This Passover soup from Rhodes is very much like *purrusalda,* a Spanish leek soup, although the Spanish recipe includes paprika and occasionally salt cod. *Agristada,* a mixture of egg and lemon, is whisked in at the end of cooking to thicken the mixture.

Serves 4 TO 6

6 MEDIUM LEEKS

$1/4$ CUP VEGETABLE OIL

4 LARGE BOILING POTATOES, PEELED AND DICED

$1/2$ POUND FRESH MUSHROOMS, BRUSHED
  CLEAN AND SLICED (OPTIONAL)

8 CUPS CHICKEN STOCK OR WATER

1 EGG

3 TABLESPOONS FRESH LEMON JUICE

SALT AND FRESHLY GROUND BLACK PEPPER

Trim off the root end and all but about 2 inches of the green tops from the leeks and cut in half lengthwise. Cut the halves crosswise into pieces about $3/4$ inch wide. Place the pieces in a sink full of cold water, swish them around to loosen any dirt, remove with a slotted spoon, and drain well in a colander.

Warm the vegetable oil in a large saucepan over medium heat. Add the leeks, potatoes, and the mushrooms, if using, and sauté for about 5 minutes, stirring occasionally. Raise the heat to high, add the stock or water, and bring to a boil. Reduce the heat to low, cover, and simmer until the vegetables are soft, about 40 minutes.

In a bowl, beat together the egg and lemon juice until quite frothy. Whisk in a little of the hot soup to temper the egg, then gradually stir the egg into the soup over very low heat. Cook very gently for about 1 minute, but do not boil. Season with salt and pepper. Ladle into bowls and serve at once.

: : : : : :

VEGETABLES AND GRAINS

chapter 4

✹

VEGETABLES AND GRAINS

Vegetables are the cornerstone of the Sephardic kitchen. Traditionally, they were served at almost every meal except breakfast, and even then they sometimes appeared in savory pastries. Most vegetables were cooked slowly in oil, with water added little by little, until they were very tender, a technique producing a result that probably is too soft for the contemporary palate. In Spain, a *sofrito* is a mixture of sautéed onions and tomato, but in the Sephardic kitchen the same term is used for this classic method of cooking vegetables. In Italy, the term is *soffrito,* or in dialect *sofegae,* meaning "suffocated." Some vegetable dishes are sweet and sour, with additions of vinegar and lemon for the sour component and honey, sugar, or fruits for the sweet.

Vegetable gratins, of which there are many, go under a variety of different names. They may be called *sfongo, encusa, almodrote, fritada,* and *quajado.* The variables are generally the number of eggs, the amount of cheese, and what is used to give the dish body: bread, matzoh, or cooked potatoes, or a combination.

Grains are not a major category in Sephardic cooking. Although they have always been a part of the local pantry, the recipe selection is small. Traditionally, rice and bread were served at every meal. In addition, various savory pastries was served to satisfy the need for grain in the diet, plus many vegetable dishes were bound together by bread.

Bulgur and cracked wheat appear on the table from time to time, but rice is the main story, and its preparation is inevitably simple: a few pine nuts, some tomato or spinach, or grated carrots are added and little more. I prefer to use basmati rice for most recipes that call for long-grain rice because it is fragrant and holds its shape well. Short-grain rice is reserved for puddings, and in Italy for risotto. Noodles, in contrast, are served only occasionally in Turkey and Greece. They are added to soup, but mostly they take the form of a Middle Eastern–style macaroni and cheese or of fried noodles based on the Spanish tradition. Some Sephardic families maintain the early Arabic name for pasta, *itriya,* but most call it *fidellos,* derived from the Spanish *fideos.*

In the past, the serving of meat and fish was not an everyday occurrence. So grains and vegetables were given equal importance at the table, often becoming the meal itself, rather than simply side dishes.

KEFTES *de* PRASA

LEEK FRITTERS

Both Gilda Angel and Méri Badi suggest serving leek fritters for Rosh Hashanah. Matzoh meal in the recipe makes them a good choice for Passover as well. And, of course, because they are fried they would be ideal for Hanukkah. The mixture of leeks, bread, and eggs also can be baked as a gratin. This baked version, called *prasifutchi,* can be thickened with potatoes instead of bread or matzoh.

Makes about 16 *fritters; serves* 6 TO 8

3 POUNDS LEEKS (12 SMALL, 8 MEDIUM, OR
    4 VERY LARGE)

4 MATZOHS OR SLICES RUSTIC BREAD

3 EGGS, LIGHTLY BEATEN

$1^{1}/_{2}$ TEASPOONS SALT, PLUS MORE TO TASTE

$^{1}/_{2}$ TEASPOON FRESHLY GROUND BLACK PEPPER

$^{1}/_{2}$ CUP CHOPPED WALNUTS (OPTIONAL)

MATZOH MEAL, AS NEEDED

OLIVE OR VEGETABLE OIL FOR DEEP-FRYING

LEMON WEDGES

Cut away the roots and most of the green part from the leeks and discard. Peel away any loose layers, cut the leeks in half lengthwise, and then cut crosswise into $^{1}/_{2}$-inch-wide pieces. Soak them in a sink full of cold water, swish them around to loosen any dirt, remove with a slotted spoon, and drain well in a colander. You will have about 6 cups chopped leeks. Put them in a saucepan with lightly salted water to cover, bring to a boil over high heat, reduce the heat to low, and simmer until the leeks are very tender, about 20 minutes. Drain well and squeeze out any excess moisture. You will have about 2 cups cooked leeks. Soak the matzohs or bread slices (remove the crusts) in water and squeeze dry.

In a large bowl, combine the leeks, soaked matzoh or bread, eggs, $1^{1}/_{2}$ teaspoons salt, pepper, and the nuts, if using. Mix well and, if the mixture seems too moist, add matzoh meal until it holds together. You may then need a bit more salt. Form the mixture into patties about 2 inches in diameter and $^{1}/_{2}$ to $^{3}/_{4}$ inch thick.

Pour oil to a depth of about 1 inch into a large sauté pan and heat to 350 degrees F on a deep-frying thermometer. Meanwhile, spread some matzoh meal on a plate and dip the patties in it, coating both sides and tapping off the excess.

When the oil is hot, add the patties, in batches, and fry, turning once, until golden on both sides, 6 to 8 minutes total. Using a slotted spatula or tongs, transfer to paper towels to drain briefly. Sprinkle with salt and serve piping hot with lemon wedges.

Variation: To make spinach fritters, use 3 pounds spinach, stems removed, wilted, drained, squeezed dry, and finely chopped, or 3 packages (10 ounces each) frozen chopped spinach, thawed and squeezed dry, for the leeks. If you like, add 1 onion, finely chopped and sautéed, with the eggs; it will impart a depth of flavor to the mixture. A little grated nutmeg will add a pleasant sweetness.

Note: The fritters can be fried ahead of serving and kept warm in a 250 degree F oven for up to 30 minutes. They also can be fried and then reheated in a light tomato sauce.

: : : : : :

KACHKARIKAS *de* KALAVASA *kon*
AJO *i* PIMYENTA

ZUCCHINI PEEL WITH GARLIC AND PEPPER

Méri Badi's recipe for cooked zucchini peel is
unusual in two ways: it has lots of garlic, reminiscent of the old days of Spanish cooking rather than
the garlic-reticent Sephardic repertoire as it
evolved in Turkey, and it uses just the outer layer of
the zucchini, not the seeds and center. I have shortened the cooking time considerably to keep the
zucchini from disintegrating, although it will still
seem a bit soft to some eaters. You can cook the
zucchini even less, but you will have to give the
garlic a good head start, as it will take 20 minutes
to soften.

Serves 4 TO 6

3 POUNDS ZUCCHINI (ABOUT 8 LARGE)

2 SMALL HEADS GARLIC, SEPARATED INTO
    CLOVES AND PEELED

1/4 CUP EXTRA-VIRGIN OLIVE OIL

3 CUPS WATER

1 TEASPOON FRESHLY GROUND BLACK PEPPER

GENEROUS PINCH OF SUGAR

1 TEASPOON SALT

Trim the ends from the zucchini and then remove the
outer layer in strips about 1 inch wide and about 1/3
inch thick. You want a thin layer of flesh attached to
every strip. Cut the strips crosswise into 1-inch
squares. Save the centers of the zucchini for another
dish. If the garlic cloves are very large, cut them in
half lengthwise. If not, leave them whole.

Combine the garlic, olive oil, water, pepper, sugar,
and salt in a saucepan. Bring to a boil over high heat,
stir well, reduce the heat to low, cover, and cook for

about 10 minutes. Uncover, add the zucchini pieces,
stir well, cover partially, and continue to simmer for
10 minutes. Check the amount of liquid left in the
pan. Most of it should have been absorbed. If the
mixture is too soupy and the zucchini and garlic are
already tender, remove them from the pan with a
slotted spoon and place in a serving dish. Bring the
liquid in the pan to a boil and reduce to a syrupy
consistency. If the zucchini and garlic are still firm,
uncover the pan and simmer to reduce the excess liquid and finish cooking the vegetables.

Taste and adjust the seasonings. Serve warm or at
room temperature.

Variations: Other recipes for braised zucchini
peel omit the garlic and pepper and cook the zucchini
squares directly in a sauce of fresh or dried Greengage
plums (called golden prunes) or sour raisins, using a
pinch of sugar, some lemon juice, oil, and water.
Those cooked with fruit are called *kachkarikas de
kalavasa kon avramila* or *kon agras.*

: : : : : :

KOMIDA *de* BALKABAK *kon* PRUNAS

PUMPKIN WITH PRUNES

Including dried fruits in savory dishes is typical of Arab-Moorish cuisine. This heritage is present in Méri Badi's Sephardic recipe for sweet pumpkin (*bal* is "honey" and *kabak* is "pumpkin") and prunes. This dish resembles *blou,* the Moroccan-Jewish compote of pumpkin and apricots, and would be an ideal accompaniment to roast chicken or grilled lamb. Originally cooking time for the pumpkin and prunes was one hour. I ended up with homely mush. Therefore, I have reduced the cooking time drastically so that both the pumpkin and prunes hold their shape. I also have used the prune soaking liquids instead of water, as they enrich the flavor of the dish.

Serves 6 TO 8

1 PUMPKIN OR BUTTERNUT SQUASH, ABOUT
   2 POUNDS, HALVED, SEEDED, PEELED,
   AND CUT INTO $1^{1}/_{2}$-INCH CUBES
$1^{1}/_{2}$ CUPS PITTED PRUNES, PLUMPED IN
   2 CUPS HOT WATER FOR 1 HOUR
3 TABLESPOONS OLIVE OIL
GRATED ZEST AND JUICE OF 1 LEMON
2 TABLESPOONS CONFECTIONERS' SUGAR
$1^{1}/_{2}$ TEASPOONS SALT
$^{1}/_{2}$ TEASPOON GROUND CINNAMON (OPTIONAL)

In a large, heavy saucepan, combine the squash cubes, plumped prunes and their soaking liquid, olive oil, lemon zest and juice, sugar, salt, and the cinnamon, if using. Stir well, bring to a boil over medium heat, reduce the heat to low, and cook uncovered, stirring from time to time, until the squash is tender and the liquid has been absorbed, 15 to 20 minutes. Check occasionally to make sure there is enough liquid in the pan, or the squash will scorch. Add a little water as needed to prevent burning.

Taste and adjust the seasonings. Serve warm or at room temperature.

: : : : : :

SFONGO *di* ESPINAKA

SPINACH AND POTATO GRATIN, IZMIR STYLE

A *sfongo* is a gratin of vegetables thickened with potatoes, eggs, and cheese. This *sfongo* is unusual in appearance, as additional mashed potato is formed into little mounds that are interspersed in the spinach-and-potato base. You could also make this with Swiss chard, for a *sfongo di pasi*. In *Sefarad Yemekleri*, the spinach is chopped and added uncooked. I find that it is easier to mix in the spinach after it has been wilted. Other versions of this recipe omit the potato mounds and arrange the spinach and potatoes in alternating layers.

Serves 8

4 POUNDS SPINACH

4 LARGE BOILING POTATOES, PEELED AND
    CUT INTO QUARTERS

$1/4$ CUP MILK

$1^{1}/_2$ CUPS MIXED GRATED CHEESES SUCH AS
    KASHKAVAL, GRUYÈRE, AND PARMESAN

6 EGGS

$1^{1}/_2$ TEASPOONS SALT

$1/2$ TEASPOON FRESHLY GROUND BLACK PEPPER

PLAIN YOGURT

Rinse the spinach well and remove the stems (reserve them for salad, page 43). Chop the leaves finely. Place the spinach in a large sauté pan with only the rinsing water clinging to the leaves, and cook briefly over medium heat, turning as needed, until wilted, just a few minutes. Drain well and squeeze dry. You should have about 4 cups cooked spinach.

Place the potatoes in a saucepan with lightly salted water to cover generously. Bring to a boil and cook until tender, about 30 minutes. Drain well, return to the pan, and place over low heat briefly to cook away any remaining moisture. Add the milk and mash until smooth. You should have about 4 cups mashed potatoes. Add 1 cup of the cheese, the eggs, the salt, and the pepper. Mix well.

Preheat the oven to 350 degrees F. Brush a 9-by-12-by-2-inch baking dish with warm olive oil.

Divide the potato mixture in half. Add half of it to the cooked spinach and mix well. Spread the spinach-potato mixture in the bottom of the prepared dish. Make $1/2$-inch-deep indentations in the layer at regular intervals, spacing them about $1^{1}/_2$ inches apart. Fill with rounded mounds of the remaining mashed potatoes. Top evenly with the remaining $1/2$ cup grated cheese.

Bake the gratin until golden, 35 to 40 minutes. Serve hot directly from the dish. Pass a bowl of yogurt at the table.

Note: In the cookbook from Temple Or Ve Shalom in Atlanta, this dish is called *quajado de spinaka* with potato nests. Bread is added to the spinach along with eggs and half the cheese. Then the potatoes are mashed with eggs and the remaining cheese and become the little mounds nested in the spinach layer.

: : : : : :

TORTINO *di* SPINACI

SPINACH GRATIN

The anchovies, pine nuts, and raisins are clues to the Sicilian origin of this dish. Baking the seasoned spinach with the eggs makes this rich and filling. If you prefer a lighter dish, omit the eggs and the baking and serve this as highly seasoned sautéed spinach.

Serves 6

FINE DRIED BREAD CRUMBS FOR DUSTING

3 POUNDS SPINACH

4 TO 6 TABLESPOONS OLIVE OIL

3 ANCHOVY FILLETS, MINCED

4 TO 5 TABLESPOONS CHOPPED FRESH
   FLAT-LEAF PARSLEY

2 TABLESPOONS CAPERS, RINSED AND CHOPPED

2 CLOVES GARLIC, MINCED

$^1/_2$ CUP PINE NUTS, TOASTED AND COARSELY CHOPPED

$^1/_2$ CUP RAISINS, PLUMPED IN HOT WATER
   AND WELL DRAINED

SALT

3 EGGS, LIGHTLY BEATEN

Preheat an oven to 350 degrees F. Oil an 8-by-11-by-2-inch baking dish or a 2-quart casserole, then dust it with the bread crumbs, tapping out the excess.

Rinse the spinach well and remove the stems (reserve them for salad, page 43). Place the spinach in a large sauté pan with only the rinsing water clinging to the leaves, and cook over medium heat, turning as needed, until wilted, just a few minutes. Empty the contents of the pan into a colander and drain the spinach well.

Add the olive oil to the now-empty pan along with the anchovies, parsley, capers, and garlic. Place over medium heat and sauté for 2 minutes. Return the drained spinach to the pan, mix well, and fold in the pine nuts and raisins. Season with salt. Remove from the heat. Fold the eggs into the spinach mixture, then turn it into the prepared baking dish.

Bake the gratin until lightly golden, about 30 minutes. Serve hot directly from the dish.

: : : : : :

ALMODROTE *de* BERENJENA

EGGPLANT GRATIN

Almodrote, which appears in every Sephardic cook-book, dates back to early Spain. The word is of Arab origin, and in medieval Catalonia, *almodroc* referred to a dish with garlic, eggs, and cheese. Somewhere along the way the garlic disappeared, but the cheese and eggs remained. I found that the variables for this recipe have to do with the proportion of egg-plant, cheese, and egg. Some recipes include bread as a thickener, while others contain no bread at all. If you want to return the garlic to the original con-cept, add a clove or two, well minced, to the mashed eggplant. Some chopped parsley or dill is a nice addition, too.

Serves 8

4 GLOBE EGGPLANTS, 1 POUND EACH

4 SLICES RUSTIC BREAD, CRUSTS REMOVED,
    SOAKED IN WATER, AND SQUEEZED DRY

4 EGGS

6 OUNCES FRESH WHITE CHEESE SUCH AS
    $^3/_4$ CUP RICOTTA OR $1^1/_2$ CUPS NOT-TOO-SALTY
    CRUMBLED FETA

$^1/_2$ POUND KASHKAVAL OR GRUYÈRE CHEESE,
    GRATED (ABOUT 2 CUPS)

$^1/_3$ CUP SUNFLOWER OR OLIVE OIL

$1^1/_2$ TO 2 TEASPOONS SALT

$^1/_2$ TEASPOON FRESHLY GROUND BLACK PEPPER

For a smoky taste, preheat the broiler and broil the eggplants, turning often, until they are very soft and have collapsed, about 20 minutes. Alternatively, cook them slowly on a stove-top cast-iron griddle, turning them often. You also can bake them in a 400 degree F oven until they are soft throughout, about 45 minutes. Transfer the eggplants to a colander.

When cool enough to handle, strip away the skin and remove the large seed pockets. Place the pulp on a cutting board and chop coarsely. Return it to the colander and let drain for 10 to 20 minutes to release the bitter juices. You should have 2 to 2 $^1/_2$ cups pulp.

Preheat the oven to 350 degrees F. Oil a 7-by-11-by-2-inch baking dish.

Transfer the eggplant to a bowl and mash well with a fork. Add the bread, eggs, ricotta or feta cheese, and all but $^1/_4$ cup of the kashkaval or Gruyère cheese, all but 2 tablespoons of the oil, the $1^1/_2$ teaspoons salt, and the pepper. Taste and adjust with more salt, if needed. Spread the mixture in the prepared baking dish. Sprinkle evenly with the remaining $^1/_4$ cup grated cheese and drizzle the remaining 2 tablespoons oil over the top.

Bake until golden and set, 30 to 40 minutes. Serve hot directly from the dish.

Note: In the cookbook from Temple Or Ve Shalom in Atlanta, this same dish is called *fretada de berenjena.*

: : : : : :

FRITADA *de* KALAVASA

SQUASH OMELET

Fritada is related in name and style to the better-known Italian *frittata*. While this version adds bread for thickening, other recipes use mashed potatoes or a little cheese to firm up the omelet, in the style of the *encusa* or *almodrote,* and some use only eggs to bind, as in a classic omelet. I have taken the liberty of adding dill to the basic recipe, as it fits with the flavor profile and is used in a zucchini *almodrote* recipe. Mint would also be a nice contrast. The original Turkish recipe called for peeling the squash, but I don't think it is necessary if you salt the squash to remove the bitterness.

Serves 6

2 POUNDS ZUCCHINI OR SUMMER SQUASH, GRATED ON
  THE LARGE HOLES OF A CHEESE GRATER
  (ABOUT 6 CUPS LOOSELY PACKED)
SALT FOR SPRINKLING, PLUS 1$^1/_2$ TEASPOONS
2 RIPE TOMATOES, PEELED, SEEDED, AND CHOPPED
6 TABLESPOONS CHOPPED FRESH FLAT-LEAF PARSLEY
$^1/_4$ CUP CHOPPED FRESH DILL
4 SLICES RUSTIC BREAD, CRUSTS REMOVED,
  SOAKED IN WATER, AND SQUEEZED DRY
1 SMALL YELLOW ONION, GRATED OR FINELY MINCED,
  OR 1 BUNCH GREEN ONIONS,
  WHITE PART ONLY, MINCED
8 EGGS, LIGHTLY BEATEN
$^1/_2$ TEASPOON FRESHLY GROUND BLACK PEPPER
2 TABLESPOONS SUNFLOWER OR OLIVE OIL
PLAIN YOGURT

Place the grated squash in a colander, sprinkling the layers with salt, and let drain for 30 minutes. Rinse and squeeze dry.

Preheat the oven to 350 degrees F. Place a 9-by-12-by-2-inch baking dish in the oven to warm.

Place the squash in a large bowl. Add the tomatoes, parsley, dill, soaked bread, onion, eggs, 1$^1/_2$ teaspoons salt, and pepper and mix well.

Remove the baking dish from the oven and brush with the oil. Pour in the egg mixture. Return the dish to the oven and bake until set and golden, 30 to 40 minutes. Remove from the oven and serve warm or at room temperature directly from the dish. Pass the yogurt at the table.

Variation: You can mix together the ingredients, except the onion, as directed. Place two 8-inch sauté pans on top of the stove over medium heat and warm 2 tablespoons oil in each pan. Add half of the onion to each pan and sauté until translucent, about 5 minutes. Divide the squash mixture between the pans and fry, in the manner of a Spanish *tortilla,* until the bottom of each omelet is set and golden, about 8 to 10 minutes. Turn out, cooked side up, onto 2 large plates and slide the omelets back in the pans to cook the other sides until set and golden, 3 to 4 minutes longer. Slide onto serving plates and serve warm or at room temperature, cut into wedges. (If you do not have 2 pans, cook 1 omelet at a time, or cook the entire mixture in 1 large flameproof sauté pan and set the top by slipping the pan under a hot broiler for a few minutes. Serve warm or at room temperature.)

: : : : : :

QUAJADO *de* TOMATE

TOMATO BREAD PUDDING

This delectable cross between an omelet and a bread pudding is one of the joys of the summer tomato season. It is called a *fritada* in *Sefarad Yemekleri*, but in other cookbooks it is known as *quajado de tomate*. *Quajado* can mean "congealed," or it may be related to *queijado*, the Portuguese word for "cheesecake." The Arab word for the earthenware cooking vessel called a *cazuela* by the Spanish was *qas'ah*, so the term is very ancient indeed. Janet Mendel, in her award-winning book *Traditional Spanish Cooking*, has a recipe for *cuajado de almendra*, an almond bread pudding, so the word is still in use in Spain. For this wonderful dish, only full-flavored seasonal tomatoes need apply.

Serves 6 TO 8

3 POUNDS RIPE TOMATOES, PEELED, SEEDED,
   AND CHOPPED (ABOUT 6 CUPS)
SALT
SUGAR
4 SLICES RUSTIC BREAD, CRUSTS REMOVED,
   SOAKED IN WATER, AND SQUEEZED DRY
6 EGGS, LIGHTLY BEATEN
4 TO 6 TABLESPOONS CHOPPED FRESH
   FLAT-LEAF PARSLEY
$1/2$ POUND KASHKAVAL CHEESE, OR HALF
   GRUYÈRE CHEESE AND HALF PARMESAN
   CHEESE, GRATED (ABOUT 2 CUPS)
FRESHLY GROUND BLACK PEPPER

Place the chopped tomatoes in a colander, sprinkling the layers with a little salt and a bit of sugar to draw out the excess moisture, and let drain for 1 hour.

Preheat the oven to 350 degrees F. Oil a 9-by-12-by-2-inch baking dish.

Transfer the tomatoes to a bowl and add the soaked bread, eggs, parsley, and all but about $1/2$ cup of the cheese. Mix well and season with salt and pepper. Transfer the mixture to the prepared dish and evenly sprinkle the remaining $1/2$ cup over the top.

Bake the pudding until golden and set, 25 to 30 minutes. Serve warm directly from the dish.

: : : : : :

TURLU

TURKISH RATATOUILLE

Méri Badi identifies *turlu* as a Judeo-Spanish dish. It resembles Spanish *pisto* dishes from Murcia or La Mancha, but with the Turkish addition of okra. *Pisto* evolved from an ancient stew called *alboronia,* Moorish for "eggplant." Over time, vegetables from the New World were introduced into the mix. Although no herbs are added to the recipe, oregano, marjoram, parsley, or mint would not be out of place.

If you have eaten okra before but have not liked its texture, try this recipe. The okra pods are put in a bowl of vinegar for 30 minutes and then are rinsed in a colander. This step rids them of their unpleasant sliminess.

Serves 8

$1/2$ POUND OKRA

$1/2$ CUP WINE VINEGAR

6 TABLESPOONS OLIVE OIL

2 LARGE ONIONS, CHOPPED

SALT

7 RIPE TOMATOES, PEELED, SEEDED, AND CHOPPED

2 GLOBE EGGPLANTS, PEELED IN A VERTICALLY STRIPED
    PATTERN, QUARTERED LENGTHWISE, AND THEN CUT
    CROSSWISE INTO 2-INCH PIECES

4 SMALL NEW POTATOES, PEELED AND HALVED IF VERY
    SMALL OR QUARTERED IF LARGER

2 RED OR YELLOW BELL PEPPERS, SEEDED AND CHOPPED

2 TEASPOONS TOMATO PASTE

PINCH OF SUGAR (OPTIONAL)

2 LARGE ZUCCHINI, QUARTERED LENGTHWISE AND CUT
    CROSSWISE INTO $1^1/2$-INCH LENGTHS

1 POUND GREEN BEANS, TRIMMED AND HALVED
    CROSSWISE OR CUT INTO 2-INCH LENGTHS

A FEW TABLESPOONS CHOPPED FRESH HERB OF YOUR
    CHOICE (SEE RECIPE INTRODUCTION; OPTIONAL)

Trim off the stems from the okra and soak the pods in water to cover to which the vinegar has been added. Let stand for 20 minutes, then drain, rinse well, and set aside.

Meanwhile, warm the olive oil in a large, deep sauté pan over medium heat. Add the onions and sauté until translucent, about 5 minutes. Season with salt. Add 4 of the chopped tomatoes and cook, stirring occasionally, for 3 minutes. Layer the eggplants, potatoes, and bell peppers on top of the tomatoes and onions. Mix the remaining 3 tomatoes with the tomato paste and scatter over the top. Add the sugar, if using, and season with salt. Pour in water to a depth of $1/2$ inch, cover, and cook over low heat until half-cooked, 20 to 30 minutes.

Uncover and add the okra, the zucchini, and the green beans. Re-cover and continue to cook over low heat for another 20 minutes. Test for doneness: the eggplant should have absorbed some pan juices and be translucent and tender, and the potatoes should be tender. If the vegetables are not yet cooked, return the pan to low heat, adding a little water if the mixture is dry, re-cover, and cook until tender. If the vegetables are tender but a lot of sauce remains, remove the vegetables with a slotted spoon and boil the sauce until it is reduced. Then return the vegetables to the pan and add the herb, if using.

Taste and adjust the seasonings. Spoon into a serving dish and serve warm.

: : : : : :

CROCHETTE *de* PATATE
ALLA SICILIANA

SICILIAN POTATO CROQUETTES

While they are not the classic Ashkenazic *latkes,* these potato croquettes would be ideal at the Hanukkah table. They are also called *bimuelos de patata* in the Balkans, *keftikes de patata* in Greece, or *fritas de patata kon kezo* in Ladino, and they are affectionately known as *patates toplar* by the Sephardim in Turkey. Although the word *toplar* means "cannonball," they are not heavy, just round. Turkish Jews dip them in broken noodles rather than bread crumbs. While these are delicious seasoned with just parsley and cheese, the green onion and garlic add a deeper flavor note, the mint contributes brightness, and the pine nuts deliver texture.

Serves 6

2 POUNDS BOILING POTATOES, PEELED AND
   QUARTERED OR HALVED

2 EGGS, SEPARATED

3 TABLESPOONS CHOPPED FRESH FLAT-LEAF PARSLEY

$^1/_3$ CUP GRATED PARMESAN OR PECORINO CHEESE

3 TO 4 TABLESPOONS CHOPPED FRESH MINT (OPTIONAL)

$^1/_4$ CUP FINELY MINCED GREEN ONION, INCLUDING
   TENDER GREEN TOPS (OPTIONAL)

1 CLOVE GARLIC, MINCED (OPTIONAL)

$^1/_4$ CUP PINE NUTS (OPTIONAL)

SALT AND FRESHLY GROUND BLACK PEPPER

VEGETABLE OR OLIVE OIL FOR DEEP-FRYING

ALL-PURPOSE FLOUR FOR COATING

FINE DRIED BREAD CRUMBS FOR COATING

Place the potatoes in a saucepan with lightly salted water to cover generously. Bring to a boil and cook until tender, 15 to 20 minutes. Drain well and, while still warm, pass them through a potato ricer placed over a bowl or mash them. Add the egg yolks, parsley, cheese, and the mint, green onion, garlic, and pine nuts, if using. Stir well to combine. Season with salt and pepper. Form into 1-inch balls or ovals.

Pour the oil to a depth of 3 inches into a saucepan or a deep sauté pan, and heat to 375 degrees F on a deep-frying thermometer. Meanwhile, in a bowl, beat the egg whites until soft peaks form. Spread a little flour on one plate and some bread crumbs on a second plate. Dip the balls or ovals first into the flour, then into the egg whites, and finally into the crumbs, coating evenly at each step. Place on racks or parchment paper–lined baking sheets. (These croquettes can be prepared up to this point a few hours ahead of serving and covered and refrigerated until you are ready to fry them.)

When oil is hot, add the croquettes, in batches, and deep-fry until golden, about 5 minutes. Using tongs or a slotted spoon, transfer to paper towels to drain, then keep warm in the oven preheated to 250 degrees F until all the croquettes are fried. Serve hot.

Note: You can also use baked russet potatoes for the croquettes, scooping the cooked flesh from the skins into a bowl, then mixing with the other ingredients as directed.

: : : : : :

ANGINARAS

SWEET-AND-SOUR ARTICHOKES

Artichokes are a Passover specialty all over the Mediterranean, as spring brings the best and most tender specimens. This is a Turkish recipe, but a similar dish, called *enginares,* appears in Nicholas Stavroulakis's *The Cookbook of the Jews of Greece* and is attributed to the town of Drama.

Serves 8

3 LARGE, JUICY LEMONS

8 LARGE ARTICHOKES

3 CUPS WATER

2 TO 3 TABLESPOONS SUGAR OR HONEY

3 TABLESPOONS OLIVE OIL

1 TEASPOON SALT

Squeeze the juice from the lemons and set it aside. Squeeze any remaining juice into a large bowl of cold water and then drop in the spent halves. Working with 1 artichoke at a time, remove almost all of the leaves until you reach the pale green heart. Pare away the dark green area from the base and from an inch or so of the stem. Cut the artichoke in quarters lengthwise, and scoop out and discard the choke from each piece. Drop the quarters into the lemon water to prevent discoloration.

In a saucepan or a large, deep sauté pan, combine the 3 cups water, lemon juice, sugar or honey, oil, and salt. Bring to a boil over high heat, add the artichokes, and reduce the heat to low. Cover and simmer until the artichokes are tender, 20 to 30 minutes. The timing will depend upon the size of the artichokes. Test with the point of a knife or with a fork.

When the artichokes are tender, remove from the heat and drain off most of the liquid, leaving only enough to cool the artichokes in liquid to cover (about 1 cup). Serve at room temperature.

Variations: Add the juice of 2 oranges and a pinch of red pepper flakes to the braising liquid. Or add a few thyme sprigs or 1 or 2 thyme sprigs and a bay leaf to the braising liquid.

: : : : : :

AVAS FRESKAS

FAVA BEANS WITH FRESH CORIANDER

This Sephardic dish is almost identical to a Portuguese ragout of favas cooked with garlic and coriander—minus the bacon, of course. The Spanish version of this same stew uses mint instead of coriander and substitutes sausage for the bacon. If you cannot find fresh favas, frozen baby limas can be substituted.

Serves 4 TO 6

4 POUNDS FAVA BEANS, SHELLED (ABOUT 2 CUPS), OR
   1 PACKAGE (1 POUND) FROZEN BABY LIMA BEANS
2 TABLESPOONS OLIVE OIL
1 ONION, CHOPPED
2 CLOVES GARLIC, FINELY MINCED
³/4 TO 1 CUP WATER
1 SMALL BAY LEAF
SALT AND FRESHLY GROUND BLACK PEPPER
2 TEASPOONS GROUND CUMIN (OPTIONAL)
¹/3 CUP CHOPPED FRESH CORIANDER

For the optional yogurt sauce:
1 CUP PLAIN YOGURT, DRAINED IN A SIEVE FOR 4 HOURS
2 CLOVES GARLIC, GREEN SPROUTS REMOVED
   AND MINCED
SALT AND FRESHLY GROUND BLACK PEPPER

If using the fava beans, bring a saucepan filled with water to a boil. Add the beans and blanch for about 1 minute, then drain and, when cool enough to handle, slip each bean free from its tough skin. If using frozen limas, reserve until needed.

Warm the olive oil in a saucepan over medium heat. Add the onion and sauté until translucent and tender,

about 10 minutes. Add the garlic and sauté for a minute or two. Then add the fava or lima beans, water, and bay leaf and simmer until tender, 10 to 15 minutes for fresh favas or 8 to 10 minutes for frozen limas.

Meanwhile, make the yogurt sauce, if using: In a bowl, stir together the yogurt and garlic. Season with salt and pepper.

Drain the beans and place in a bowl. Season with salt and pepper and add the cumin, if using. Mix well, then toss in the coriander. Mix gently and serve hot. If serving the yogurt sauce, pass it at the table.

Notes: If you want to serve the beans as a salad, add 3 to 4 tablespoons wine vinegar and 2 to 3 tablespoons olive oil to the drained beans while they are still warm. Let cool, cover, and chill. You will need to heighten the salt and cumin before serving, as the chilling will mute the flavors.

A similar recipe in *La table juive, avikas freskas* or *avas de misraim,* calls for cooking green onions in olive oil, then adding the fava beans, some cut-up romaine lettuce, and a bit of sugar. No water is needed, as the romaine breaks down and releases sufficient moisture.

: : : : : :

APYO

BRAISED CELERY ROOT

In Turkey, celery root is a favorite vegetable among the Sephardim and may appear on the table for the first night of Passover. It is often combined with other vegetables in a light and lemony stew. *Apyo* is usually served at room temperature. Artichokes may be prepared the same way.

Serves 4 TO 6

4 CUPS COLD WATER

JUICE OF 1 LEMON, PLUS LEMON JUICE TO TASTE
    (OPTIONAL)

1 LARGE OR 2 MEDIUM CELERY ROOTS, ABOUT
    2 POUNDS TOTAL

$^1/_3$ CUP OLIVE OIL

2 ONIONS, CHOPPED

4 CUPS HOT WATER OR VEGETABLE STOCK, HEATED

3 CARROTS, PEELED AND DICED

1 TABLESPOON SUGAR

SALT AND FRESHLY GROUND BLACK PEPPER

$^1/_2$ CUP CHOPPED FRESH DILL

Combine the cold water and the juice of 1 lemon in a saucepan. Peel the celery root(s) and cut into $^1/_2$-inch-thick slices. Add the celery root to the pan, bring to a boil, and cook for 10 minutes. Drain and set aside.

Warm the olive oil in a large sauté pan over medium heat. Add the onions and sauté until translucent, about 5 minutes. Add the hot water or vegetable stock, celery root, carrots, sugar, and salt to taste and cook until the vegetables are tender and some of the liquid has evaporated, 20 to 25 minutes.

Season with salt and pepper and a little lemon juice to taste, if desired. Transfer to a serving dish and let cool. Sprinkle with the dill. Serve at room temperature.

Variation: If you want to serve this dish warm, thicken the juices with *agristada*. Beat 2 eggs with $^1/_2$ cup fresh lemon juice until quite frothy. Whisk a little of the hot pan juices into the eggs to temper them, and then stir the eggs into the pan and heat gently for 1 minute. Do not allow to boil.

: : : : : :

PIPIRIZAS *con* QUESO

CHEESE-STUFFED PEPPERS

Green peppers are grilled over a flame, peeled, carefully seeded, stuffed, and then fried until golden crisp on the outside, while the cheese within is meltingly creamy. Don't worry if the peppers should tear a bit, however; the flour-and-egg coating acts as a seal. Pepper size and the amount of filling needed to stuff each pepper are the only variables, so make enough filling. If you have some filling left over, spread it on bread and toast it, or use it in a gratin like the *almodrote* on page 96. These peppers could be served with a light tomato sauce if you like, although it is not traditional.

Serves 8

8 LARGE GREEN BELL PEPPERS, OR 16 SMALLER
   GREEN PEPPERS OR POBLANO CHILES
4 EGGS
1 1/2 CUPS CRUMBLED FETA CHEESE
1 1/2 CUPS FARMER CHEESE, RICOTTA CHEESE,
   OR FROMAGE BLANC
3/4 CUP GRATED KASHKAVAL OR GRUYÈRE CHEESE
2 TO 3 TABLESPOONS CHOPPED FRESH
   FLAT-LEAF PARSLEY
ALL-PURPOSE FLOUR
SALT AND FRESHLY GROUND BLACK PEPPER
VEGETABLE OIL FOR FRYING
TOMATO SAUCE, HEATED (OPTIONAL; SEE EGGPLANT
   ROLLS WITH TOMATO SAUCE, PAGE 162)

Place the peppers over an open flame on a gas stove or in a broiler until they are charred almost black on all sides and are softened. Slip the peppers into a plastic bag or covered container and let steam for 15 minutes, then scrape off the charred peel with a knife. Do not peel under running water, or you will lose much of the roasted flavor. Carefully cut a slit in the side of each pepper and scoop out the seeds.

In a bowl, lightly beat 2 of the eggs. Add the cheeses and parsley and mix well. Stuff the peppers with the mixture. Spread the flour on a plate and season it with salt and pepper. In a shallow bowl, lightly beat the remaining 2 eggs.

Pour the vegetable oil to a depth of about 1/2 inch into a large sauté pan and place over medium-high heat. Dip the peppers in flour, then in the beaten eggs. Add to the hot oil, in batches, and fry, turning once to crisp and color on all sides, until golden brown, about 5 minutes. Using a slotted spatula, transfer the peppers to a platter. Serve hot. If desired, pass the tomato sauce at the table.

Cheese-Stuffed Tomatoes Variation: Cut 8 large tomatoes in half, scoop out the centers, sprinkle the interiors with salt and a pinch of sugar, and fill with this cheese mixture. Top the filling with a bit of extra Gruyère. Arrange in a baking dish, add a bit of water to the dish, cover, and bake in a 350 degree F oven until the tomatoes are tender, 25 to 45 minutes, depending on their size. Serve hot.

Cheese-Stuffed Eggplants Variation: Cut 8 to 10 long, slender (Japanese) eggplants in half lengthwise, and peel in a striped pattern lengthwise. Scoop out and reserve the flesh. Boil the cases for 3 to 5 minutes to soften slightly, then drain well. Chop the reserved eggplant pulp and sauté in olive oil until soft, about 5 minutes, then let cool a bit. Add to the cheese-and-egg mixture. Stuff the filling into the eggplant cases, and top with some extra grated Gruyère. Arrange in a baking dish, add a bit of water to the dish, and bake until tender, 15 to 20 minutes. Serve hot.

: : : : : :

PAPEYADA *de* BERENJENA
FRIED EGGPLANT WITH SUGAR

This Sephardic dish from Edirne, in Turkey, is of Hispano-Arabic origin. The giveaway is the sprinkling of sugar on the fried eggplant. Some recipes direct you to salt the eggplant or soak it in salted water for 10 to 15 minutes, then squeeze it dry before dipping it in the egg and frying it. Claudia Roden believes that no soaking is needed if you dip the slices in egg before frying. The recipe also appears in *La table juive* as a Rosh Hashanah dish. What is unusual in this recipe is that the eggplants are fried and then cooked again in the oven. This is probably not necessary, as the slices are certainly cooked through after the frying. So, you could stop immediately after the frying and just sprinkle the slices with salt and sugar and eat them. Sugar and eggplant seem like an odd combination, but in the Middle East baby eggplants are also preserved in sugar syrup and eaten as a sweet at the end of the meal.

Serves 6 TO 8

2^1/$_2$ POUNDS GLOBE EGGPLANTS
2 EGGS
OLIVE OR SUNFLOWER OIL FOR FRYING AND DRIZZLING
^{1}/$_2$ CUP SUGAR
SALT

Preheat the oven to 350 degrees F. Oil a 9-by-12-by-2-inch baking dish.

Peel the eggplants and slice them vertically about ^{1}/$_3$ inch thick. Place the slices in a bowl filled with lightly salted water. Let stand for 15 minutes, then drain and squeeze dry.

In a shallow bowl, lightly beat the eggs. Pour oil to a depth of 2 inches into a large sauté pan and place over medium heat. When the oil is hot, dip the eggplant slices in the beaten eggs, in batches, and slip them into the oil. Fry until golden, 5 to 7 minutes. Using tongs or a slotted spatula, transfer to paper towels to drain briefly, then place in the prepared baking dish.

When the bottom of the dish is completely covered, sprinkle the eggplant with sugar and salt. Repeat, sprinkling each layer with more sugar and salt, until all the eggplant slices have been used. Drizzle the surface with oil.

Bake until the eggplant is very tender when pierced with a fork, about 25 minutes. Serve hot or warm directly from the dish.

: : : : : :

ARROZ *con* PIÑONES

RICE WITH PINE NUTS

This classic Sephardic rice pilaf is the typical accompaniment for Fish with Abraham's Fruit (page 125).

Serves 6 TO 8

$1/4$ CUP OLIVE OIL

1 SMALL ONION, CHOPPED

2 CUPS LONG-GRAIN WHITE RICE, RINSED AND DRAINED

1 CUP PINE NUTS

4 CUPS WATER

$1^1/2$ TEASPOONS SALT

PINCH OF SAFFRON THREADS (OPTIONAL)

Warm the olive oil in a saucepan over medium heat. Add the onion and sauté until translucent, about 5 minutes. Add the rice and pine nuts, reduce the heat to low, and stir until the grains are well coated with the oil, about 5 minutes. Add the water, salt, and the saffron, if using, and raise the heat to high. Bring to a boil, cover, reduce the heat to low, and cook until the liquid is absorbed and the rice is tender, 18 to 20 minutes. Remove from the heat and let rest, covered, for 5 to 10 minutes, then serve.

: : : : : :

ARROZ *kon* TOMATE

RICE WITH TOMATOES

Here is a basic Turkish pilaf that is suitable for serving at nearly any meal. *Le feste ebraiche* describes a more elaborate tomato pilaf enjoyed by Jews in Italy. It omits the tomato sauce, cooking the rice simply with stock and braising tomatoes separately. The tomatoes are made by slipping a mixture of parsley, garlic, salt, sugar, and margarine into a slit made in each small whole tomato, and simmering the tomatoes in a saucepan until tender, 10 to 15 minutes. The pilaf is served in a deep platter with the tomatoes surrounding it.

2 CUPS LONG-GRAIN WHITE RICE, RINSED AND DRAINED

1 CUP TOMATO SAUCE

3 TABLESPOONS OLIVE OIL

$1^1/2$ TEASPOONS SALT

3 CUPS WATER

In a saucepan, combine the drained rice, tomato sauce, oil, salt, and water and bring to a boil over high heat. Reduce the heat to low, cover, and cook until all liquid is absorbed and the rice is tender, 18 to 20 minutes. Fluff with a fork and serve.

: : : : : :

KOMIDA *de* SEFANORYA

RICE WITH CARROTS AND LEMON

Méri Badi's original Judeo-Spanish recipe for this dish calls for cooking the grated carrots for 30 minutes and then cooking them 30 minutes longer with the rice. By then, I suspect they will have disintegrated, so I have shortened the cooking time. I also have added a bit of grated lemon zest to brighten the flavors and suggest a sprinkling of parsley or mint for contrast. This is a pretty dish, with the strips of golden carrots and grains of rice in about equal amounts.

Serves 6 TO 8

2 POUNDS CARROTS

$1/4$ CUP OLIVE OIL

GRATED ZEST AND JUICE OF 2 LEMONS

3 CUPS WATER

2 TEASPOONS SALT

1 CUP LONG-GRAIN WHITE RICE, RINSED AND DRAINED

2 TO 3 TABLESPOONS CHOPPED FRESH FLAT-LEAF
    PARSLEY OR MINT (OPTIONAL)

Peel the carrots and grate them on the largest holes of a box grater or with the shredder disk on a food processor. You should have about 6 lightly packed cups.

Warm the olive oil in a large saucepan over medium heat. Add the carrots, lemon zest and juice, water, and salt, reduce the heat to low, and cook, stirring from time to time, until the carrots are softened, 8 to 10 minutes.

Add the rice, stir well, cover the pan, and continue to cook over low heat until all the liquid has been absorbed and the rice is tender, 18 to 20 minutes.

Remove from the heat and let rest, covered, for 5 to 10 minutes.

Spoon the rice and carrots into a serving dish and top with the parsley or mint, if desired. Serve at once.

Variation: For a sweet-and-sour dish, add $1/3$ cup raisins or dried currants, plumped in hot water, when adding the rice. If adding toasted nuts, stir them in just before serving the rice.

: : : : : :

ARROZ *kon* SPINAKA

RICE WITH SPINACH

You can eat this rustic pilaf hot or at room temperature. Sometimes it is served topped with chopped hard-cooked eggs or a little crumbled feta cheese. In Greece it is called *spanakorizo* and remains a popular dish today.

Serves 6

6 TABLESPOONS OLIVE OIL

2 ONIONS, CHOPPED

1 LARGE CLOVE GARLIC, MINCED

1 CUP LONG-GRAIN WHITE RICE

8 CUPS COARSELY CHOPPED SPINACH

$^1/_2$ CUP CHOPPED FRESH DILL

2 RIPE TOMATOES, PEELED, SEEDED, AND
    CHOPPED (OPTIONAL)

$1^1/_2$ TEASPOONS SALT

$^1/_2$ TEASPOON FRESHLY GROUND BLACK PEPPER

$1^1/_2$ CUPS WATER

2 TABLESPOONS FRESH LEMON JUICE

Warm 3 tablespoons of the olive oil in a large sauté pan over medium heat. Add the onions and sauté until translucent, about 5 minutes. Add the garlic and rice and sauté, stirring often, until the grains are well coated with the oil, about 5 minutes. Add the spinach, dill, tomatoes (if using), salt, pepper, and water and raise the heat to high. Bring to a boil, stirring and pushing the spinach down into the pan as it wilts. Reduce the heat to low, cover, and cook until the liquid is absorbed and the rice is tender, 15 to 18 minutes. Remove from the heat and let rest, covered, for 5 to 10 minutes.

Spoon the rice into a serving dish. In a cup, stir together the remaining 3 tablespoons olive oil and the lemon juice and drizzle the mixture over the rice. Serve hot or at room temperature.

Note: If aesthetics are important to you, cook the rice and the spinach separately and fold them together when they are done. The spinach fades in color when it is cooked together with the rice for such a long time. Of course the dish will not taste quite the same, but it will look brighter.

: : : : : :

TORTINO *di* MACCHERONI
con CARNE

PASTA AND MEAT GRATIN

In her book *The Sephardic Kosher Kitchen,* Suzy David calls this same dish *mussaka de macarons.* In the cookbook from Temple Or Ve Shalom in Atlanta, Georgia, it is named *maccaron reinado.* Keeping with the spirit of a classic moussaka, a layer of sautéed eggplant slices can be added. Simply fry the slices in oil or bake them in the oven until soft, and then arrange them on top of the meat layer. In traditional Greek cooking, this dish is known as *pastitsio.* This version comes from a Sephardic menu in *Le feste ebraiche.*

Serves 4 TO 6

1 POUND MACARONI

5 TO 6 TABLESPOONS OLIVE OIL

1 LARGE ONION, CHOPPED

1 POUND GROUND BEEF OR VEAL, OR A MIXTURE

SALT AND FRESHLY GROUND BLACK PEPPER

3 RIPE TOMATOES, PEELED, SEEDED, AND
    CHOPPED (OPTIONAL)

5 EGGS

1/4 CUP CHOPPED FRESH FLAT-LEAF PARSLEY

1 CUP TOMATO SAUCE, HEATED (OPTIONAL; SEE
    EGGPLANT ROLLS WITH TOMATO SAUCE, PAGE 162)

Bring a large pot filled with salted water to a boil. Add the macaroni and cook until al dente, about 10 minutes or according to package directions. Drain well and set aside in a bowl.

Preheat the oven to 350 degrees F. Oil a 9-by-12-inch baking dish.

Warm 3 tablespoons of the oil in a sauté pan over medium heat. Add the onion and sauté until tender and translucent, about 10 minutes. Add the meat and salt and pepper to taste and sauté until the meat is lightly browned, about 5 minutes. Add the tomatoes, if using, stir well, and remove from the heat. Mix in 2 of the eggs. Add the parsley. Whisk the remaining 3 eggs until blended and then stir them into the pasta.

Spread half of the pasta in the bottom of the prepared dish and top with all of the meat mixture. Arrange the remaining pasta over the top. Drizzle the remaining 2 to 3 tablespoons olive oil evenly over the top.

Bake the gratin until golden on the surface, 30 to 40 minutes. Serve directly from the dish. If desired, pass the tomato sauce at the table.

Variation: Melt 3 tablespoons margarine in a saucepan over medium heat and whisk in 3 tablespoons all-purpose flour. Cook, stirring, for 2 to 3 minutes, then gradually add 1 1/2 cups meat stock, whisking constantly. Cook, stirring often, until thickened, about 5 minutes, and remove from the heat. Whisk 3 eggs until blended, then whisk in about 1/2 cup of the hot sauce. Whisk the egg mixture into the remaining sauce. Omit the 3 eggs added to the cooked pasta. Layer the gratin as follows: half of the pasta, one-third of the sauce, all of the meat mixture, half of the remaining sauce, the remaining pasta, and finally the remaining sauce. Bake as directed.

: : : : : :

FIDELLOS TOSTADOS ★ FRIED NOODLES

FIDELLOS TOSTADOS

FRIED NOODLES

In Spain, *fideos* is a classic noodle dish prepared in the manner of paella. The noodles are sautéed to give them some color, then they are cooked in stock until the liquid is absorbed in the manner of rice. In the Turkish book *Sefarad Yemekleri,* these fried noodles are called *skulaka,* and in some Greek cookbooks they are called *fideikos. Fidellos* is a Ladino term. Coiled vermicelli or *fedelini* are the noodles of choice. If you are using the coils, there is no need to break them up, but if you are using long pasta, you will need to snap it into shorter lengths. Some recipes add tomatoes to the cooking liquid. Use vegetable stock or water for a dairy meal, meat or poultry stock for a meat meal.

Serves 4 TO 6

1 PACKAGE (12 OUNCES) COILED VERMICELLI
    OR STRAIGHT *FEDELINI*
$^1/_2$ CUP OLIVE OR SUNFLOWER OIL
2 CUPS PEELED, SEEDED, AND CHOPPED FRESH
    OR CANNED TOMATOES (OPTIONAL)
3 CUPS STOCK, WATER, OR PART WATER AND PART
    TOMATO LIQUID IF USING CANNED TOMATOES
1 TEASPOON SALT

If using *fedelini,* break it into 3-inch lengths. Warm the oil in a large sauté pan over medium heat. Add the noodles and fry, turning once, until golden, about 5 minutes. Add the tomatoes, if using, and the stock or other liquid and the salt. Cover partially and cook, stirring occasionally, until the liquid is absorbed and the noodles are tender, 8 to 10 minutes. Remove the pan from the heat and let rest, covered, for 5 minutes, then serve hot.

: : : : : :

MAKARONIA *kon* LECHE

MACARONI AND CHEESE FROM THRACE

Although this dish will seem remarkably familiar to most Americans, *makaronia kon leche* was a specialty of the town of Komotini, in Thrace, and was often served at Shavuot. The Greeks did not use elbow macaroni, instead preferring a long noodle. The dish can be cooked on top of the stove or baked in the oven.

Serves 4 TO 6

1 POUND MACARONI, ZITI, OR PENNE
1 CUP MILK
$^1/_4$ CUP CRUMBLED FETA CHEESE
$^1/_4$ CUP GRATED PARMESAN CHEESE
ADDITIONAL FETA AND PARMESAN CHEESE IF BAKING

Bring a large pot filled with salted water to a boil. Add the pasta and cook until al dente, 8 to 10 minutes or according to the package directions. Drain well.

Pour the milk into a saucepan and bring just to a boil over medium heat. Add the cheeses, reduce the heat to low, and add the cooked pasta. Cook over low heat, stirring often, until all the milk has been absorbed and the pasta is very tender, about 10 minutes. Spoon into a serving bowl and serve immediately.

Alternatively, preheat the oven to 350 degrees F. Boil the pasta as directed, transfer to a well-buttered baking dish, add the cheeses and milk, stir well, and then sprinkle with additional feta and Parmesan cheeses. Bake until browned, about 20 minutes. Serve directly from the dish.

: : : : : :

CIPOLLINE *in* AGRODOLCE

SWEET-AND-SOUR PEARL ONIONS

You can serve these Venetian sweet-and-sour pearl onions hot or at room temperature. Note the classic Levantine addition of pine nuts and raisins.

Serves 6

2 1/2 POUNDS SMALL WHITE, YELLOW, OR RED
  ONIONS, EACH ABOUT 1 INCH IN DIAMETER
6 TABLESPOONS UNSALTED BUTTER OR OLIVE OIL
2 TABLESPOONS SUGAR
6 TABLESPOONS RED WINE VINEGAR
1/4 CUP RAISINS
1/4 CUP PINE NUTS
SALT

Trim the root ends of the onions carefully, leaving the bottom of each bulb intact. Cut a cross in each root end to prevent the onion from telescoping during cooking. Bring a large saucepan filled with water to a boil. Add the onions and boil until cooked but still firm, 5 to 10 minutes, depending upon their size. Drain and, when cool enough to handle, slip off the skins.

Warm the butter or olive oil in a large sauté pan over medium heat. Add the onions and sauté, stirring occasionally, until golden brown, about 8 minutes. Reduce the heat to low and add the sugar, vinegar, raisins, and pine nuts. Stir well, cover tightly, and simmer until the onions are completely tender, about 15 minutes longer. Season with salt and transfer to a serving dish.

Note: La cucina nella tradizione ebraica suggests a splash of Marsala for plumping the raisins before adding them to the onions.

: : : : : :

BULGUR *or* PILAV

WHEAT PILAF

Bulgur and cracked wheat are staples of the Sephardic Turkish kitchen and are used in Greece as well, primarily in soups. Cracked wheat is whole wheat berries that have been crushed with steel blades. Bulgur is wheat berries that have been steamed, dried, and then crushed. American markets are not always careful about labeling these two products, but either one will work in this recipe.

Most recipes for wheat pilaf cook the grain as if it were rice, steaming it in stock to cover. More often than not this results in a mixture that is heavy and soggy, with the grains sticking together. To have the wheat dry out properly, start cooking it in the same manner as you cook risotto, then finish it in the oven.

Serves 6 TO 8

1/4 CUP MARGARINE OR OLIVE OIL
1 ONION, FINELY CHOPPED
SALT
1 1/2 CUPS MEDIUM-GRIND BULGUR OR CRACKED WHEAT
3 CUPS CHICKEN STOCK OR WATER, HEATED
OPTIONAL GARNISHES: CHOPPED GREEN ONIONS,
  CHOPPED FRESH MINT OR CORIANDER, DRIED
  CURRANTS PLUMPED IN HOT WATER AND DRAINED,
  OR CHOPPED TOASTED ALMONDS OR PINE NUTS

Preheat the oven to 350 degrees F.

Warm the margarine or olive oil in a heavy sauté pan over medium heat. Add the onion and a sprinkling of salt and sauté until the onion is tender and translucent, about 10 minutes. Add the bulgur or cracked wheat and stir until the grains are well coated with the fat, about 3 minutes. Add half of the hot chicken stock or water, reduce the heat to low, and stir until the liquid is absorbed, about 10 minutes. Add the remaining liquid, raise the heat to high, and bring to a boil. Reduce the heat to low, cover tightly, and cook for 15 minutes.

Uncover, transfer the pilaf to a baking dish, and place in the oven. Bake, uncovered, for 15 to 20 minutes. Stir the pilaf and test for doneness. It should be ready, but if the grains seem sticky, return the dish to the oven for about 10 minutes longer, or until the grains are dry and separate.

Remove from the oven and fold in one of the garnishes, if desired. Serve directly from the dish.

: : : : : :

FISH

chapter 5

✦

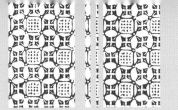
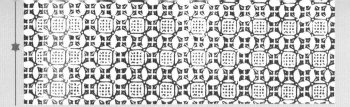

FISH

Fish holds a central place on the Sephardic table. It is served on Friday night of the Sabbath and is often part of the meatless Thursday dinner as well. A whole fish with head intact is traditionally served for Rosh Hashanah, to commemorate the head, that is, the beginning, of the new year.

The most popular fish preparations are poached, baked or braised with a sauce, or fried. Probably the most common accompanying sauce is *agristada,* an egg-and-lemon mixture. Today, as in the past, it is a common thickener for sauces in Spain, Italy, Greece, and Turkey, especially those for fish and vegetable dishes. (In the kosher kitchen, however, *agristada* is also used in place of béchamel, *beurre manié,* or cream in meat dishes in which dairy products are prohibited.) Usually *agristada* is assembled in the pan, using the warm fish cooking liquids, but a second version, thickened with cornstarch or flour and served cold like a mayonnaise, is also served. The other classic sauce for fish, especially for dishes that are served cold, is *ajada,* a garlic mayonnaise that is a relative of aioli.

Hispano-Arabic–inspired nut sauces and sweet-and-sour sauces, often fruit based (plum, rhubarb, or fruit and tomato), are used on fish, too. Tomato sauce is yet another typical accompaniment. In many cases, the sauce is not cooked separately, but instead is one that occurs in the pan as the fish cooks with chopped tomatoes. The tomatoes are often enhanced with onion, sometimes with garlic, and usually with a good squeeze of lemon juice, a piquant finish consistent with the tart flavors favored by the Sephardic Turkish and Greek palate.

PESHKADO PLAKI

FISH, PLAKI STYLE

In Greece, *plaki* style is one of the most popular ways for preparing baked fish. Variations on this recipe are found in Italy, France, and Spain as well. In *The Sephardic Kitchen,* Rabbi Robert Sternberg includes a version called *peshkado ahilado kon legumbres.* In Temple Bikur Holim's *Sephardic Cookbook,* a similar recipe called fish *plaqui* adds a red pepper to the green one and a few diced carrots.

Serves 4

6 TABLESPOONS OLIVE OIL

2 TABLESPOONS FRESH LEMON JUICE

1 TEASPOON DRIED OREGANO (OPTIONAL)

KOSHER OR SEA SALT AND FRESHLY
    GROUND BLACK PEPPER

4 FIRM WHITE FISH FILLETS SUCH AS COD,
    FLOUNDER, SEA BASS, OR HALIBUT,
    ABOUT 6 OUNCES EACH

2 ONIONS, HALVED AND THINLY SLICED

2 CLOVES GARLIC, FINELY MINCED

1/4 CUP CHOPPED FRESH FLAT-LEAF PARSLEY

1 POUND BOILING POTATOES, COOKED UNTIL
    TENDER BUT STILL FIRM, PEELED, AND SLICED
    (OPTIONAL)

4 LARGE, RIPE TOMATOES, PEELED AND SLICED

1/2 CUP FISH STOCK OR DRY WHITE WINE,
    OR AS NEEDED

In a small cup, stir together 2 tablespoons of the olive oil, 2 tablespoons of the lemon juice, the oregano (if using), and salt and pepper to taste. Rub the fish fillets with the mixture, cover, and refrigerate for 1 hour.

Preheat the oven to 400 degrees F. Oil a baking dish large enough to hold the fish fillets in a single layer.

Warm 3 tablespoons of the olive oil in a large sauté pan over medium heat. Add the onions and sauté until tender and translucent, about 10 minutes. Add the garlic and sauté for 1 minute longer. Stir in half of the parsley and season with salt and pepper.

If using potatoes, arrange them in a layer on the bottom of the dish and season with salt and pepper. Top with the onions, then the fish fillets, and finally the tomato slices. If not using potatoes, arrange the fillets in the bottom of the dish and top with the onions and then the tomatoes. Pour on any marinade remaining from the fish and add the 1/2 cup fish stock or wine. Bake until the fillets test done with the point of a knife inserted into the thickest part, 12 to 18 minutes. If the mixture seems dry during baking, add more stock, wine, or water to the dish. Remove the dish from the oven, sprinkle with the remaining parsley, and serve immediately directly from the dish.

Note: A more baroque version of this recipe, called *gewetch di pescado,* appears in Suzy David's *The Sephardic Kosher Kitchen.* She adds green bell peppers, carrots, celery, peas, and green beans, creating a kind of *primavera* sauce, seasoned with allspice and bay. She layers the precooked vegetables with sliced potatoes, places the fish fillets on top, covers them with lemon slices, and adds a good drizzle of olive oil. The dish is covered and baked for 20 to 30 minutes and served warm or cold. In the cookbook from Atlanta's Temple Or Ve Shalom, this dish is called *capama,* from the Turkish word for "to cover," and, in its English translation, fish Creole.

: : : : : :

PESHKADO AHILADO *kon* SALSA COLORADO

FISH WITH RED PEPPER SAUCE

Instead of a red sauce made with tomatoes and lemon, this Turkish recipe from *La table juive* uses roasted red peppers and paprika, a nod to its Spanish origin. The original recipe called for "Arab parsley," a colloquial term for fresh coriander. To accent the smokiness of the roasted peppers, you may want to use the imported Spanish paprika called pimentón de La Vera, available at some specialty stores.

Serves 6

2 POUNDS FIRM WHITE FISH FILLETS SUCH AS
    SEA BASS, COD, FLOUNDER, SNAPPER, OR
    HALIBUT
KOSHER OR SEA SALT AND FRESHLY GROUND
    BLACK PEPPER
3 RED BELL PEPPERS, ROASTED, PEELED,
    SEEDED, AND CHOPPED
6 CLOVES GARLIC, MINCED
$1/2$ TO $3/4$ CUP WATER
1 TABLESPOON SWEET PAPRIKA
1 TEASPOON GROUND CUMIN (OPTIONAL)
$1/4$ CUP CHOPPED FRESH CORIANDER
OLIVE OIL

Place the fish fillets on a plate, sprinkle with salt and pepper, cover, and refrigerate for 30 minutes.

In a food processor or mortar, combine the peppers, garlic, and $1/2$ cup water and process or mash to make a spoonable sauce, adding more water as needed. You should have about $1 1/2$ cups pepper puree. Season with salt, pepper, paprika, and the cumin, if you like. Stir in the coriander.

Place the fish fillets in a single layer in a large sauté pan and pour the pepper sauce over them. Drizzle with olive oil. Place the pan over low heat, cover, and cook gently until the fillets test done with the point of a knife inserted into the thickest part, 10 to 15 minutes, depending upon the thickness of the fish.

Transfer the fillets and sauce to a platter and serve at once.

Note: In *La table juive,* a version of this dish, called *peshkado con tomat y pimientón,* appears. In that recipe, tomatoes are sautéed together with 3 roasted red peppers, sliced, in 3 tablespoons olive oil and then seasoned with salt and pepper. The juice of 4 lemons is added, the fish is placed in the sauce, the pan is covered, and the fish is simmered until it tests done, about 15 minutes. In his recipe for *peshkado ahilado con tomate* in *The Sephardic Kitchen,* Rabbi Robert Sternberg uses roasted green peppers instead of red ones, while in some variations of the recipe, chopped medium-hot chiles similar to poblanos are added to the sauce.

: : : : : :

MOUSSAKA *di* PESCE

BAKED FISH WITH RICE AND EGGPLANT

Moussaka is typically a Greek or Turkish dish of lamb and eggplant seasoned with tomatoes. Versions made with potatoes, artichoke stems, and cauliflower also exist. This Sephardic recipe for fish moussaka appears in *La cucina nella tradizione ebraica,* a cookbook assembled by an Italian women's group. It also appears in the collection of recipes from Temple Or Ve Shalom in Atlanta, but without the rice. In Salonika, *peshe* is adopted from *pesce,* the Italian word for fish.

Serves 6

12 EGGPLANT SLICES, EACH $^1/_2$ INCH THICK

SALT

4 CUPS WATER, LIGHTLY SALTED

1 CUP LONG-GRAIN WHITE RICE

ALL-PURPOSE FLOUR

FRESHLY GROUND BLACK PEPPER

OLIVE OIL

3 CLOVES GARLIC, MINCED

1 TABLESPOON GROUND CUMIN

2 $^1/_2$ CUPS TOMATO SAUCE OR PUREED
    CANNED PLUM TOMATOES

6 FIRM FISH FILLETS SUCH AS SWORDFISH,
    TUNA, HALIBUT, OR SEA BASS, EACH 5
    TO 6 OUNCES AND $^1/_2$ INCH THICK

1 EGG, LIGHTLY BEATEN (OPTIONAL)

Sprinkle the eggplant slices generously with salt and place in a colander to drain for about 30 minutes.

Meanwhile, bring the salted water to a boil. Add the rice and boil until al dente, 10 to 12 minutes. Drain in a sieve and rinse with cold water to stop the cooking. Drain again and set aside.

Preheat the oven to 375 degrees F. Oil a 9-by-12-inch baking dish.

When the eggplant is ready, rinse well and squeeze dry. Spread some flour on a plate. Season with salt and pepper. Pour olive oil to a depth of $^1/_2$ inch into a large sauté pan, and warm over medium-high heat. Working in batches, dip the eggplant slices into the flour, tapping off the excess, and slip them into the hot oil. Fry, turning once, until golden and cooked through, 6 to 8 minutes total. Transfer to paper towels to drain, then sprinkle with salt. Repeat until all the slices are fried, adding oil to the pan as needed.

In a small saucepan, warm 1 tablespoon olive oil over medium heat. Add the garlic and cumin and warm through. Add the tomato sauce or pureed tomatoes and simmer, stirring occasionally, for 3 minutes to blend the flavors. Season with salt and pepper and remove from the heat.

Pour oil to a depth of $^1/_4$ inch in a large sauté pan and heat over medium-high heat. Spread the remaining seasoned flour on a plate. Working in batches, dip the fish fillets into the flour, tapping off the excess, and slip them into the hot oil. Fry, turning once, until golden on both sides, about 3 to 4 minutes on each side. Transfer to a plate.

Season the rice generously with salt and pepper and layer it in the bottom of the prepared baking dish. Cover it with the fried fish in a single layer, then top with the eggplant slices and finally the tomatoes. If you like, pour the beaten egg evenly over the top. Bake until the fish tests done when the point of a knife is inserted into the thickest part, about 20 minutes. Serve hot directly from the dish.

: : : : : :

PESHKADO AVRAMILA

FISH WITH ABRAHAM'S FRUIT

According to Sephardic folklore, after Abraham was circumcised, he sat under a sour plum tree, and thus the plum has come to be called Abraham's fruit. In Turkey, this dish is prepared for Rosh Hashanah, an autumn holiday when a whole fish is customarily served. At that time of year, many kinds of plums are at the market, and although yellow plums are traditional, you can use another tart plum. The amount of moisture plums contain varies, so you will have to see how much water you need to add, or conversely how much you will need to reduce the sauce. If you have a craving for this dish in the dead of winter, dried plums, that is, prunes, can be used along with the same ingredients (see note). The fish can be served warm or at room temperature and is usually accompanied with Rice with Pine Nuts (page 109).

Serves 4

1 WHOLE FISH SUCH AS SALMON, COD, OR SNAPPER,
    4 TO 5 POUNDS, CLEANED
COURT BOUILLON (SEE POACHED FISH WITH
    ALMOND SAUCE OR WALNUT SAUCE, PAGE 126)

For the plum sauce:
2 POUNDS TART PLUMS, PREFERABLY A YELLOW
    VARIETY, PITTED AND CUT INTO PIECES
1 CUP WATER
3 TABLESPOONS VEGETABLE OIL
ABOUT $^1/_2$ CUP RED WINE, A SWEET WINE LIKE
    MARSALA, OR WATER
GRATED ZEST AND JUICE OF 2 LEMONS
SALT AND FRESHLY GROUND BLACK PEPPER
PINCH OF GROUND ALLSPICE OR CLOVES (OPTIONAL)
SUGAR, IF NEEDED

Measure the thickness of the whole fish at its thickest point and set the fish aside. Prepare the court bouillon as directed.

Meanwhile, begin making the plum sauce. In a saucepan, combine the plums and water and bring to a simmer over medium heat. Cook the plums, uncovered, until they become quite soft, 15 to 20 minutes. If the skins are not too tough, transfer the contents of the pan to a food processor and puree until smooth. If the skins are tough, pass the mixture through a food mill placed over a bowl. You should have about $1^1/_3$ cups puree.

Return the pureed plums to the saucepan, add the vegetable oil, the wine or water as needed to thin the mixture, and some of the lemon juice and zest to balance the plums' sweetness. Place over medium heat, bring to a simmer, and cook, stirring from time to time, until thickened. Season with salt, a generous amount of black pepper, and the allspice or cloves, if using. Taste the sauce and, if it is too tart, do not add any more lemon; instead, stir in a little sugar. You are looking for a nice balance between sweet and sour. Cover and keep warm.

Slip the fish into the court bouillon and cook as directed. Using 2 slotted spatulas, carefully transfer the fish to a platter. Reheat the sauce gently and spoon it over the fish. Serve warm or at room temperature.

Note: For a wintertime prune sauce, place 1 pound pitted prunes in a saucepan with water to cover and simmer over medium heat until tender, about 30 minutes. Using a slotted spoon, transfer the plums to a food processor and puree until smooth.

Pour the puree into a clean saucepan and thin with the wine or water and the lemon juice. Add the lemon zest, sugar to taste, and the oil and simmer for 10 minutes to blend the flavors. Season with salt and pepper and a pinch of cinnamon or cloves. Adjust the lemon or sugar. Serve as you would the plum sauce.

There are times when you won't want to cook a whole fish, but you can bake fish fillets in the sauce. Place the fish fillets in an oiled baking dish, top with the sauce, and bake, in a 400 degree F oven until the fish tests done, 10 to 15 minutes for each inch of thickness. Fish fillets may also be simmered covered in the sauce on top of the stove. Finally, although it is not traditional, you can broil or grill fish fillets and spoon the warm sauce over the cooked fish.

: : : : : :

CEVIZLI BALIK *or* BADEMLI BALIK

POACHED FISH WITH WALNUT SAUCE OR ALMOND SAUCE

In the Sephardic community, carp was considered the special holiday fish, especially for Rosh Hashanah, as it represented good luck and longevity. In Salonika, the carp, or *sazan,* came from a lake the Sephardim called Goyvasidi, a Ladino corruption of Agios Vasilios (Saint Basil), the Greek name for the lake. While the fish could be served very simply, with just the court bouillon reduced to a shimmering jelly or thickened with the egg-and-lemon *agristada,* it also was sometimes covered with a fragrant nut sauce, in the manner of a Turkish *tarator.* Here, I have provided a walnut sauce and an almond sauce, each sufficient to cover the fish.

Serves 6

1 WHOLE FISH SUCH AS CARP, SALMON, COD, FLOUNDER, OR SNAPPER, 5 TO 7 POUNDS, CLEANED

For the court bouillon:

4 CUPS WATER

1 CUP DRY WHITE WINE

1 LARGE ONION, HALVED

2 CARROTS, PEELED AND SLICED

2 CELERY STALKS WITH LEAVES ATTACHED, AND/OR 2 LARGE SLICES CELERY ROOT, PEELED AND SLICED

3 FRESH FLAT-LEAF PARSLEY SPRIGS

10 TO 12 BLACK PEPPERCORNS

3 LEMON SLICES

For the walnut sauce:

1 CUP GROUND WALNUTS

1 OR 2 SLICES DAY-OLD RUSTIC BREAD, CRUSTS REMOVED, SOAKED IN WATER, AND SQUEEZED DRY

6 TABLESPOONS CHOPPED FRESH FLAT-LEAF PARSLEY

3 TO 4 CLOVES GARLIC, MINCED (OPTIONAL)

¼ CUP WINE VINEGAR

¼ CUP WATER, OR AS NEEDED

3 TO 4 TABLESPOONS OLIVE OIL, OR AS NEEDED

SALT AND FRESHLY GROUND BLACK PEPPER

For the almond sauce:

1 CUP GROUND ALMONDS

2 SLICES DAY-OLD RUSTIC BREAD, CRUSTS REMOVED, SOAKED IN WATER, AND SQUEEZED DRY

6 TABLESPOONS CHOPPED FRESH FLAT-LEAF PARSLEY OR DILL

3 TABLESPOONS WINE VINEGAR

¼ CUP WATER

3 TO 4 TABLESPOONS OLIVE OIL, OR AS NEEDED

SALT AND FRESHLY GROUND BLACK PEPPER

Measure the thickness of the whole fish at its thickest point and set the fish aside.

In a fish poacher (or, lacking a poacher, a roasting pan), combine all of the ingredients for the court bouillon. Bring to a boil over high heat, reduce the heat to medium, and simmer for 10 minutes. Slip the whole fish into the simmering liquid, cover, reduce the heat to very low so that bubbles barely break on the surface, and poach until the fish tests done when the point of a knife is inserted into the thickest part, about 10 minutes for each inch of thickness.

With 2 slotted spatulas, carefully transfer the fish to a platter. Let it cool, then carefully remove the skin. Clean the platter, removing any extra juices that may have settled on it.

While the fish is cooling, make one of the nut sauces. To make the walnut sauce *(cevizli balik),* put the walnuts, soaked bread, parsley, and the garlic, if using, in a food processor. Pulse well to combine. Transfer to a bowl and stir in the vinegar, water, and olive oil. Season with salt and pepper. Add more water or oil as needed to create a spoonable sauce. Taste and adjust the seasonings.

To make the almond sauce *(bademli balik),* put the almonds, soaked bread, and parsley or dill in a food processor. Pulse well to combine. Transfer to a bowl and stir in the vinegar, water, and oil. Season with salt and pepper. Add more water or oil as needed to create a spoonable sauce. Taste and adjust the seasonings.

Mask the fish with the walnut or almond sauce and serve at room temperature.

Notes: Fish fillets such as salmon, cod, sea bass, or flounder can be used in place of the whole fish. Use 6 thick fillets, each weighing about 6 ounces. This recipe can be made into a Passover dish by substituting $1/2$ cup matzoh meal for the bread in either sauce. Nicholas Stavroulakis describes another fish with nut sauce in *The Cookbook of the Jews of Greece.* For that recipe, fish fillets are dipped in egg, coated with matzoh meal, and then fried in olive oil. Once the fish is removed from the pan, ground nuts, water, and vinegar are added to it and simmered together until a sauce forms, and then the fillets are reheated in the sauce.

: : : : : :

PESHKADO *kon* RUIBARBARO

FISH WITH RHUBARB SAUCE

Spring marks the arrival of rhubarb at the market and of Passover. Thus, it is not surprising that fish in sweet-and-sour rhubarb sauce appears on the Seder table in Greece and Turkey. The major difference between the preparations favored in the two countries is in the proportion of rhubarb to tomato. In Greece, one part rhubarb to two parts tomato rules, while in Turkey the proportions are reversed. The original version of this recipe, from the Jewish community of Rhodes, calls for swordfish, but some rabbis forbid its use as it does not have scales for the first six months of its life. Sea bass, cod, flounder, and salmon are excellent alternatives. This dish was a great favorite at my San Francisco restaurant, Square One. We served it during Passover and then off and on throughout the rhubarb season. Although not authentic, you can also grill the fish fillets and spoon the sauce over them at the table.

Serves 4 TO 6

For the rhubarb sauce:

1 1/2 POUNDS RHUBARB

3 CUPS WATER

2 TABLESPOONS OLIVE OIL

1 1/2 POUNDS RIPE TOMATOES, PEELED, SEEDED, AND CHOPPED, OR ABOUT 3 CUPS CHOPPED, SEEDED CANNED PLUM TOMATOES

1 CUP DRY RED WINE

1 TO 2 TABLESPOONS HONEY

ZEST AND JUICE OF 1 LEMON (OPTIONAL)

SALT AND FRESHLY GROUND BLACK PEPPER

PINCH OF GROUND CINNAMON (OPTIONAL)

2 POUNDS FIRM FISH FILLETS SUCH AS COD, SEA BASS, FLOUNDER, OR SALMON

To make the rhubarb sauce, clean the rhubarb stalks by pulling off the heavy filaments, much as you would pull strings from celery. Cut crosswise into 1 1/2-inch pieces. Place the pieces in a saucepan and add the water. Bring to a boil over high heat, reduce the heat to low, and simmer, uncovered, until the rhubarb has melted into a puree and is tender, 8 to 10 minutes.

Warm the olive oil in a sauté pan over medium heat. Add the tomatoes and cook, stirring occasionally, until the tomatoes are reduced to a thick sauce, about 15 minutes. Add the wine, 1 tablespoon honey, and the lemon juice and zest, if using, and stir well. Add the tomatoes to the rhubarb puree, or vice versa, and mix well. Simmer, uncovered, over low heat until the sauce is thick and rich, about 20 minutes. Season with salt, pepper, and the cinnamon, if using. Taste and adjust the sweet-and-sour balance, adding a bit more honey if needed. Keep warm.

While the sauce is cooking, preheat the oven to 400 degrees F.

Arrange the fish fillets in a single layer in a baking dish. Spoon some of the sauce over them, covering them completely. Cover and bake until the fish tests done when the point of a knife is inserted into the thickest part, about 15 minutes. Transfer the fillets to a platter and spoon the rest of the warm sauce over them. Serve at once.

: : : : : :

SAZAN *en* SALTSA

CARP WITH SWEET-AND-SOUR SAUCE

While the Italians use pine nuts and raisins for an *agrodolce,* or sweet-and-sour sauce, the Greeks use dried currants and walnuts, along with red wine and vinegar, for this Passover specialty from Salonika.

Serves 6

1 WHOLE CARP, ABOUT 6 POUNDS, CLEANED, OR

    6 FISH FILLETS SUCH AS COD, SNAPPER, HALIBUT,

    OR SEA BASS, ABOUT 6 OUNCES EACH

KOSHER OR SEA SALT

6 TO 8 TABLESPOONS OLIVE OIL

2 TO 3 TABLESPOONS FRESH LEMON JUICE

1 ONION, FINELY CHOPPED

$^3/_4$ CUP DRY RED WINE

$^1/_4$ CUP RED WINE VINEGAR

$^1/_2$ CUP DRIED CURRANTS

$^1/_2$ CUP WALNUTS, TOASTED AND CHOPPED

$^1/_2$ CUP CHOPPED FRESH FLAT-LEAF PARSLEY

FRESHLY GROUND BLACK PEPPER

If using a whole fish, clean and fillet the fish, or have your fishmonger do it for you. Divide each fillet into 3 equal pieces. Place the fillets on a platter and sprinkle with salt. In a small bowl, whisk together 2 tablespoons of the olive oil and 2 tablespoons of the lemon juice and pour evenly over the fish. Cover and refrigerate for at least 1 to 3 hours.

Warm 2 to 3 tablespoons of the oil in a large sauté pan over medium-high heat. Add the fish and sauté, turning once, until browned on both sides, about 6 minutes total. Transfer to a plate and set aside. Discard the oil in the pan and wipe the pan clean.

Return the pan to medium heat and add 2 tablespoons oil. Add the onion and sauté until tender, about 8 minutes. Add the wine, vinegar, currants, and walnuts and simmer until a rich sauce forms, about 10 minutes.

Return the fish to the pan and simmer it in the sauce over low heat, basting with the sauce a few times, until the fish tests done when the point of a knife is inserted into the thickest part, about 10 minutes. Using a spatula, transfer the fish to a platter, spoon the sauce over the top, and sprinkle with the parsley and pepper. Serve at once.

: : : : : :

SOGLIOLE *al* LIMONE *per il* SABATO

SOLE WITH LEMON FOR THE SABBATH

Poached fish is a specialty of the Sabbath meal, either a large whole carp or striped bass or one small fish for each person. In Italy, each diner is served a whole sole, with its head and tail intact. Of course, you can make this favorite Sabbath dish from Ancona with $1^1/_2$ pounds sole fillets, poaching them for only 4 to 5 minutes, but you will miss the delicate flavor that the bones impart.

Serves 4

4 WHOLE DOVER SOLES, ABOUT 1 POUND EACH, CLEANED

KOSHER OR SEA SALT

3 CUPS WATER, DRY WHITE WINE, OR FISH STOCK

OLIVE OIL

FRESH LEMON JUICE

CHOPPED FRESH FLAT-LEAF PARSLEY (OPTIONAL)

Sprinkle the fish with kosher salt. In a wide saucepan, bring the water, wine, or stock to a boil over high heat. Slip in the fish, cover the pan, adjust the heat to very low, and poach until the fish tests done when the tip of a knife is inserted into the thickest part of each one, about 10 minutes. Using a slotted spatula, carefully transfer the fish to a platter.

Remove the skin from each fish, then cut along the central bone and carefully remove the top fillets and place them on another platter. With a fork, lift up and discard the central bone, then transfer the bottom fillets to the platter. Dress with olive oil, lemon juice, and the parsley, if using.

Variations: Poach the fish as directed, then remove from the pan, peel away the skin, and fillet the fish. Add a pinch of saffron threads and a little fresh lemon juice to the poaching liquid and boil to reduce to 1 cup. Pour the reduced liquid over the fillets, cover, and refrigerate until the juices form a jelly. Serve chilled.

For a Greek version of this same sauce, omit the saffron and reduce the poaching liquid to 1 cup. Add the juice of 1 lemon and 2 cloves garlic, finely minced, to the pan and simmer for 5 minutes. Season with salt and freshly ground black pepper, and stir in 3 tablespoons chopped fresh dill. Pour over the fish and chill as directed.

To serve warm, as for the classic *peshkado kon huevos y limon,* transfer the fish to a platter, remove the skin, and fillet. Measure out $1/2$ cup of the poaching liquid and reserve for the sauce. Save the rest for another use. In a small bowl, beat 2 eggs with the juice of 3 lemons until quite frothy.

Gradually whisk the $1/2$ cup hot poaching liquid into the eggs to temper them. Pour the egg mixture back into the pan and place over very low heat. Do not stir, but do shake the pan back and forth until the egg mixture thickens. Spoon over the warm fish and serve at once.

: : : : : :

KEFTES *de* PESCADO
FISH CAKES

In the Sephardic kitchen, the use of leftovers is raised to a high art. Cooked fish is combined with mashed potatoes for delicious fish cakes, which are made special with the addition of *agristada* or *ajada* sauce. For leftover salmon, I love dill and *agristada.* For halibut or other mild-flavored fish, I add about $1/2$ teaspoon sweet paprika to the onions, and parsley or marjoram is my herb of choice. In Greece and especially in Turkey, Sephardic cooks like to make croquettes with "blue" fish, slightly oily, full-flavored fish (not to be confused with the white-fleshed bluefish of the north Atlantic).

Serves 4

1 SMALL YELLOW ONION, GRATED, OR $1/2$ CUP
    MINCED GREEN ONION, INCLUDING GREEN TOPS
1 TABLESPOON OLIVE OIL (OPTIONAL), PLUS
    OIL FOR FRYING
1 POUND COOKED FISH, FLAKED
$1^1/2$ TO 2 CUPS MASHED POTATOES
2 EGGS
2 TO 3 TABLESPOONS CHOPPED FRESH FLAT-LEAF
    PARSLEY OR DILL (OPTIONAL)
SALT AND FRESHLY GROUND BLACK PEPPER
MATZOH MEAL OR ALL-PURPOSE FLOUR
GARLIC MAYONNAISE OR EGG-AND-LEMON SAUCE
    (SEE FRIED FISH, PAGE 131)

If you think the raw onion will be too sharp tasting, warm the 1 tablespoon olive oil in a small frying pan and sauté the onion until barely softened, 3 to 5 minutes. Remove from the heat.

In a bowl, combine the fish, potatoes, onion, eggs, and the herb, if using. Mix well and season with salt and pepper. Form the mixture into 8 chubby cakes each about 3 inches in diameter. If the mixture does not hold together easily, fold in a little matzoh meal. (The croquettes can be formed up to 4 hours ahead of cooking, covered, and refrigerated.)

Pour olive oil to a depth of ¼ inch into a large sauté pan and place over medium heat. Spread matzoh meal or flour on a plate. Working in batches, dip the fish cakes in the matzoh meal or flour, coating evenly, and place in the hot oil. Fry, turning once, until golden on both sides and heated through, 4 to 6 minutes total.

Transfer to a platter and serve at once. Pass the sauce at the table.

: : : : : :

PESCADO FRITO

FRIED FISH WITH GARLIC MAYONNAISE OR EGG-AND-LEMON SAUCE

Fried fish is popular all over the Mediterranean. Andalusia, where a large Jewish community once resided, was known both then and now as the "zone of frying," as there always have been innumerable *freidurías,* or fish-frying shops, in the region. Although many people equate fried fish with greasy fish-and-chip emporia, frying, if properly done, can be a wonderful way to capture the sweetness of fish. In Spain, olive oil was the traditional frying medium, but in Turkey its high cost saw it eventually replaced with sunflower oil. The fish may be dipped in lightly seasoned flour and fried, or it may be dipped in lightly beaten eggs and then in flour and fried. A squeeze of lemon at the table is all it needs, or perhaps a dollop of *ajada,* the Sephardic garlic mayonnaise known as *alioli* in Spain and *agliata* in Italy. The fish also can be served with *agristada,* an egg-and-lemon sauce that is called *avgolemono* in Greece and *terbiyeli* in Turkey.

Serves 4 TO 6

For the garlic mayonnaise:
5 OR 6 CLOVES GARLIC, GREEN SPROUTS REMOVED AND MINCED
KOSHER OR SEA SALT
1 EGG YOLK, AT ROOM TEMPERATURE
1 CUP VEGETABLE OIL, OR PART OLIVE OIL AND PART VEGETABLE OIL
2 TO 3 TABLESPOONS FRESH LEMON JUICE

For the egg-and-lemon sauce:
2 TABLESPOONS CORNSTARCH (SEE NOTE)
2 CUPS FISH STOCK OR WATER (OR PART STOCK AND PART WATER)
3 EGGS, LIGHTLY BEATEN
JUICE OF 2 LEMONS (⅓ TO ½ CUP)
SALT

2 POUNDS FISH FILLETS, SUCH AS SOLE, SNAPPER, OR COD, OR BONED WHOLE SMELTS
KOSHER OR SEA SALT
ALL-PURPOSE FLOUR
FRESHLY GROUND BLACK PEPPER
SWEET PAPRIKA (OPTIONAL)
2 EGGS
VEGETABLE OIL FOR FRYING

You can make either the garlic mayonnaise or the egg-and-lemon sauce for serving with the fish. To make the garlic mayonnaise *(ajada),* combine the garlic and salt on a cutting board and mash with the side of a knife to a fine puree. Transfer to a blender or food processor, add the egg yolk, and pulse to combine. With the motor running, slowly add the oil, drop by drop, until a thick emulsion forms. Then add the remaining oil in a very slow, steady stream and process until the mixture is the consistency of mayonnaise. Add lemon juice to taste, and thin with a little cold water if the mixture is too thick. Transfer to a bowl, cover, and refrigerate until serving.

To make the egg-and-lemon sauce *(agristada),* in a small saucepan, combine the cornstarch with a few tablespoons of the stock or water and stir to make a smooth paste. Add the remaining stock and/or water and bring to a boil over high heat, stirring constantly so no lumps form. Reduce the heat to medium and simmer, stirring often, until thickened, about 10 minutes. Remove from the heat. In a bowl, beat together the eggs and lemon juice until quite frothy. Whisk in a little of the hot stock to temper the eggs, then gradually stir the eggs into the liquid remaining in the pan. Simmer over very low heat, stirring often, until the sauce thickens, just a few minutes. Remove from the heat and season with salt. Transfer to a bowl and cover to keep warm, or let cool and serve cold.

Place the fish fillets or boned smelts on a plate, sprinkle with salt, cover, and refrigerate for 30 minutes.

Spread the flour on a plate and season with salt, pepper, and the paprika, if using. Beat the eggs in a wide, shallow bowl. Pour vegetable oil to a depth of 2 inches into a deep sauté pan and heat to 375 degrees F on a deep-frying thermometer. Working in batches, dip the fish fillets or smelts into the eggs and then into the flour and slip them into the hot oil. Fry, turning once, until golden and crisp, 3 to 4 minutes total for the fillets and a little less for the smelts. Using a slotted spatula, transfer to paper towels to drain briefly. Keep warm until all the fish is fried.

Arrange the fish on a platter and serve piping hot. Pass the sauce at the table.

Notes: Some versions of *ajada* (also called *azada*) add 1 slice rustic bread, crusts removed, soaked in water, and squeezed dry, to the mixture, making it more like a Greek *skordalia.* Other recipes add mashed potato or finely chopped walnuts or almonds.

When the *agristada* is served cold, it has the consistency of a mayonnaise. The cornstarch helps it to hold its emulsion.

: : : : : :

PESCADO FRITO ★ FRIED FISH WITH GARLIC MAYONNAISE OR EGG-AND-LEMON SAUCE

POULTRY AND MEAT

chapter 6

✡

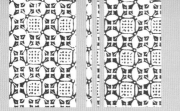

POULTRY AND MEAT

In the past, chickens were more expensive than meat and, more importantly, they were valued primarily for their eggs. Thus, the repertoire of traditional Sephardic poultry dishes is rather small. Chicken was served almost only on special occasions, such as the day before Yom Kippur, or when a hen became too old to lay eggs, at which point it was slaughtered for the table. Eggs, in contrast, were the basis of many preparations, such as *fritadas* and *almodrotes,* or they were used to make the sauces that accompanied dishes.

A roast chicken was often the centerpiece of a holiday table. It might be stuffed with apples and onions or with a currant-studded matzoh meal mixture for Passover. At other times, the bird would be cut up and braised with peppers, okra, tomatoes, eggplant, or dried fruits.

Of course, today chicken is much more readily available, and the contemporary chicken is considerably more tender than the birds of the past. Because of this change in quality, I'd also suggest using chicken thighs for the braising recipes, as they hold their juiciness better than the breasts, which have a tendency to dry out quickly. Whether you brown the thighs before braising them is up to you. That step will give them better color, but any crispiness that is gained will be lost once they are braised.

As with poultry, meat was not served every day at the Sephardic table. For the most part, it was reserved for holiday meals and other special occasions. Lamb, beef, and occasionally veal formed the basis of stews, meat loaves, meatballs, and fillings for hollowed-out vegetables and grape, cabbage, spinach, and Swiss chard leaves. The Sephardim are famous for their repertoire of *albóndigas,* or "meatballs." For economy's sake ground meat was stretched with cooked vegetables such as eggplant, leeks, spinach, or potatoes. In the same spirit of frugality, stews were extended with the addition of okra, eggplant, peppers, pearl onions, and fruit.

With kosher laws forbidding the use of the hindquarter of an animal unless the sciatic vein has been removed, most traditional recipes used shoulder, breast, and shank cuts, as well as ground meat for the ubiquitous *albóndigas.* Sauces might be tomato based, sweet and sour, or thickened with egg and lemon.

GAYNA *al* ORNO

ROAST CHICKEN WITH APPLES AND POMEGRANATE

Cooking chicken with fruit is part of a long established Hispano-Arabic tradition. In this Turkish
recipe from *Sefarad Yemekleri,* green apples and
pomegranate combine to make a festive winter dish
for the Sabbath or the holidays. A similar recipe
also appears in *Le feste ebraiche,* published by the
Jewish community of Rome. Upon reading this
recipe, my concern was that the chicken would fall
apart if roasted for 1½ hours and then roasted again
for another 30 minutes to cook the potatoes. So I
decided to roast the chicken in the first phase for
only 1 to 1¼ hours, and to parboil the potatoes so
that the second cooking phase would be shorter as
well. After making the recipe the first time, I
discovered that the onions in the stuffing had a
slightly unpleasant raw taste that remained even
after all that time in the oven. To solve the problem,
I now sauté the onions briefly before adding them
to the apples.

Serves 4 TO 6

1 ROASTING CHICKEN, 4½ TO 5 POUNDS

SUNFLOWER OR OLIVE OIL FOR RUBBING ON
    CHICKEN, PLUS 6 TABLESPOONS

SALT AND FRESHLY GROUND BLACK PEPPER

1 LARGE LEMON, HALVED

2 ONIONS, GRATED

2 TART GREEN APPLES SUCH AS GRANNY SMITH

SEEDS OF 1 POMEGRANATE

¼ CUP WATER

2 POUNDS NEW POTATOES, PEELED, HALVED
    IF SMALL, QUARTERED IF LARGE, AND THEN
    PARBOILED FOR 8 MINUTES

Preheat the oven to 375 degrees F.

Rinse the chicken and rub the outside and the cavity
with the oil, salt, pepper, and the cut sides of the
halved lemon. Squeeze the juice from the lemon
halves and reserve. You should have about 4 tablespoons.

Warm 2 tablespoons of the oil in a sauté pan over
medium heat. Add the onion and sauté until translucent and the raw taste is gone, almost 5 minutes.
Remove from the heat, transfer to a bowl, and let
cool for a few minutes. Meanwhile, core and grate the
apples. When the onions have cooled a bit, add the
apples, 2 tablespoons of the lemon juice, the pomegranate seeds, and a nice sprinkle of salt. Mix well
and stuff the mixture into the cavity. Truss closed and
place on a rack in a roasting pan. In a small bowl, stir
together the remaining 4 tablespoons oil and the
remaining 2 tablespoons lemon juice.

Place the chicken in the oven and roast, basting every
10 minutes or so with the oil mixture, for 1 to 1¼
hours, using the longer time for a larger bird. Remove
the pan from the oven and transfer the chicken to a
cutting board. Leave the oven set at 375 degrees F.
Remove the rack from the pan, and add the water to
the roasting pan.

Scoop the stuffing into a bowl. Cut the chicken into
serving pieces and place it in the baking pan. Spoon
the stuffing into the center of the chicken pieces, and
surround with the potatoes. Sprinkle the potatoes
with salt and pepper. Return the pan to the oven and
roast until the potatoes are tender and the chicken is
cooked through, about 15 minutes, turning the potatoes over once after they begin to take on color.

Remove the pan from the oven and transfer the chicken, stuffing, and potatoes to a platter. Serve at once.

Note: You can make this recipe with a 3-pound chicken and keep the initial roasting time to 1 hour. Leave the rest of the recipe as is.

: : : : : :

GAYNA *kon* MANZANA

CHICKEN WITH APPLES AND APRICOTS

La table juive calls this Turkish recipe "chicken with apples," but the apricots are an integral part of the dish and an important flavoring for the sauce; thus I have included them in the English title. Although the original recipe calls for marinating the chicken and dried fruits in the same bowl, I think it is better to soak the fruits separately. They don't need much time to soften, but you might want the chicken to marinate longer, even as long as overnight, to pick up the flavors of the spices and wine. Sometimes dried prunes are added along with the apricots and sometimes only prunes are used. Occasionally, no fresh apples are added! I imagine that this dish could be made with mixed dried fruits, including dried apples, and be delicious as well.

Serves 4 TO 6

1 ROASTING CHICKEN, 4 TO 5 POUNDS, CUT INTO
   SERVING PIECES, OR 8 CHICKEN PIECES
3 CUPS DRY WHITE WINE, OR AS NEEDED
1 TABLESPOON HONEY
1 TEASPOON GROUND GINGER
2 TEASPOONS GROUND CINNAMON
1 TEASPOON FRESHLY GROUND BLACK PEPPER
1/2 TEASPOON GROUND MACE

1/2 POUND DRIED APRICOTS
3 POUNDS TART GREEN APPLES SUCH AS GRANNY SMITH
   OR PIPPIN, PEELED, CORED, AND QUARTERED
2 TABLESPOONS FRESH LEMON JUICE
1 CINNAMON STICK
1 TABLESPOON SUGAR
1/4 CUP OLIVE OIL
3 ONIONS, CHOPPED
SALT
1/4 CUP SESAME SEEDS, TOASTED

Rinse the chicken pieces and place in a shallow bowl. In a small bowl, stir together about 1 1/2 cups of the wine, the honey, ginger, ground cinnamon, pepper, and mace. Rub this mixture over the chicken pieces, cover, and refrigerate for a few hours or as long as overnight.

Place the apricots in another bowl and add the remaining 1 1/2 cups wine or as needed to cover. In a saucepan, combine the apples, lemon juice, cinnamon stick, sugar, and water to cover. Bring to a simmer over medium heat and parboil for 8 minutes. Drain, reserving the poaching liquid. Discard the cinnamon stick and set the apples and liquid aside separately.

Warm the oil in a large stew pot or other large pan over medium heat. Add the onions, season with salt, and sauté until golden, about 15 minutes. Add the chicken pieces and their marinade, the soaked apricots and their soaking liquid, and the apple poaching liquid. Bring to a boil over high heat, reduce the heat to low, cover, and simmer until the chicken is almost cooked, 25 to 30 minutes. Check the level of the liquid from time to time and add water as needed to prevent the apricots from scorching.

Add the apples and continue to simmer until the chicken and apples are tender, 5 to 10 minutes longer. Transfer to a deep platter, sprinkle with the sesame seeds, and serve.

: : : : : :

KOTOPOULO PSITO
STUFFED ROAST CHICKEN FOR PASSOVER

Dried currants, walnuts, and matzoh meal make for a rich and savory stuffing for the Passover roast chicken. The recipe is based on one from the Greek community of Ioannina, as transcribed by Nicholas Stavroulakis in his wonderful *The Cookbook of the Jews of Greece.*

Serves 4 TO 6

1 ROASTING CHICKEN, INCLUDING GIZZARD
    AND LIVER, ABOUT 5 POUNDS
5 TABLESPOONS OLIVE OIL
1 CUP MATZOH MEAL
$1^2/_3$ CUPS DRY WHITE WINE
3 EGGS, LIGHTLY BEATEN
$^1/_2$ CUP WALNUTS, COARSELY CHOPPED
2 CUPS DRIED CURRANTS
SALT AND FRESHLY GROUND BLACK PEPPER
JUICE OF 1 LEMON

Preheat the oven to 350 degrees F. Remove the gizzard and liver from the cavity of the chicken, then rinse the chicken and set aside. Warm 2 tablespoons of the olive oil in a sauté pan over medium heat. Add the gizzard and sear well on all sides. Add the liver and cook, turning as needed, to sear well on all sides; this should take only a few minutes. Transfer the gizzard and liver to a cutting board, chop finely, and

place in a bowl. Add the matzoh meal, $^1/_3$ to $^1/_2$ cup of the white wine, the eggs, walnuts, and currants to the chopped innards and stir well. Add 2 tablespoons of the olive oil, season with salt and pepper, and mix well again.

Stuff the chicken cavity loosely with the matzoh mixture. Reserve any extra stuffing. Truss the chicken closed and rub with the remaining 1 tablespoon olive oil and the lemon juice, then sprinkle with salt and pepper. Place on a rack in a roasting pan.

Roast the chicken, basting occasionally with the remaining wine and the pan drippings, until the juices run clear when a thigh joint is pierced, about $1^1/_2$ hours. If any stuffing remains, put it in the roasting pan during the last 15 minutes of roasting so it takes on color.

Transfer the chicken to a platter and let rest for 8 to 10 minutes. Scoop the stuffing into a serving bowl. Carve the bird and serve.

: : : : : :

POYO *kon* BIZELAS

CHICKEN WITH SPRING PEAS

When fresh peas are sweet, they are a seasonal delight that make this dish both beautiful to look at and delicious to eat. Even in spring, however, not all fresh peas are tender and sweet, so if the sample pea you taste at the market is starchy, it is fine to use frozen peas, as they are usually consistently sweet and tender. The celery is not essential, but it does contribute moisture and a certain leafy character to the dish. This chicken preparation is very much like an old Portuguese recipe called *frango com ervilhas*. In that recipe, sautéed onions are added, as well as a bit of dry port or Madeira. The dill or mint used here is clearly a Turkish touch. I think some sautéed green onions would enhance this dish, and I would add them when I add the celery and fresh peas. Serve the chicken with rice or noodles.

Serves 6 TO 8

1 LARGE FRYING CHICKEN, ABOUT 4 POUNDS,
    OR 2 YOUNG FRYING CHICKENS, EACH ABOUT
    2 1/2 POUNDS, CUT INTO SERVING PIECES
ALL-PURPOSE FLOUR
SALT AND FRESHLY GROUND BLACK PEPPER
VEGETABLE OIL FOR FRYING
1 CUP WATER OR CHICKEN STOCK, OR AS NEEDED
1/2 CUP CHOPPED GREEN ONION, INCLUDING
    GREEN TOPS (OPTIONAL)
8 CELERY STALKS, CUT INTO 2-INCH LENGTHS
4 POUNDS ENGLISH PEAS, SHELLED, OR 2 PACKAGES
    (10 OUNCES EACH) FROZEN PEAS, THAWED
4 TO 6 TABLESPOONS CHOPPED FRESH DILL OR MINT
2 TEASPOONS SUGAR, IF NEEDED

Rinse the chicken pieces and pat dry. Spread the flour on a plate and season with salt and pepper. Pour vegetable oil to a depth of 1/4 inch into a large, heavy sauté pan and place over medium-high heat. One at a time, dip the chicken pieces in the seasoned flour, shaking off the excess flour, and slip them into the hot oil. Fry, turning as needed, until golden on all sides. If necessary, do this in batches to avoid crowding the chicken pieces in the pan. As the pieces are ready, transfer them to a large stew pot. Add the 1 cup water or stock, and bring to a boil over high heat. Reduce the heat to low, cover, and simmer for 20 minutes. Check the water level after about 10 minutes, and add water if the level has dropped.

Add the green onions, if using, the celery, the fresh peas, and the dill or mint and continue to simmer, covered, until the chicken is tender, 15 to 20 minutes longer. If using thawed frozen peas, add them during the last 5 minutes. Taste and adjust the seasonings, adding the sugar if you think the peas warrant the additional sweetness.

Arrange the chicken pieces on a serving platter and spoon the sauce, peas, and celery over the top. Serve immediately.

: : : : : :

KEFTAS *de* GAYNA

CHICKEN MEATBALLS WITH EGG AND LEMON

While we usually think of all meatballs as being made with meat, Sephardic Jews are equally enamored of chicken "meatballs." In Italy, chicken balls are added to stock for Passover, using matzoh meal instead of bread. The Turkish touch in this recipe from *La table juive* is the ground almonds, which add a fragrant sweetness to the mild poultry. I would play up this exoticism by adding a bit of cinnamon or nutmeg. Nicholas Stavroulakis adds ¹/₂ pound ground beef to the chicken in a Greek recipe he calls *keftikes de poyo.* Cook a pot of rice to serve with the meatballs.

Serves 4

1 POUND GROUND CHICKEN, FROM THE
  BREAST OR THIGH
1 CUP BLANCHED ALMONDS, GROUND
1 SMALL SLICE RUSTIC BREAD, CRUSTS REMOVED,
  SOAKED IN WATER AND SQUEEZED DRY
  (ABOUT ¹/₄ CUP CRUMBS)
3 EGGS
2 TEASPOONS SALT
¹/₂ TEASPOON FRESHLY GROUND BLACK PEPPER
¹/₂ TEASPOON GROUND CINNAMON OR NUTMEG
  (OPTIONAL)
ABOUT 3 CUPS CHICKEN STOCK
JUICE OF 2 LEMONS
4 TO 6 TABLESPOONS CHOPPED FRESH DILL OR
  PARSLEY, FLAT-LEAF OR A MIXTURE

In a bowl, combine the chicken, almonds, soaked bread, 1 egg, salt, pepper, and the cinnamon or nutmeg, if using. Mix well with your hands. In a wide saucepan, bring chicken stock to a boil over medium heat. Adjust the heat to a gentle simmer. Form a small sample ball of the chicken mixture, and drop it into the simmering stock. Poach until cooked through, then remove it and taste to see if the seasoning is balanced. Adjust as needed, then form the rest of the mixture into balls about 1 inch in diameter. Add all the balls to the stock, cover, and poach until cooked through, 10 to 15 minutes.

For the *agristada* enrichment, in a bowl, whisk together the remaining 2 eggs and the lemon juice until quite frothy. Whisk in a little of the hot stock to temper the eggs, then gradually stir into the stock. Simmer over very low heat for 1 to 2 minutes until thickened; do not allow to boil. Transfer the meatballs and sauce to a serving bowl and sprinkle with parsley and/or dill. Serve at once.

Note: You can make the meatballs smaller, poach them in a chicken stock, and serve them as the soup called *tavuk kefta corbasi.* Accompany the soup with lemon wedges. You can make this soup even more of a meal by adding cooked rice to the stock.

: : : : : :

POLLO *kon* BAMIYA

CHICKEN WITH OKRA

Here is a dish found in Sephardic kitchens in both Greece and Turkey. The chicken is braised in tomato sauce to which okra is added and then they are simmered together. The seasoning is elementary: salt and pepper. If you like, you could add garlic or an herb for a bit more complexity. Serve with rice pilaf.

Serves 6 TO 8

2 POUNDS OKRA

$1/2$ CUP WINE VINEGAR

OLIVE OIL FOR FRYING

2 YOUNG FRYING CHICKENS, ABOUT $2 1/2$ POUNDS
    EACH, CUT INTO SERVING PIECES

SALT AND FRESHLY GROUND BLACK PEPPER

1 ONION, CHOPPED

6 RIPE TOMATOES, PEELED, SEEDED, AND CHOPPED

PINCH OF SUGAR

PINCH OF GROUND CINNAMON

PINCH OF GROUND CLOVES

1 CUP DRY RED WINE

$1/2$ CUP WATER, OR AS NEEDED

FRESH LEMON JUICE OR WINE VINEGAR, IF NEEDED

Trim off the stems from the okra and soak the pods in water to cover to which the vinegar has been added. Let stand for 20 minutes to rid the okra of its slipperiness. Drain well.

Meanwhile, pour olive oil to a depth of $1/4$ inch into a heavy sauté pan large enough to hold the chicken and vegetables and place over high heat. Sprinkle the chicken pieces with salt and pepper, add to the pan, and fry, turning as needed, until golden on all sides,

8 to 10 minutes. Using tongs or a slotted spoon, transfer to a plate and set aside.

Add the onion to the oil remaining in the pan and cook over medium heat, stirring often until softened and pale gold, 10 to 12 minutes. Then add the tomatoes, sugar, cinnamon, cloves, wine, and $1/2$ cup water and simmer over medium heat for 5 minutes to soften the tomatoes.

Return the chicken to the pan, cover, and cook over low heat for 20 minutes. Add the okra and continue to cook until the chicken and vegetables are tender, 15 to 20 minutes longer. Check the pan from time to time, and if the pan juices evaporate, add more water. When the chicken is ready, taste and add a bit of lemon juice or vinegar if you think it needs a bit of acid to cut the richness, then season to taste with salt and pepper.

Transfer the chicken and vegetables to a platter and serve immediately.

Variation: A similar dish is called *pollo kon berenjena*. The only variable is the vegetable, with eggplant replacing the okra. To prepare it, trim the ends from the eggplants, but do not peel them. Cut the eggplants into 2-inch cubes. Sprinkle the cubes with salt and layer them in a colander for 30 minutes to drain. Rinse well and squeeze dry. Pour olive oil to a depth of $1/4$ inch into a large, deep sauté pan and place over medium-high heat. Working in batches, add the eggplant pieces to the hot oil and fry, turning as needed, until golden brown on all sides and nearly tender, 10 to 15 minutes. Using tongs or a slotted spoon, transfer to paper towels to drain. Proceed as directed in the recipe, adding the eggplant to the pan in place of the okra.

ARMI *do* GAYNA

CHICKEN WITH PEPPERS, ONIONS, AND PAPRIKA

Armi do gayna resembles *pollo al chilindrón* from Rioja and Navarre in Spain, the regions famous for peppers. But the addition of allspice is a decidedly Turkish one. I also like a bit of hot pepper here—a subtle hint of heat in the background. Suzy David calls this *gaina kon zarzavat* and adds dill for a leafy touch. Serve with rice and pass lemon wedges to brighten the taste.

Serves 4 TO 6

3 TABLESPOONS OLIVE OIL

1 LARGE FRYING CHICKEN, ABOUT 4 $1/2$ POUNDS,
    CUT INTO SERVING PIECES

4 OR 5 LARGE ONIONS, THINLY SLICED

3 LARGE RED BELL PEPPERS, SEEDED AND
    SLICED LENGTHWISE

2 $1/2$ TABLESPOONS SWEET PAPRIKA

$3/4$ TEASPOON GROUND ALLSPICE

1 BAY LEAF

PINCH OF CAYENNE PEPPER OR HOT PAPRIKA (OPTIONAL)

SALT AND FRESHLY GROUND BLACK PEPPER

$1/2$ CUP WATER OR CHICKEN STOCK, OR AS NEEDED

CHOPPED FRESH FLAT-LEAF PARSLEY (OPTIONAL)

LEMON WEDGES (OPTIONAL)

Warm the olive oil in a large heavy sauté pan over high heat. Working in batches if necessary, add the chicken pieces and fry, turning as needed, until golden on all sides. With tongs or a slotted spoon, transfer the chicken to a plate and set aside.

Add the onions to the oil remaining in the pan and sauté over medium heat until softened, for about 10 minutes. Add the bell peppers, sweet paprika, all-spice, bay leaf, and the cayenne or hot paprika, if using. Sprinkle generously with salt and pepper and cook, stirring often, until the onions are golden, about 10 minutes. Return the chicken pieces to the pan and add the $1/2$ cup water or stock. (If the pan is not large enough to hold all of the chicken, transfer its contents to a stew pot along with the chicken.)

Cover tightly and simmer over low heat until chicken is tender, 30 to 40 minutes. Check the pan from time to time, and if the pan juices evaporate, add more water or stock. Taste the pan juices and adjust the seasonings.

Transfer the chicken and pan sauce to a platter. If you like, sprinkle with a bit of parsley and pass the lemon wedges.

: : : : : :

PILICLI PATLICAN

CHICKEN WITH ROASTED EGGPLANT PUREE

Hunkar begendi is a classic Turkish dish of roasted eggplant puree enriched with a creamy béchamel and Parmesan cheese. In the nonkosher kitchen, this rich puree is often spread on a platter and surrounded by meatballs in a tomato sauce. Esin Eden's recipe for *pilicli patlican* adds richness to the eggplant puree without the addition of dairy. The braising juices from the chicken are incorporated into the roasted eggplant, adding body and concentrated flavors and staying kosher, too. This same eggplant puree can be served surrounded by little meat or chicken balls that have been braised in tomato sauce.

Serves 4

OLIVE OIL FOR FRYING
1 SMALL FRYING CHICKEN, 2 TO 3 POUNDS,
    CUT INTO SERVING PIECES
SALT AND FRESHLY GROUND BLACK PEPPER
1 LARGE ONION, GRATED OR FINELY CHOPPED
2 LARGE, RIPE TOMATOES, PEELED, SEEDED,
    AND CHOPPED
JUICE OF 3 LEMONS
1 CUP WATER OR CHICKEN STOCK
3 GLOBE EGGPLANTS, ABOUT 1 POUND EACH
4 OR 5 CLOVES GARLIC, MINCED (OPTIONAL)
4 TO 6 TABLESPOONS CHOPPED FRESH
    FLAT-LEAF PARSLEY

Pour olive oil to a depth of $1/4$ inch into a large sauté pan and place over high heat. Working in batches if necessary, add the chicken pieces and fry, turning as needed and sprinkling with salt and pepper, until golden on all sides, 8 to 10 minutes. Using tongs or a slotted spoon, transfer to a plate and set aside.

Add the onion to the oil remaining in the pan, adding more oil if the pan is dry, and cook over medium heat, stirring often, until softened and pale gold, 10 to 12 minutes. Then add the tomatoes, the juice of 2 lemons, and water or stock and return the chicken to the pan. Bring to a boil over high heat, reduce the heat to low, cover, and simmer until the chicken is tender, 30 to 40 minutes.

Meanwhile, preheat the broiler and broil the eggplants, turning often, until they are very soft and have collapsed, about 20 minutes. Alternatively, cook them slowly on a stove-top cast-iron griddle, turning them often. Transfer the eggplants to a colander to drain. When cool enough to handle, strip away the skin and remove the large seed pockets. Fill a bowl with water, add the remaining lemon juice, and drop the pulp into it. After 10 minutes, drain the pulp, squeeze dry, and place in a bowl. (The lemon-water soak keeps the eggplant light colored, which is important to the Turkish cook.) Mash the eggplant with a fork to form a thick puree. Do not use a food processor, as you want some texture here.

When the chicken is ready, using tongs or a slotted spoon, transfer it to a plate; keep warm. Add the eggplant puree to the pan juices along with the garlic, if using, and simmer over low heat 5 minutes to blend with the pan juices. Season with salt and pepper. If the puree seems dry, add a few tablespoons water.

To serve, spoon the puree onto the center of a platter. Surround it with the chicken pieces. Top the puree and the chicken with the parsley. Serve at once.

: : : : : :

HAMIM *de* KASTANYA

LAMB STEW WITH CHESTNUTS

This recipe is adapted from a Turkish cookbook, *Sefarad Yemekleri.* Its origins, however, are Spanish. The sweet and starchy chestnuts pair equally well with lamb or beef. Most of the work is in peeling the chestnuts. I have found that the ease of peeling chestnuts varies from batch to batch, with some a breeze to peel and some maddeningly frustrating. So if you can find vacuum-packed, peeled and cooked chestnuts, use them instead. If not, be patient and have a very sharp knife and asbestos-tipped fingers at the ready, because the chestnuts must be peeled while hot. Cut a deep cross on the flat side of each nut and roast in a hot oven, turning once, for 30 to 45 minutes. Alternatively, cut the cross and boil the nuts in salted water until the shell starts to split and the edges of the cross begin to curl, about 20 minutes. Then, as soon as you can handle the hot nuts, cut away the outer shells and the thin, brown peel covering them.

Serves 6 TO 8

$^1/_4$ CUP OLIVE OR SUNFLOWER OIL

2 ONIONS, CHOPPED

2 POUNDS BONELESS LAMB SHOULDER,
    CUT INTO 1$^1/_2$-INCH CUBES

1 TEASPOON GROUND CINNAMON

$^1/_2$ TEASPOON GROUND ALLSPICE

2 CUPS MEAT STOCK OR WATER, OR AS NEEDED

1 TABLESPOON TOMATO PASTE

SALT AND FRESHLY GROUND BLACK PEPPER

1 POUND NEW POTATOES, PEELED AND CUT
    INTO $^1/_2$-INCH DICE

1 POUND CHESTNUTS, PEELED (SEE RECIPE
    INTRODUCTION)

3 TO 4 TABLESPOONS CHOPPED FRESH
    FLAT-LEAF PARSLEY

Warm the oil in a stew pot or other large pan over medium heat. Add the onions and sauté until softened and golden, about 15 minutes. Add the meat and brown it well on all sides, turning often. Add the cinnamon and allspice and stir well. Measure the 2 cups stock or water and dissolve the tomato paste in them. Pour into the stew pot and add stock or water if needed just to cover the meat. Season with salt and pepper, cover the pot, bring to a gentle boil, reduce the heat to low, and simmer until the meat is almost tender, about 1 hour.

Add the potatoes and chestnuts and continue to simmer until all of the ingredients are tender, 20 to 30 minutes longer. Taste and adjust the seasonings. Spoon the stew into a deep platter, sprinkle with the parsley, and serve.

Variation: Beef chuck can be used in place of the lamb shoulder. Treat it the same way.

: : : : : :

ROLLO *me* HAMINADOS

MEAT LOAF WITH SWEET-AND-SOUR TOMATO SAUCE

Nicholas Stavroulakis attributes this recipe to the
towns of Arta and Previza in Greece. Similar meat
loaf recipes are found in Italian and Persian Jewish
kitchens, however. Here as elsewhere, the word
hamin suggests a Sabbath dish, baked in the *hamin*
or oven and served at room temperature. This meat
loaf is especially succulent served hot, however,
with a sweet-and-sour tomato sauce.

Serves 4 TO 6

For the tomato sauce:

2 TABLESPOONS OLIVE OIL

3 OR 4 LARGE TOMATOES, PEELED, SEEDED,
    AND CHOPPED

2 TABLESPOONS HONEY

1 CUP DRY RED WINE

1/2 TEASPOON GROUND CINNAMON

JUICE OF 2 LEMONS

SALT AND FRESHLY GROUND BLACK PEPPER

For the meat loaf:

1 1/2 POUNDS GROUND BEEF

2 EGGS, LIGHTLY BEATEN

1/2 CUP MATZOH MEAL OR DRIED BREAD CRUMBS

2 ONIONS, GRATED OR MINCED

2 LARGE, RIPE TOMATOES, PEELED, SEEDED,
    AND CRUSHED

2 CLOVES GARLIC, MINCED

2 TABLESPOONS CHOPPED FRESH FLAT-LEAF PARSLEY

2 TABLESPOONS CHOPPED FRESH BASIL

SALT AND FRESHLY GROUND BLACK PEPPER

3 ONION SKIN EGGS, PEELED (PAGE 44)

2 TABLESPOONS OLIVE OIL

To make the tomato sauce, warm 1 tablespoon of the
olive oil in a sauté pan over medium heat. Add the
tomatoes and 1 tablespoon of the honey and cook,
stirring occasionally, until the tomatoes are reduced
to a purée, 20 to 30 minutes. Add the wine, the
remaining 1 tablespoon each oil and honey, and the
cinnamon and simmer for a few more minutes to
blend the flavors. Add the lemon juice and season
with salt and pepper. Remove from the heat and set
aside.

Preheat the oven to 350 degrees F. Oil a baking pan
large enough to hold the meat loaf.

To make the meat loaf, in a bowl, combine the beef,
eggs, matzoh meal or bread crumbs, onions, tomatoes, garlic, parsley, basil, salt, and pepper. Mix well
with your hands. Form half the meat into a long, flattened roll. Top with the eggs, arranging them in a
line down the center. Cover with the remaining meat.
Seal the seams well and pat into a roll. Place in the
prepared baking pan. Rub the roll with the olive oil.

Bake the meat loaf, basting from time to time with
the sauce, until it is cooked through, about 1 hour.
Remove from the oven, transfer the meat loaf to a
platter, and let rest for 10 minutes.

Just before serving, gently reheat the remaining sauce
and transfer to a bowl. Slice the meat loaf and serve.
Pass the sauce at the table.

: : : : : :

PATATAS KAVAKADAS
MEAT-STUFFED BAKED POTATOES

When many people hear "stuffed baked potato," they usually think of fast-food restaurants and a giant russet potato overflowing with assorted toppings. This recipe from *Sefarad Yemekleri* uses uncooked boiling potatoes as the shells for a savory meat filling. I have suggested the addition of a little grated onion because it adds a depth of flavor and plays off the starchiness of the potatoes. Although it is not part of the traditional recipe, you might want to serve the stuffed potatoes with a bit of tomato sauce swirled into the pan juices.

Serves 8

3 POUNDS NEW POTATOES (ABOUT 8 LARGE)

1 POUND GROUND BEEF OR LAMB

1 THICK SLICE RUSTIC BREAD, CRUSTS REMOVED,
    SOAKED IN WATER, AND SQUEEZED DRY

$^1/_2$ SMALL ONION, GRATED (OPTIONAL)

3 TABLESPOONS CHOPPED FRESH FLAT-LEAF
    PARSLEY (OPTIONAL)

$1^1/_2$ TEASPOONS SALT, PLUS MORE TO TASTE

$^1/_2$ TEASPOON FRESHLY GROUND BLACK PEPPER,
    PLUS MORE TO TASTE

VEGETABLE OIL FOR FRYING

$1^1/_2$ CUPS ALL-PURPOSE FLOUR

3 EGGS, BEATEN

$1^1/_2$ TO 2 CUPS BEEF STOCK

Peel the potatoes and cut them in half lengthwise. With a melon baller or small, sharp knife, scoop out or carve a pocket in the center of each potato half, leaving a shell about $^1/_3$ inch thick.

In a bowl, combine the meat, the soaked bread, the onion and parsley, if using, the $1^1/_2$ teaspoons salt,

and $^1/_2$ teaspoon pepper. Mix well, then fill the potatoes with the mixture.

Preheat the oven to 400 degrees F.

Pour vegetable oil to a depth of 1 inch into a deep sauté pan and place over medium heat. Meanwhile, place the flour in a bowl and season with salt and pepper. Break the eggs in a bowl and beat them lightly until blended.

Working in batches, dip the potatoes in flour and then into the eggs and slip them into the hot oil. Fry, turning as needed, until golden on all sides, about 5 minutes. As the potatoes are ready, lift them out with a slotted spatula, drain briefly on paper towels, and arrange in a baking dish.

Add the beef stock to the baking dish to a depth of about 1 inch and sprinkle the potatoes with salt and pepper. Cover and bake until the potatoes are tender, about 20 minutes.

Note: In *The Sephardic Kosher Kitchen,* Suzy David parboils the potatoes, then peels them, cuts them in half, and scoops out the centers to make cavities, which she fills with a mixture of cheese, egg, and bread crumbs.

: : : : : :

MOUSSAKA

EGGPLANT AND LAMB CASSEROLE

Moussaka is the ideal winter dish—a rich stick-to-your-ribs concoction. According to John Cooper, in his estimable *Eat and Be Satisfied,* it was served during Rosh Hashanah. Most of us associate moussaka with a topping of cheesy béchamel custard. According to kosher laws, however, no cheese or dairy may be used with meat, so this Turkish Sephardic moussaka from *La table juive* takes on a totally different character. Instead of the richness of cheese and cream, it is rich and smoky from the chopped grilled eggplant added to the meat filling. While most recipes suggest frying the eggplant in oil, you can cut back on fat by slicing the eggplant, placing the slices on oiled baking sheets, brushing them with additional oil, and baking them until they are tender and translucent in a 400 degree F oven. Similar recipes appear in books by Esin Eden and Gilda Angel, but I liked this one the best because of the added texture and richness of the grilled eggplant.

In Turkey, moussaka is usually layered in a rather deep, cylindrical mold, much like a charlotte tin or soufflé dish, for baking and then unmolded. This makes for a dramatic presentation, but it is harder to serve. If the moussaka has not compacted well, after the first cut it may collapse. So I have taken the coward's way out and prepared it in a baking dish: no stress, no unmolding necessary, and definitely easier to serve. Incidentally, while this dish is very tasty after the first baking, it becomes even tastier reheated on the second day, when the flavors have had a chance to meld and mellow.

Serves 6 TO 8

4 POUNDS GLOBE EGGPLANTS (4 OR 5)

OLIVE OIL FOR FRYING

SALT

$1^{1}/_{4}$ TO $1^{1}/_{2}$ POUNDS BONELESS LAMB SHOULDER, FINELY DICED OR GROUND

2 LARGE ONIONS, FINELY CHOPPED

1 POUND RIPE TOMATOES, PEELED, SEEDED, AND CHOPPED, OR 1 CAN (16 OUNCES) PLUM TOMATOES, DRAINED, SEEDED, AND CHOPPED

4 CLOVES GARLIC, MINCED

1 TABLESPOON DRIED OREGANO (OPTIONAL)

1 TEASPOON GROUND CINNAMON

FRESHLY GROUND BLACK PEPPER

4 TO 6 TABLESPOONS FINE DRIED BREAD CRUMBS

Peel 2 of the eggplants vertically in a striped pattern. Cut the peeled eggplants crosswise into $^{1}/_{3}$-inch-thick slices. Pour olive oil to a depth of $^{1}/_{4}$ inch into a sauté pan and place over medium-high heat. Add the eggplant slices, in batches, and fry, turning once, until golden, 6 to 8 minutes total. Be sure that the eggplant is cooked through and translucent but not falling apart. Undercooked eggplant will taste bitter. Using tongs or a slotted spatula, transfer to paper towels to drain and sprinkle lightly with salt. Repeat with the remaining slices, adding more oil to the pan as needed.

Preheat the broiler and broil the remaining 2 or 3 eggplants, turning often, until they are very soft and have collapsed, about 20 minutes. Alternatively, cook them slowly on a stove-top cast-iron griddle, turning them often. Transfer the eggplants to a colander to drain. When cool enough to handle, strip away the skin and remove the large seed pockets. Drain the pulp in the colander for 20 minutes to release the bitter juices, then transfer to a chopping board and chop. You will want about 2 cups coarse puree.

Warm 2 or 3 tablespoons of olive oil in a large sauté pan over high heat. Add the lamb and brown well. Using a slotted spoon, transfer to a plate. Add the onions to the fat remaining in the pan and sauté over medium heat until translucent, 5 to 8 minutes. Add the tomatoes, garlic, oregano (if using), and cinnamon, and season with salt and pepper. Return the lamb to the pan, cover, and simmer until the meat is tender, 15 to 20 minutes. Stir in the chopped eggplant pulp, then taste and adjust the seasonings.

Preheat the oven to 350 degrees F. Brush a 7^1/$_2$-by-12-by-2-inch baking dish or a large oval gratin dish with oil. Sprinkle the dish lightly with some of the bread crumbs.

Line the bottom of the dish with one-third of the fried eggplant slices. Layer half of the meat mixture on top and sprinkle with half of the bread crumbs. Layer on half of the remaining eggplant slices and top with remaining meat mixture. Sprinkle with remaining bread crumbs and arrange the remaining eggplant slices on top. Cover the dish with aluminum foil and place in a large roasting pan. Pour hot water into the roasting pan to reach halfway up the sides of the baking dish.

Bake until browned and bubbling, 35 to 45 minutes. Remove from the oven and let stand for 10 minutes before cutting into squares. Serve very warm.

Notes: Some cooks suggest dipping the eggplant slices in beaten egg before frying them, believing that they will absorb less oil. In *La cucina nella tradizione ebraica,* compiled by an Italian Jewish women's

organization, the moussaka calls for a fake béchamel sauce made by cooking 2 tablespoons flour in 2 tablespoons fat, then adding 2 cups meat stock and simmering until thickened. This is poured on top of the moussaka before baking. Nicholas Stavroulakis suggests topping the moussaka with sliced tomatoes.

Finally, in the tradition of wasting nothing, even artichoke stems are used in a moussakalike dish, which is known as *enginar sapi musakkasi.* The meat is cooked with onions and tomatoes in the customary way. Artichoke stems that have been peeled, sliced, and parboiled in acidulated water are then arranged in a well-oiled baking dish, topped with the meat mixture, and drizzled with ^{1}/$_2$ cup water or 1 or 2 beaten eggs. The dish is baked for about 25 minutes at 350 degrees F. Some cooks believe that adding the eggs makes the moussaka easier to unmold.

: : : : : :

PATLICAN SILKME

SHAKEN LAMB

Like a James Bond martini, this Turkish stew should be shaken, not stirred. The lamb and vegetables are layered in a stew pot with virtually no liquid save for a bit of water and the tomatoes. They cook to a melting tenderness, needing just a quick shake from time to time to prevent sticking.

Serves 4

$^1/_2$ POUND PEARL ONIONS

ABOUT 2 TABLESPOONS OLIVE OIL

1 POUND BONELESS LAMB SHOULDER, CUT
    INTO 1-INCH CUBES

2 YELLOW ONIONS, CHOPPED

2 TOMATOES, PEELED, SEEDED, AND FINELY
    CHOPPED OR GRATED

JUICE OF 1 LEMON

1 LARGE EGGPLANT, ABOUT 1$^1/_2$ POUNDS

SALT AND FRESHLY GROUND BLACK PEPPER

2 SMALL GREEN BELL PEPPERS, SEEDED
    AND QUARTERED LENGTHWISE

1 TABLESPOON RED WINE VINEGAR

$^1/_2$ CUP WATER

Fill a saucepan with water and bring to a boil. Meanwhile, carefully trim the roots from the pearl onions, being careful not to cut too deeply into the bases. Add to the boiling water and parboil for 5 minutes. Drain, rinse in cold water, and remove the skins. Cut a cross in the root end of each onion to prevent the onions from telescoping while cooking. Set aside.

Warm the olive oil in a large sauté pan over high heat. Add the lamb, in batches, and brown well on all sides. Using a slotted spoon, transfer to a plate and set aside.

Add the chopped onions to the oil remaining in the pan and sauté over medium heat until translucent, about 5 minutes. Return the meat to the pan and add the tomatoes. Stir well, cover, and cook over low heat, stirring from time to time, until almost all of the liquid from the tomatoes has been absorbed, about 15 minutes. Check from time to time to make sure it doesn't all evaporate, and add water if needed.

Meanwhile, fill a large bowl with water and add the lemon juice. Peel the eggplant vertically in a striped pattern, then cut it in half lengthwise. Cut the halves into $^1/_2$-inch-thick slices. Immerse the slices in the lemon water. Let soak for 20 minutes, then drain, rinse, and pat dry with paper towels.

Lightly oil a stew pot or other large, heavy pan and place the eggplant slices in the bottom. Sprinkle with salt and pepper. Add the pearl onions and then the meat mixture. Sprinkle with salt and pepper. Top with the quartered peppers and sprinkle again with salt and pepper. Mix together the vinegar and water and pour over the peppers.

Cover the pot and place over medium heat. Cook until the meat is tender, 35 to 40 minutes, shaking the pan from time to time to prevent sticking. Serve hot.

: : : : : :

KODRERO *con* AJO FRESCO

LAMB WITH GREEN GARLIC

Spring is the season for green garlic, fragrant shoots with tiny young bulbs. Before individual cloves are formed, the green garlic resembles large green onions or baby leeks. Combined with springtime's young onions, they make a delicate and aromatic stew. The slow cooking results in the cloves becoming mild and creamy. This stew was a great favorite at Passover dinners at my restaurant, Square One. Serve with rice or noodles.

Serves 6 TO 8

ALL-PURPOSE FLOUR
SALT AND FRESHLY GROUND BLACK PEPPER
OLIVE OIL, AS NEEDED
3 TO 4 POUNDS BONELESS LAMB SHOULDER,
    CUT INTO 1½-INCH PIECES
2 TABLESPOONS TOMATO PASTE
2 TABLESPOONS RED WINE VINEGAR
1 CUP WATER OR MEAT STOCK
½ POUND GREEN GARLIC, OR 2 HEADS MATURE GARLIC
2 POUNDS GREEN ONIONS (5 OR 6 BUNCHES)
CHOPPED FRESH MINT, DILL, OR FLAT-LEAF PARSLEY

Spread the flour on a plate and season with salt and pepper. Warm about 2 tablespoons olive oil in a large, heavy sauté pan over high heat. Coat the lamb pieces in the seasoned flour, shaking off the excess flour. Add to the hot oil, in batches, and brown well on all sides.

Transfer the lamb to a stew pot and add the tomato paste, vinegar, water or stock, and salt and pepper to taste. Bring to a boil over high heat, reduce the heat to low, cover, and simmer gently until the lamb is almost tender, 50 to 60 minutes.

Meanwhile, prepare the garlic and onions: Do not peel the green garlic. Instead, snip off the root end and slice into 2-inch lengths, using all of the green. If using heads of garlic, peel the cloves. Set aside. Trim the roots off the green onions and cut them into 2-inch lengths as well. Bring a saucepan filled with salted water to a boil. Add the green onions and green garlic and blanch for 2 minutes, then drain. Warm 2 or 3 tablespoons olive oil in a sauté pan over medium heat. Add the garlic and green onions and sauté until they begin to take on color, about 5 minutes, seasoning them with salt and pepper as they cook. Remove from the heat.

After about 1 hour, when the lamb is almost cooked, add the sautéed garlic and green onions to the pot, re-cover, and continue to cook until the lamb is tender, 20 to 30 minutes longer. Taste and adjust the seasonings. Spoon into a deep platter, sprinkle with the mint, dill, or parsley, and serve.

: : : : : :

TERNERA *kon* ESPINAKA
AVGOLEMONO

VEAL AND SPINACH STEW WITH EGG AND LEMON

Veal and spinach stew is served on the Sabbath and, according to Gilda Angel in *Sephardic Holiday Cooking,* is a perfect dish for Hanukkah. It has a velvety texture. Suzy David's version of this recipe calls for braising lamb chops with spinach and omits the egg and lemon. Serve with rice.

Serves 8

OLIVE OIL FOR FRYING

3 POUNDS BONELESS VEAL SHOULDER OR SHANK,
    CUT INTO 1½-INCH PIECES

2 ONIONS, CHOPPED

SALT AND FRESHLY GROUND BLACK PEPPER

FRESHLY GRATED NUTMEG (OPTIONAL)

1½ TO 2 CUPS WATER OR MEAT STOCK

2 POUNDS SPINACH, BLANCHED FOR 1 MINUTE, DRAINED
    WELL, CHOPPED, AND SQUEEZED DRY, OR 2 PACKAGES
    FROZEN CHOPPED SPINACH, THAWED

3 EGGS

JUICE OF 2 LEMONS

Pour olive oil to a depth of ¼ inch into a large stew pot or wide, deep frying pan and place over high heat. Add the meat, in batches, and brown well on all sides, adding more oil as needed. Using a slotted spoon, transfer the meat to a plate. Set aside.

Add about 2 tablespoons oil to the same pan if none remains, and place over medium heat. (Unlike lamb, veal does not release any fat and may absorb all of the fat in the pan.) Add the onions and sauté until tender and translucent, about 10 minutes. Return the veal to the pan. Season with salt and pepper and with the

nutmeg, if using, and add the water or stock. The liquid should just cover the meat. Bring to a boil over high heat, reduce the heat to low, cover, and simmer gently until the veal is almost tender, about 1 hour. Check after 35 or 40 minutes to make sure that all the liquid has not evaporated. If it has, add more stock or water and shake the pan or stir well to dislodge all of the meat juices and any brownish bits. Add the spinach and continue to cook until the veal is tender, 15 to 20 minutes longer.

In a bowl, beat together the eggs and lemon juice until quite frothy. Whisk in a little of the hot stew liquid to temper the eggs, then gradually stir the eggs into the stew. Stir well for a minute or two over low heat (or you could shake the pan back and forth over the burner), then serve immediately.

: : : : : :

ALBÓNDIGAS *de* PRASA
LEEK AND MEAT FRITTERS

Meat patties extended with cooked vegetables are common on the Sephardic table. The classic combination of leeks and meat is associated with Izmir, and of spinach and meat with Salonika. The mixture may be thickened with fresh bread crumbs or with mashed potatoes. Nicholas Stavroulakis adds chopped *haminado* eggs and dill, while Esin Eden adds cinnamon. Sometimes grated walnuts are added for *albóndigas de prasa kon muez,* a recipe from *Sefarad Yemekleri.* And, as we have seen in the vegetable chapter, the patties can be reheated in tomato sauce.

Makes 36 TO 40 *meatballs; serves* 6 TO 8

3 POUNDS LEEKS (12 SMALL, 8 MEDIUM, OR 4 LARGE)

3/4 POUND GROUND BEEF OR LAMB

3 SLICES RUSTIC BREAD, CRUSTS REMOVED, SOAKED IN WATER, AND SQUEEZED DRY, OR 2 POTATOES, PEELED, BOILED, AND MASHED (ABOUT 1 CUP)

2 EGGS, SEPARATED

3/4 TEASPOON GROUND CINNAMON (OPTIONAL)

2 TO 3 TABLESPOONS GRATED WALNUTS (OPTIONAL)

1/2 CUP CHOPPED FRESH DILL (OPTIONAL)

2 ONION SKIN EGGS, PEELED AND FINELY CHOPPED (OPTIONAL; PAGE 44)

1 1/2 TEASPOONS SALT, PLUS SALT TO TASTE

1/2 TEASPOON FRESHLY GROUND BLACK PEPPER

OLIVE OIL FOR FRYING

ALL-PURPOSE FLOUR OR MATZOH MEAL

LEMON WEDGES

Cut away the root ends from the leeks and most of the green and discard. Peel away loose layers, cut the leeks in half lengthwise, and then cut crosswise into 1/2-inch-wide pieces. Soak them in a sink full of cold water, swish them around to loosen any dirt, remove with a slotted spoon, and drain well in a colander. You will have about 6 cups chopped leeks. Put them in a saucepan with salted water to cover, bring to a boil, reduce the heat to low, and simmer until the leeks are very soft, about 20 minutes. Drain very well. You will have about 2 cups cooked leeks.

In a bowl, combine the leeks, meat, bread or mashed potatoes, egg yolks, and the cinnamon, walnuts, or dill and chopped eggs, if using. Add the salt and pepper, then knead with your hands until the mixture holds together well. Form into balls about 1 1/4 inches in diameter. You may keep them round or you can flatten them a bit, as they will cook more quickly.

Pour olive oil to a depth of 1 1/2 inches into a large sauté pan and heat to 350 degrees F on a deep-frying thermometer. Meanwhile, spread some flour or matzoh meal on a plate. In a bowl, beat the egg whites until very frothy but not stiff. When the oil is hot, dip the meatballs in the flour or matzoh meal, then in the egg whites. Add to the oil, in batches, and fry until golden, 8 to 10 minutes. Using a slotted spoon, transfer to paper towels to drain. Keep warm. When all the fritters are fried, arrange on a platter and sprinkle lightly with salt. Serve with lemon wedges.

Variations: For *albóndigas de espinaka* (spinach meatballs), use 3 pounds spinach, wilted, drained, squeezed dry, and finely chopped, in place of the leeks. Use the bread instead of potatoes. Roll the meatballs in the matzoh meal or flour, let stand briefly, and then roll them again in the meal or flour. They are fairly moist, and this will make it easier to brown them. Fry as directed.

: : : : : :

ALBÓNDIGAS *al* BUYOR ★ MEATBALLS WITH TOMATO SAUCE

ALBÓNDIGAS *or* KOFTE

MEATBALLS IN SIX STYLES

The Spanish word *albóndiga* comes from the Arabic *al bundaq,* meaning "round." *Kofte,* or *keftikes* in the diminutive, are Spanish *albóndigas,* or "meatballs," but with a Turkish name. The meat mixture can be formed into oblongs or patties, as well as balls, and it is usually bound with softened bread crumbs, except during Passover when matzoh meal is used. Grated onion is sometimes added to the meat mixture to boost the flavor. The meatballs can be simply fried in oil or served in or with a sauce. On Crete, they are fried and topped with onions and parsley and sprinkled with lemon juice. Obviously, meatballs are versatile, given the sauce variations that follow. *Albóndigas al buyor* are served with a tomato sauce scented with a bit of cinnamon, *terbiyeli* uses egg and lemon juice. The plum sauce, of Spanish origin, dates back to the fifteenth century and shows the Moorish influence on the food of the Andalusian Jews. The nut-thickened sauces are also of Hispano-Arabic origin.

Serves 4

For the basic meatballs:

$^1/_2$ TO $^3/_4$ POUND GROUND BEEF OR LAMB

2 SLICES RUSTIC BREAD, CRUSTS REMOVED,
   SOAKED IN WATER, AND SQUEEZED DRY

$^1/_2$ ONION, GRATED (OPTIONAL)

1 EGG, LIGHTLY BEATEN

3 TABLESPOONS CHOPPED FRESH FLAT-LEAF PARSLEY

SALT AND FRESHLY GROUND BLACK PEPPER

OLIVE OIL FOR FRYING

For the tomato sauce:

1 SMALL ONION, MINCED

2 CLOVES GARLIC, MINCED

4 LARGE, RIPE TOMATOES, PEELED, SEEDED,
   AND CHOPPED

$^1/_4$ TEASPOON GROUND CINNAMON, OR TO TASTE

SALT AND FRESHLY GROUND BLACK PEPPER

1 TABLESPOON HONEY

2 TABLESPOONS CHOPPED FRESH FLAT-LEAF PARSLEY

For the egg-and-lemon sauce:

$^1/_2$ CUP WATER

1 TABLESPOON ALL-PURPOSE FLOUR MIXED WITH
   2 TO 3 TABLESPOONS WATER

2 EGGS

JUICE OF 2 LEMONS

2 TABLESPOONS CHOPPED FRESH FLAT-LEAF PARSLEY

For the fruit sauce:

25 SMALL TART PLUMS (3 TO 4 POUNDS TOTAL WEIGHT;
   SEE NOTES), PITTED PRUNES, OR DRIED APRICOTS

ABOUT 1 CUP WATER FOR FRESH PLUMS, OR ABOUT
   2 CUPS FOR DRIED FRUIT

DASH OF FRESH LEMON JUICE

For the almond sauce:

1 CUP WATER, OR AS NEEDED

$^1/_2$ CUP GROUND ALMONDS

2 TABLESPOONS CHOPPED FRESH FLAT-LEAF PARSLEY

For the walnut sauce:

3 TO 4 TABLESPOONS GRATED ONION (OPTIONAL)

$^1/_2$ CUP DRY RED WINE

$^1/_2$ CUP CHOPPED WALNUTS

For the garlic sauce:

2 TABLESPOONS OLIVE OIL

2 HEADS GARLIC, CLOVES SEPARATED AND PEELED

JUICE OF 3 LEMONS

$1^1/_2$ CUPS WATER

PINCH OF SUGAR

To make the meatballs, in a bowl, combine the meat, soaked bread, onion, egg, parsley, and salt and pepper to taste. Knead with your hands until the mixture holds together well. Form into walnut-sized balls or into oblong patties about 2 inches long.

Pour in just enough olive oil to form a film on the bottom of a sauté pan and place over medium-high heat. Add the meatballs and fry until lightly browned on all sides. Using a slotted spoon, transfer to a platter.

To make meatballs with tomato sauce *(albóndigas al buyor),* prepare and brown the meatballs as directed. Remove from the pan. Add the onion and garlic to the same pan, adding more oil if needed, and sauté over medium heat until translucent, about 5 minutes. Add the tomatoes and cinnamon, season with salt and pepper, and stir well. Add the honey and simmer, uncovered, until the tomatoes break down and form a sauce, about 15 minutes. Add a little water if the sauce is very thick, then return the meatballs to the pan. Cover, reduce the heat to low, and simmer in the sauce until the meatballs are cooked through and the flavors are blended, 10 to 15 minutes. Transfer to a dish, sprinkle with the parsley, and serve.

To make meatballs with egg-and-lemon sauce *(terbiyeli kofte),* prepare and brown the meatballs as directed, then reduce the heat to medium and continue to cook, turning as necessary, until cooked through, about 10 minutes. Remove from the pan and keep warm. Add the water to the pan over medium heat and deglaze the pan, stirring to dislodge any browned bits. Stir in the diluted flour and simmer for a few minutes. In a bowl, beat together the eggs and lemon juice until quite frothy. Gradually whisk some of the hot pan juices into the eggs, then stir

the eggs into the pan juices. Cook over very low heat, stirring constantly, until the mixture thickens and coats a spoon, a few minutes. Do not allow to boil. Pour the sauce over the meatballs, sprinkle with the parsley, and serve.

To make meatballs with fruit sauce *(bobotkali kofte),* halve and pit the fresh plums, if possible. (The plums are small and can be difficult to pit when raw.) Alternatively, place the prunes or dried apricots in a bowl with the 2 cups water or as needed to cover generously and let soak overnight. Prepare and brown the meatballs as directed. Remove from the pan. Add the fresh plums and the 1 cup water or the soaked prunes or apricots and their soaking liquid to the pan over medium heat, bring to a gentle simmer, and cook until fruit breaks down, almost 20 minutes. Remove the pits from the fresh plums now if they were too difficult to pit when raw. Return the meatballs to the pan, add the lemon juice, and simmer until the sauce is reduced, the meatballs are cooked through, and the flavors are blended, 10 to 15 minutes, then serve.

Note: Bobota are a small green plum—the size of cherries—and are therefore difficult to pit when raw. You can use larger plums, too. Plan on 3 to 4 pounds.

To make meatballs with almond sauce *(bademli kofte),* prepare and brown the meatballs as directed. Remove from the pan. Add 1 cup water to the pan over medium heat and deglaze the pan, stirring to dislodge any browned bits. Add the almonds and chopped parsley and simmer, stirring occasionally, until thickened, 10 to 15 minutes. Return the meatballs to the pan and simmer in the sauce for 10 minutes. Add water if needed to thin the sauce, then serve.

To make meatballs with walnut sauce *(nugada kofte),* prepare the meatballs, adding the grated onion to the meat mixture, if desired. Brown the meatballs as directed, then remove from the pan. Add the wine to the pan over medium heat and deglaze the pan, stirring to dislodge any browned bits. Add the walnuts and simmer, stirring occasionally, until thickened, about 10 minutes. Return the meatballs to the pan and simmer in the sauce until the meatballs are cooked through, 10 to 15 minutes, then serve.

To make meatballs with braised garlic *(kofte kon ajo sofrito),* prepare and brown the meatballs as directed. Remove from the pan. Add the olive oil, garlic, lemon juice, water, and sugar to the pan, bring to a boil, reduce the heat to low, cover, and simmer until the garlic is tender, about 25 minutes. Return the meatballs to the pan and simmer in the sauce until the meatballs are cooked through, 10 to 15 minutes, then serve.

: : : : : :

YAPRAKES *de* BERENJENA
EGGPLANT ROLLS WITH TOMATO SAUCE

Instead of hollowing out eggplants and carving them into shells to hold the meat mixture, try Méri Badi's wonderful recipe for fried eggplant slices rolled around little meatballs, which are then baked with tomato sauce. A word about eggplant size: Our average eggplants are larger than those found in Spain, Greece, and Turkey. They usually seem to weigh about a pound. So where the recipe called for four, two sufficed. The cooking time seemed excessively long, too, as the eggplants are already cooked and so is the tomato sauce. All you need is time to cook the meat filling. I would suggest getting ground meat that is not too lean, as you want the filling to be moist. I might like the sauce to be sweeter, with a touch of cinnamon, but that is my Greek-inspired palate talking. You can decide for yourself if you want this more Spanish in taste or more Middle Eastern.

Serves 4 TO 6

For the meatballs:

$1/2$ POUND GROUND BEEF, NOT TOO LEAN

$1/4$ CUP FRESH BREAD CRUMBS

2 TO 3 TABLESPOONS OLIVE OIL

1 TEASPOON SALT

$1/2$ TEASPOON FRESHLY GROUND BLACK PEPPER

1 SMALL ONION, GRATED (OPTIONAL)

$1/3$ CUP PINE NUTS, TOASTED (OPTIONAL)

For the eggplant:

2 LONGISH GLOBE EGGPLANTS, ABOUT 1 POUND EACH,
    OR 4 SMALLER EGGPLANTS, ABOUT $1/2$ POUND EACH

OLIVE OIL FOR FRYING

2 EGGS

SALT

For the tomato sauce:

8 RIPE TOMATOES, PEELED, SEEDED, AND CHOPPED
    (ABOUT 3 POUNDS)

2 TEASPOONS SUGAR, OR MORE TO TASTE

SALT AND FRESHLY GROUND BLACK PEPPER

2 TABLESPOONS OLIVE OIL

PINCH OF GROUND CINNAMON (OPTIONAL)

1 RIPE TOMATO, SLICED

To make the meatballs, combine the meat, bread crumbs, olive oil, salt, and pepper. If you like, add the onion or pine nuts as well. Mix well and form into walnut-sized balls, making them slightly oval. Set aside.

Peel the eggplants vertically in a striped pattern. Cut in half lengthwise and then cut each half crosswise into slices about $1/3$ inch thick. If you want the rolls to be larger, do not cut the eggplants in half. With full slices you will get 14 to 16 rolls. If you cut the wider ones in half, you will get about 26 rolls (the end pieces are already small enough).

Pour olive oil to a depth of $1/2$ inch into 1 or 2 large sauté pans and heat over medium-high heat. Meanwhile, beat the eggs in a small bowl until blended. In batches, dip the eggplant slices in the beaten eggs and slip them into the hot oil. Fry, turning once, until golden on both sides and cooked through, about 8 minutes, adding more oil to the pans as needed. Using tongs or a slotted spatula, transfer to paper towels to drain. Sprinkle lightly with salt and let cool.

To make the tomato sauce, combine the tomatoes, sugar, and salt and pepper to taste in a small

saucepan. Place over medium heat, bring to a simmer, and cook, stirring occasionally, until the tomatoes break down and form a sauce, about 15 minutes. Stir in the olive oil and the cinnamon, if using. You will want 2½ to 3 cups of tomato sauce.

When the eggplant slices are cool, place 1 meatball at the bottom of each slice and roll up. As you roll, you may need to reshape the meatball slightly to make it fit in the eggplant slice.

Place the eggplant rolls, seam side down, in a wide sauté pan. Cover with the tomato sauce and then with the tomato slices. Place over very low heat, cover, and simmer until the filling is cooked, 20 to 30 minutes. Serve hot.

Notes: You can instead place the rolls in a baking dish and bake in a 350 degree F oven for about 30 minutes. In the recipe in *Sefarad Yemekleri,* before cooking, each assembled eggplant roll is decoratively topped with a piece of green pepper and tomato skewered on a toothpick.

: : : : : :

OJAS *de* PARRA *kon* AVAS

STUFFED GRAPE LEAVES WITH WHITE BEANS

Given the title of this recipe, which comes from *Sefarad Yemekleri,* you might think you are getting vine leaves stuffed with white beans, but that would be off the mark. These are the traditional meat-and-rice-stuffed vine leaves, also called *yaprakes* or *sarmas.* (In Atlanta's Temple Or Ve Shalom cookbook, they are called *yaprakes de oja.*) After the stuffed grape leaves have simmered, cooked white beans are added to the pan, and the grape leaves and beans are cooked together, their rich juices commingling.

Even though this recipe looks like a good deal of work, you can prepare both the beans and the grape leaves separately well ahead of time. Also, remember that stuffed grape leaves and stewed white beans were kitchen staples for the Sephardic Greeks and Turks, so this dish from Izmir probably represents another creative use of leftovers.

Serves 8

For the white beans:
1½ CUPS DRIED GREAT NORTHERN OR
    OTHER WHITE BEANS
5 CUPS WATER
1 SMALL ONION, CHOPPED
1 BAY LEAF
1 CLOVE GARLIC
SALT

For the stuffed grape leaves:
½ POUND GROUND BEEF OR LAMB
¼ CUP LONG-GRAIN WHITE RICE, SOAKED IN WATER
    TO COVER FOR 30 MINUTES AND DRAINED
3 TABLESPOONS CHOPPED FRESH FLAT-LEAF PARSLEY
2 TO 3 TABLESPOONS PINE NUTS

OJAS *de* PARRA *kon* AVAS ★ **STUFFED GRAPE LEAVES WITH WHITE BEANS**

2 TO 3 TABLESPOONS DRIED CURRANTS

SALT AND FRESHLY GROUND BLACK PEPPER

2 TABLESPOONS CHOPPED FRESH DILL (OPTIONAL)

1 TEASPOON GROUND CINNAMON (OPTIONAL)

ABOUT 36 SMALL BRINE-PACKED GRAPE LEAVES, WELL
    RINSED AND PATTED DRY, PLUS EXTRA LEAVES,
    WELL RINSED, FOR LINING PAN (OPTIONAL)

1 CUP OLIVE OR SUNFLOWER OIL

JUICE OF 1 LEMON

ABOUT 2 RIPE TOMATOES, SLICED, IF NOT USING
    GRAPE LEAVES FOR LINING

LEMON WEDGES

To prepare the beans, pick over dried beans for stones or other impurities and rinse well. Place in a saucepan, add the water, and bring to a boil over high heat. Reduce the heat to medium and simmer for a few minutes, then turn off the heat, and let stand for 1 hour.

Drain the beans and return them to the saucepan with fresh water to cover by 2 to 3 inches. Add the onion, bay leaf, and garlic and bring to a boil over high heat. Reduce the heat to low, cover, and simmer until beans are tender, about 1 hour, seasoning them with salt after they begin to soften. Remove from the heat and set aside.

To prepare the stuffed grape leaves, in a bowl, combine the meat, rice, parsley, pine nuts, currants, and salt and pepper to taste. Season with the dill and cinnamon, if desired.

Lay out some of the grape leaves on a work surface, shiny side down. Snip off the stems with scissors. Place a teaspoon or so of the mixture near the stem end of a leaf. Fold the stem end over the filling, fold in the sides, and then roll up the leaf into a cylinder. Do not roll too tightly, as the rice expands during cooking.

Line the bottom of a large sauté pan with extra vine leaves, if you like, as they will prevent the stuffed leaves from sticking or scorching. Arrange the stuffed leaves, seam side down, in the pan in a single layer. Pour the oil and lemon juice over them. Add hot water just to cover. Place 1 or 2 heavy plates only slightly smaller than the diameter of the pan on top of the stuffed leaves to weight them down. Cover, reduce the heat to low, and cook gently until the filling is cooked, 35 to 40 minutes. Remove from the heat and remove the plate(s). (Alternatively, arrange the vine leaves, if using, in a large baking dish, arrange the stuffed grape leaves in it in the same manner, and bake in a 350 degree F oven for 30 minutes.)

To assemble the finished dish, line the bottom of a large stew pot or baking dish with grape leaves or with sliced tomatoes. Spoon in the beans and their cooking liquids. Top with the stuffed grape leaves in a single layer and add their juices. If you don't have a pan large enough to hold the stuffed grape leaves in one layer, place about one-third of the beans in the bottom of the pot or dish, top with half of the grape leaves, then half of the remaining beans, all of the remaining grape leaves, and finally all of the remaining beans. Cover and heat through on the stove top over low heat or in a 350 degree F oven. Add liquid if needed to prevent the beans from scorching. Serve with lemon wedges.

: : : : : :

DOLMAYANI

MEAT-STUFFED CABBAGE LEAVES WITH FRUIT

These cabbage rolls from *Sefarad Yemekleri* are part of a large repertoire of Sephardic dolmas. A delicious sweet-and-sour sauce forms during the cooking of the cabbage packets with seasonal fruit, quinces in fall or winter, and plums in summer.

Serves 6

1 LARGE HEAD CABBAGE
1 POUND GROUND BEEF OR LAMB
3 TABLESPOONS CHOPPED FRESH FLAT-LEAF PARSLEY
3 TABLESPOONS CHOPPED FRESH DILL
$1/4$ TO $1/2$ CUP LONG-GRAIN WHITE RICE, SOAKED
    IN WATER FOR 30 MINUTES AND DRAINED
2 ONIONS, GRATED
$1^1/2$ TEASPOONS SALT
$1/2$ TEASPOON FRESHLY GROUND BLACK PEPPER
2 OR 3 QUINCES, OR $1/2$ POUND PLUMS (6 TO 8 SMALL)
JUICE OF 4 LEMONS (ABOUT 1 CUP)
1 CUP TOMATO JUICE

Bring a large pot two-thirds full of salted water to a boil. Cut out the core of the cabbage with a sharp knife. Slip the cabbage into the water, reduce the heat so the water simmers, and cook until the cabbage leaves soften, about 10 minutes. Drain carefully and remove the outer large leaves. You should have 12 to 16 leaves. Reserve the remaining cabbage for another use.

In a bowl, combine the meat, parsley, dill, rice, onions, salt, and pepper. Knead the meat with your hands until the mixture holds together well.

Spread the cabbage leaves out on a work surface. Place a few tablespoons of meat on the center of a leaf. Fold over the top, fold in the sides, and then fold over the bottom part of the leaf, making a dolmalike package. Skewer closed with toothpicks. Repeat until all filling is used. Place the packages, seam side down, in a single layer in a large, wide pot or saucepan.

If using quince, peel and core them and cut into large dice or $1/2$-inch-thick slices. If using plums, cut in half, remove the pits, and then cut into quarters if large. Top the cabbage packets with the sliced fruit. (If all the packets will not fit in a single layer, you can layer them with the fruit.) Add the lemon juice and tomato juice and bring to a simmer over low heat. Cover and simmer until tender, 1 to $1^1/2$ hours. (Alternatively, place the covered pot in an oven preheated to 300 degrees F for 1 to $1^1/2$ hours.) Taste and adjust the seasonings in the pan juices. Serve hot.

: : : : : :

LEGUMBRES YENOS *de* KARNE

MEAT-STUFFED VEGETABLES

Grape leaves and cabbage leaves are one form of dolma. Equally popular in the Sephardic kitchen are the *rellenos* or *reynadas,* meat-and-rice stuffed vegetables offered as a main course and sometimes served with *agristada,* an egg-and-lemon sauce. This amount of filling will stuff about 4 pounds of vegetables. I have included directions for tomatoes, peppers, eggplants, zucchini, and onions. If you are using a medley of vegetables, select those of a similar size for a nice visual presentation. You can also use this filling for grape leaves. It will stuff about 60 leaves. See page 164 for directions on folding and cooking.

Serves 6 TO 8

For the filling:

1/4 CUP OLIVE OIL

2 ONIONS, CHOPPED

3 CLOVES GARLIC, MINCED

2 TABLESPOONS CHOPPED FRESH FLAT-LEAF PARSLEY

1 TABLESPOON SALT

1 TEASPOON GROUND ALLSPICE

1 TEASPOON FRESHLY GROUND BLACK PEPPER

1 TEASPOON GROUND CINNAMON

1/2 CUP PINE NUTS, TOASTED

1/2 CUP DRIED CURRANTS, SOAKED IN HOT WATER
    UNTIL PLUMPED AND DRAINED

1 POUND GROUND LAMB

1 CUP LONG-GRAIN WHITE RICE, SOAKED IN WATER
    FOR 30 MINUTES AND DRAINED

1 CUP WATER

ABOUT 4 POUNDS TOMATOES, BELL PEPPERS, EGG-
    PLANTS, ZUCCHINI, OR ONIONS, OR A MIXTURE

1/2 CUP OLIVE OIL

SUGAR AND SALT, IF STUFFING TOMATOES

For the egg-and-lemon sauce (optional):

1 CUP STOCK, ANY KIND

2 OR 3 WHOLE EGGS, OR 3 EGG YOLKS

JUICE OF 2 SMALL LEMONS (4 TO 5 TABLESPOONS)

To make the filling, warm the olive oil in a very large sauté pan over low heat. Add the onions and sauté until tender and translucent, about 10 minutes. Add the garlic, parsley, salt, allspice, pepper, cinnamon, pine nuts, and currants and continue to sauté for 3 minutes. Add the meat and cook, breaking up any lumps, until it is no longer pink, about 5 minutes. Add the rice and water and cook for about 5 minutes. Remove from the heat and let cool.

For *reynadas de tomat* (stuffed tomatoes): Cut off the tops of ripe tomatoes and scoop out the pulp. Reserve the tomato pulp and all juices, as well as the tops. Sprinkle the insides of the tomatoes with salt and a little sugar. Set aside. Put the tomato pulp in a blender or food processor and puree until smooth. Add to the rice mixture.

Preheat the oven to 350 degrees F. Stuff the meat mixture into the tomatoes. Do not fill too tightly, as the rice will continue to expand. Place in a baking dish and replace the tops. Pour about 1/3 cup hot water into the dish and spoon the 1/2 cup oil over the tomatoes. Bake uncovered, basting occasionally with the pan juices, until the filling is heated through and the tomatoes are tender, about 30 minutes. Serve warm or cold.

For *reynadas de pipirushkas* (stuffed peppers): Cut off the tops of the bell peppers and remove the seeds. Parboil the shells for 4 to 5 minutes and drain. Stuff and bake as directed for tomatoes. Serve warm.

For *kucaras de berenjena* (stuffed eggplant): Take eggplants, cut in half, scoop out some of the pulp to make a shell, and reserve and chop the pulp, discarding as many seeds as possible. Sauté the chopped pulp with the onions. Sauté the eggplant cases in olive oil for about 5 minutes to soften them. Stuff and bake as directed for the tomatoes. Serve warm.

For *kalavasas yenas de karne* (stuffed zucchini): If using large zucchini, cut in half, scoop out and discard the seeds to make a case. If the zucchini are small, enlarge the hollows by cutting out a bit of the pulp, and then chop the pulp and sauté with the onions. Parboil the cases for 3 minutes and drain. Stuff and bake as directed for the tomatoes. Serve warm.

For *reynadas de sevoya* (stuffed onions): Boil the onions until they are tender but not soft, about 10 minutes. Drain and, when cool enough to handle, cut in half crosswise. Scoop out part of each half to make a cavity. Chop the reserved onion and add to the meat filling. Stuff and bake as directed for tomatoes, reducing the time to about 20 minutes. The onions should be golden. Serve warm.

If you are serving the stuffed vegetables warm, you may want to accompany them with an egg-and-lemon sauce. To make the sauce, bring the stock to a simmer in a saucepan. Meanwhile, in a bowl, beat the whole eggs or egg yolks with the lemon juice until quite frothy. Gradually whisk in a little of the hot stock to temper the eggs, then stir the eggs into the remaining stock. Stir over low heat until slightly thickened. Do not allow the mixture to boil. You can also separate 3 eggs, beat together the yolks and lemon juice until frothy, and then beat the whites until stiff peaks form. Fold the yolk mixture into the

stiffly beaten whites, and then temper the mixture with the hot stock. Finally, add the egg mixture to the stock and heat gently. Spoon the sauce over the stuffed vegetables.

: : : : : :

LINGUA *di* MANZO *con le* OLIVE
BOILED TONGUE WITH OLIVE SAUCE

This Italian recipe is for tongue aficionados. You may use a fresh or corned tongue. If you use a corned tongue, bring it to a boil in water to cover, drain, and then start the recipe. This step will rid the tongue of excess salt. In her version of this recipe, which she calls *aluenga con azeitunas,* Suzy David adds 1 teaspoon ground cinnamon to the sauce and instead of tomato paste uses 1 cup tomato sauce, making a cross between an olive sauce and an *agrodolce,* or sweet-and-sour sauce.

Serves 6 TO 8

1 BEEF TONGUE, ABOUT 3 POUNDS, WELL SCRUBBED

2 ONIONS, PEELED BUT LEFT WHOLE

1 LARGE CARROT, PEELED

3 CELERY STALKS WITH LEAVES

12 BLACK PEPPERCORNS

1 BAY LEAF

6 CORIANDER SEEDS

BOILING WATER, AS NEEDED

For the olive sauce:

3 TABLESPOONS OLIVE OIL

2 CLOVES GARLIC, MINCED

2 TO 4 TABLESPOONS CHOPPED FRESH HERB OF CHOICE SUCH AS BASIL, MARJORAM, FLAT-LEAF PARSLEY, OR MINT

1¹/₂ CUPS PITTED MEDITERRANEAN-STYLE BLACK
  OLIVES, COARSELY CHOPPED
3 TABLESPOONS TOMATO PASTE
SALT AND FRESHLY GROUND BLACK PEPPER

Place the tongue in a deep pot with the onions,
carrot, celery, peppercorns, bay leaf, and coriander
seeds. Add boiling water to cover, return to a boil,
cover, reduce the heat to low, and simmer until
tender, 2 ¹/₂ to 3 hours.

Remove the tongue from the pot. Strain the cooking
liquid and reserve. When the tongue is cool enough
to handle, peel it and cut away the thick gristle and
bones at the large end. Slice the tongue and set aside.

To make the sauce, warm the olive oil in a large, deep
sauté pan over medium heat. Add the garlic and herb
and sauté until the garlic is tender, 1 to 2 minutes.
Add the olives and tomato paste and stir well. Add
the tongue slices to the pan and enough of the
strained cooking liquid to cover. Simmer over very
low heat for 20 minutes to blend the flavors. Season
with salt and pepper and serve hot.

: : : : : :

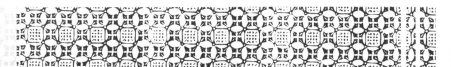
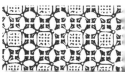

DESSERTS

chapter 7

✦

DESSERTS

When it comes to desserts, the Sephardim seem to have inherited the Hispano-Arabic sweet tooth. Traditionally, dessert was not a daily occurrence, however. More often than not a piece of fresh fruit or a handful of dried fruits and nuts were all that were eaten at the end of a meal. Although I have not unearthed a large written repertoire of recipes for cooked fruits, I do know that fruits were used in the making of the conserves and spoon sweets that were served on holidays. Quince, pumpkin, and citrus were the most popular.

Pastries are a focus at breakfast, at special coffees and teas, and at circumcisions, weddings, and holidays. In accordance with kosher laws, butter-based pastries, custard sauces, cheese-filled pastries, and milk-enriched puddings may be served only at dairy meals. Pastry doughs and cake batters served at meat-based meals are made with margarine or oil. Naturally, the desserts for Passover use matzoh meal and nuts in place of flour, with beaten eggs providing the leavening. Signature Spanish additions of orange and almond are the most popular flavorings, with vanilla and cinnamon adding other subtle dimensions. Orange-flower water or rose water add their perfume in discreet amounts. Walnuts and hazelnuts turn up in cakes and pastries, too, but it is the almond and the orange, those ancestors from Arabic Spain, that dominate the dessert menu at the Sephardic table.

ZERDE

SAFFRON RICE PUDDING

Saffron, the tiny stigmas of a type of crocus, was introduced to Spain and Portugal by the Arabs. It takes tens of thousands of flowers to yield a single pound of saffron threads, a fact that makes their high price understandable. The stratospheric cost means that this golden-hued rice pudding has always been reserved for special occasions, such as weddings and circumcisions. The ingredients— rice, pine nuts, raisins, pomegranate seeds, saffron—all symbolize either good fortune or fertility.

Toasting the saffron threads maximizes their flavor. For a meat meal, omit the milk and steep the saffron in warm water. *Zerde* is a classic Turkish dessert that came to the Jews via the Dönme, or Muslimized followers of Shabbatai Zevi.

Serves 6 TO 8

$^1/_2$ CUP SHORT-GRAIN WHITE RICE, RINSED

$1^1/_2$ CUPS SUGAR

6 CUPS WATER

2 LARGE PINCHES OF SAFFRON THREADS,
    FINELY CRUSHED

$^1/_2$ CUP MILK, WARMED

1 TABLESPOON ARROWROOT OR CORNSTARCH

3 TABLESPOONS WATER

$^1/_3$ CUP GOLDEN RAISINS

$^1/_2$ CUP PINE NUTS, TOASTED, OR POMEGRANATE SEEDS

Place the rice in a saucepan along with the sugar and water. Bring to a boil over medium heat, stirring to dissolve the sugar. Reduce the heat to low and simmer uncovered, stirring often until the rice is quite puffed but some liquid still remains in the pan, about 30 minutes.

Meanwhile, toast the saffron in a small, dry frying pan over low heat until it is fragrant, about 3 minutes. Be careful it does not burn. Add the saffron to the warmed milk in a small bowl and let steep for 15 minutes.

In a small cup, dissolve the arrowroot or cornstarch in the water. When the rice is ready, stir the mixture into it. Then add the saffron infusion and the raisins to the rice. Simmer over low heat, stirring occasionally, until thick, about 15 minutes longer.

Pour the pudding into individual bowls or 1 large serving bowl and top with the pine nuts or pomegranate seeds. Serve at room temperature or chilled.

: : : : : :

SUTLATCH

CREAM OF RICE PUDDING

Serve this creamy, delicate pudding to break the fast after Yom Kippur. *Sutlatch* may also be served at Shabbat *desayuno* after morning services. While it was usually prepared with milk, the cooking liquid was sometimes *pipitada,* made by steeping melon seeds in water and traditionally drunk to restore body fluids lost while fasting on Yom Kippur. Gilda Angel's version of this recipe in *Sephardic Holiday Cooking* uses vanilla as the aromatic flavoring for a milk-based pudding, but Nicholas Stavroulakis suggests either grated orange zest or rose water. I prefer to combine the vanilla and orange zest. Other names for this pudding are the Turkish *mahallebi* and the Greek Christian *rizogalo.*

Serves 8

6 TABLESPOONS RICE FLOUR OR CREAM OF RICE

6 TABLESPOONS SUGAR

5 TO 6 TABLESPOONS WATER

4 CUPS MILK OR *PIPITADA* (FOLLOWING)

1 TEASPOON VANILLA EXTRACT AND/OR

   1 TABLESPOON GRATED ORANGE ZEST,

   OR 2 TABLESPOONS ROSE WATER

GROUND CINNAMON

In a bowl, combine the rice flour or Cream of Rice and sugar. Gradually add the water, stirring until a thick lump-free paste forms.

In a saucepan, bring the milk or *pipitada* to a boil over medium heat. Gradually add the rice-flour paste, whisking constantly to prevent lumps from forming. Continue to whisk the mixture constantly over medium heat until it thickens, 4 to 5 minutes. Remove from the heat and stir in the vanilla and/or orange zest or the rose water. Pour the pudding into eight 4-ounce custard cups. Sprinkle with cinnamon, cover, and refrigerate until well chilled before serving.

Pipitada: Remove the seeds from 4 or 5 cantaloupes and spread them on paper towels to dry for at least 48 hours or as long as a week. If need be, dry them in a 200 degree F oven until they are free of moisture. When they are fully dried, transfer them to a blender or food processor and grind to a powder. Place on a piece of cheesecloth, bring the corners together, and tie securely. Fill a bowl or pitcher with 8 cups water, immerse the seed packet in the water, and let steep at room temperature for 24 hours. From time to time, squeeze the cheesecloth bundle to release the flavor into the water. The water will look milky. After 24 hours, discard the seed packet and add 2 to 4 tablespoons sugar, according to taste, and 2 drops of rose water or orange-flower water. Cover and chill well before drinking.

: : : : : :

REVANI

SEMOLINA CAKE WITH SYRUP

Revani was named for a sixteenth-century Turkish poet who wrote about the delights of food, and both Greek and Turkish Jews traditionally make this dessert. I love the texture of it. It has a nice crunchiness due to the use of semolina. Surprisingly, even with the syrup, it is not overly sweet. You could serve the cake without the syrup, but it would be too dry to stand alone and would need a compote of berries or fruit spooned on top.

Serves 8 TO 10

For the syrup:
2 CUPS SUGAR
2 CUPS WATER
4 TEASPOONS FRESH LEMON JUICE

For the cake:
9 EGGS, SEPARATED
$^3/_4$ CUP SUGAR
GRATED ZEST OF 2 LEMONS OR 1 LARGE ORANGE
2 CUPS FINE SEMOLINA OR CREAM OF WHEAT
$^1/_4$ CUP ALL-PURPOSE FLOUR
$^1/_4$ CUP UNSALTED BUTTER, MELTED AND COOLED

To make the syrup, combine the sugar and water in a saucepan over medium heat and bring to a simmer, stirring until the sugar dissolves. Reduce the heat to low and cook until the syrup thickens slightly, about 10 minutes. It should not be too thick. Remove from the heat, stir in the lemon juice, and let cool.

Preheat the oven to 350 degrees F. Butter a 9-by-12-by-2-inch baking pan.

To make the cake, combine the egg yolks, sugar, and zest in a bowl and beat with an electric mixer until the mixture is very thick and pale and holds a 3-second ribbon when the beaters are lifted. In a separate bowl, stir together the semolina or Cream of Wheat and the all-purpose flour.

Fold the flour mixture into the yolk mixture. In another bowl, using clean beaters, beat the egg whites until soft peaks form. Fold the egg whites in four batches into the yolk mixture alternately with the melted butter, beginning and ending with the whites. Pour the batter into the prepared pan.

Bake the cake until golden, 35 to 40 minutes. Remove from the oven and place on a rack. Pour the cooled syrup evenly over the hot cake. Let the cake cool completely before serving.

Note: Another *revani* recipe uses part all-purpose flour, part semolina, and part ground nuts.

: : : : : :

FLAN *d'*ARANCIA

ORANGE CUSTARD

Flan is the classic Spanish dessert, a custard usually prepared with cream or milk, eggs, and flavoring. This Sephardic version, however, uses orange juice instead of milk or cream, permitting it to be served after a meat-based meal. The texture may seem a bit odd at first, especially if you are partial to cream-based custards. If that is the case, you'll prefer the version made with only egg yolks, as it is richer and creamier, in the Portuguese tradition. Claudia Roden adds 1 cup ground almonds to the custard mixture. The nuts rise to the top in baking and then end up on the bottom after the custard is unmolded. The almonds add another dimension of sweetness, but their strong flavor cuts the presence of the orange.

Serves 6

1¹/₂ CUPS SUGAR
2 TABLESPOONS WATER
1 CUP BLANCHED ALMONDS (OPTIONAL)
6 WHOLE EGGS OR 8 EGG YOLKS
1 CUP FRESH ORANGE JUICE
GRATED ZEST OF 2 ORANGES
ORANGE SEGMENTS (OPTIONAL)

In a small, heavy saucepan, melt ¹/₂ cup of the sugar with the water over high heat. Cook, without stirring, until the mixture is a caramel color and is fragrant. Do not let it get too dark, or it will taste bitter. Very carefully pour the caramel into the bottom of a 1-quart flan mold or 6 custard cups. Swirl quickly to coat the bottom(s) and sides.

Preheat the oven to 350 degrees F.

If using almonds, place in a food processor with ¹/₄ cup of the remaining sugar and process until finely ground. Set aside.

In a bowl, whisk together the eggs or egg yolks and the remaining sugar. Add the orange juice and zest and mix well. (If you are not using the almonds, add the remaining ¹/₂ cup sugar at this point.) Whisk in the almonds, if using.

Pour the mixture into the prepared mold or custard cups and place the container(s) in a baking pan. Add hot water to the pan to reach halfway up the sides of the mold or cups. Cover the baking pan with aluminum foil.

Bake until a knife inserted into the center emerges clean, 35 to 40 minutes for the small custards and 1 hour for the large mold. Remove from the oven, then remove from the baking pan. Let cool a bit, then cover with aluminum foil or plastic wrap and refrigerate until well chilled.

To serve, run a thin knife blade around the inside edges of each custard cup or the mold and invert onto individual plates or a large plate. Spoon the caramel that flows onto the plate(s) over the top(s). Garnish with orange segments, if desired.

: : : : : :

INCHUSA *de* LECHE

DOUBLE-CRUSTED CUSTARD TART

Suzy David has two versions of this delicate tart in *The Sephardic Kosher Kitchen.* The word *inchusa* refers to a tart, sometimes with a single crust, sometimes with a double crust. Given the changeable nature of recipe names, I was not surprised to find *encusa,* used for a spinach gratin. One bite of this tart, however, and you will know that this is a classic Spanish dessert. Lacking a shallow tart pan you may use a 9-inch pie pan. In that case, you may not need all of the dough. When my 5 1/2-year-old granddaughter, Elena, a jaded chocoholic, tasted this tart she moaned "omigod" and asked for seconds. Grandma, of course, complied with pleasure.

Serves 8

For the dough:
3 CUPS ALL-PURPOSE FLOUR
1/4 CUP SUGAR
1/2 TEASPOON SALT
GRATED ZEST OF 1 LEMON
1 CUP MARGARINE OR UNSALTED BUTTER, CHILLED AND
    CUT INTO THIN SLICES
1 EGG, LIGHTLY BEATEN
1/2 TEASPOON VANILLA EXTRACT
1 TABLESPOON ICE WATER, IF NEEDED

For the filling:
4 EGG YOLKS
1 TABLESPOON CORNSTARCH
2 CUPS MILK
1/3 CUP SUGAR
GRATED ZEST OF 1 LEMON
1 TEASPOON VANILLA EXTRACT
1/4 CUP BUTTER, CUT INTO THIN SLICES
1 EGG YOLK, LIGHTLY BEATEN

To make the dough, put the flour, sugar, salt, and lemon zest in a bowl and stir to mix. Add the margarine or butter and, using a pastry blender, work it in until the mixture resembles coarse cornmeal. Add the egg and vanilla and stir and toss with a fork until the dough comes together in a rough mass. Add the ice water if the dough doesn't come together easily. Alternatively, combine the flour, sugar, salt, and lemon zest in a food processor and pulse a few times to blend. Add the margarine or butter and pulse until the mixture resembles coarse cornmeal. Add the egg and vanilla and process until the dough forms a rough mass, adding the ice water if the mixture seems too dry.

With your hands, form the dough into a ball, cut it into quarters, place one piece on top of the other, and work the stack into a ball. Repeat this process 3 times. Wrap the dough in plastic wrap and refrigerate for at least 1 hour or as long as 1 day.

To make the filling, in a heavy saucepan, beat the egg yolks until blended. Dissolve the cornstarch in the milk and then whisk the mixture into the yolks. Add the sugar and lemon zest and place over low heat. Cook, whisking constantly, until small bubbles begin to appear, then remove from the heat and continue to whisk, beating in the vanilla and then the butter a bit at a time until the butter melts. Cover the pan with plastic wrap and nest in an ice bath to cool. If you are not assembling the tart right away, refrigerate.

Divide the dough into 2 pieces, one slightly larger than the other. On a lightly floured board, roll out the larger portion into rounds slightly less than 1/4 inch thick. Carefully transfer to a 10-inch tart pan with a removable bottom or a 9-inch pie pan. Prick the bottom in a few places with a fork. Cover and place in the freezer until dough is very cold. (This will prevent shrinkage during baking.)

Preheat the oven to 350 degrees F.

Pour the chilled filling into the tart shell. On a floured work surface, roll out the remaining disk of dough into a round slightly less than $1/4$ inch thick. Dampen the edges of the bottom crust. Carefully place the pastry round over the filling. Trim any excessive overhang, then pinch to seal. Brush the top with the beaten egg yolk.

Bake the pie until the crust is golden brown, 35 to 40 minutes. Transfer to a rack and let cool completely before serving.

: : : : : :

PANDESPANYA
SPONGE CAKE

According to John Cooper in *Eat and Be Satisfied,* this classic orange-scented sponge cake, called *pandespanya* by Sephardim and *panaspana* by the Romaniote Greeks, dates back to medieval Spain and Portugal. The non-Passover version uses flour, but for Passover you must omit the flour and baking soda and use $1^{1}/_{2}$ cups matzoh cake meal, or 1 cup ground nuts and $1/_{2}$ cup matzoh cake meal. You will also need to increase the egg whites to 10 or 12, as they will be the only leavening.

Serves 10

8 EGGS, SEPARATED

1 CUP SUGAR

$1^{1}/_{2}$ CUPS ALL-PURPOSE FLOUR

$1/_{2}$ TEASPOON BAKING SODA

$1/_{4}$ CUP FRESH ORANGE JUICE

GRATED ZEST OF 2 ORANGES

$1/_{2}$ TEASPOON VANILLA EXTRACT

$1/_{4}$ CUP UNSALTED BUTTER, MELTED AND COOLED

Preheat the oven to 350 degrees F. Butter and flour a 10-inch springform pan.

Place the egg yolks in a bowl and beat with an electric mixer until pale yellow. Gradually beat in $1/_{2}$ cup of the sugar, beating until thick and pale. Add the flour, baking soda, orange juice, orange zest, and vanilla and mix well.

In another bowl, using the electric mixer and clean beaters, beat the egg whites until foamy. Gradually beat in the remaining $1/_{2}$ cup sugar until stiff peaks form. Fold the butter into the egg yolk mixture, then fold in the egg whites just until no white streaks remain. Pour the batter into the prepared pan.

Bake the cake until golden and the top springs back when pressed gently, about 45 minutes. Transfer to a rack and let the cake cool in the pan. Unclasp the pan sides and slide the cooled cake onto a plate to serve.

Note: You can make this cake without the butter if it is to be served at a meat meal. It will, however, be a bit drier.

: : : : : :

TISPISHTI

WALNUT CAKE

Tispishti is a classic Turkish walnut cake bathed in syrup. It has a moist texture and, surprisingly, is not too sweet. Gilda Angel's *Sephardic Holiday Cooking* uses honey syrup, but most recipes for this cake use lemon-scented sugar syrup, which is lighter. Some cooks pour cooled syrup over the hot cake. Others pour warm syrup over a cooled cake. The cake is also called *tishpishti, tishpitti, tichpichti,* and *tezpisti.* Although one recipe uses $1^1/_2$ cups walnuts and $^1/_2$ cup almonds, and another uses part walnuts and part hazelnuts, walnuts usually are the signature flavor. If you are serving the cake at a dairy meal, a dollop of whipped cream is a nice enhancement.

Serves 8 TO 10

For the syrup:

2 CUPS SUGAR

1 CUP WATER

2 TABLESPOONS FRESH LEMON JUICE

1 TABLESPOON ORANGE-FLOWER OR ROSE WATER
    (OPTIONAL)

For the cake:

10 EGGS, SEPARATED

$^2/_3$ CUP SUGAR

2 TEASPOONS BAKING SODA

2 TABLESPOONS FRESH ORANGE JUICE

1 TEASPOON VANILLA EXTRACT

$1^1/_2$ TEASPOONS GROUND CINNAMON

PINCH OF GROUND CLOVES

GRATED ZEST OF 1 ORANGE

GRATED ZEST OF 1 LEMON

2 CUPS GROUND TOASTED WALNUTS

To make the syrup, combine the sugar, water, and lemon juice in a saucepan and bring to a boil, stirring until the sugar dissolves. Reduce the heat to low and cook until the syrup thickens slightly, 8 to 10 minutes. Remove from the heat and let cool. Add orange-flower or rose water, if desired.

Butter a 10-by-14-by-3-inch baking pan. Preheat the oven to 350 degrees F.

To make the cake, place the egg yolks in a bowl and beat with an electric mixer until pale yellow. Gradually add the sugar and beat until thick and pale. Dissolve the baking soda in the orange juice and add to the egg yolks along with the vanilla, cinnamon, and cloves. Beat until combined. Stir in the grated zest and nuts.

In another bowl, using the electric mixer and clean beaters, beat the egg whites until stiff peaks form. Stir one-third of the beaten whites into the yolk-nut mixture, then fold in the remainder. Pour the batter into the prepared pan.

Bake the cake until a toothpick inserted into the center emerges clean, 25 to 35 minutes. Remove from the oven, place on a rack, and let cool for a bit. Puncture the top of the cake in several places with a toothpick or a small skewer. Pour the syrup evenly over the warm cake. Let cool completely. Cut into serving pieces and serve.

Variation: For *korydato,* a Greek Passover walnut cake from Ioannina, omit the baking soda and replace $^1/_2$ cup of the walnuts with $^1/_2$ cup matzoh cake meal. Or reduce the walnuts to 1 cup and add 1 cup matzoh cake meal for a lighter version.

: : : : : :

BAKLAVA

LAYERED FILO PASTRY

Both Greeks and Turks claim this masterpiece of Middle Eastern sweets. It can be made with walnuts, almonds, hazelnuts, or pistachios, or a combination. Sticky honey syrups are not traditional. Instead, a simple sugar syrup flavored with lemon juice and zest is poured over the baklava after baking.

Makes about 36 pieces

1 POUND BLANCHED ALMONDS, WALNUTS, OR HALF ALMONDS AND HALF WALNUTS (ABOUT 4 CUPS), COARSELY CHOPPED

1/2 CUP SUGAR

2 TEASPOONS GROUND CINNAMON

1/2 TEASPOON GROUND CARDAMOM

1/2 POUND UNSALTED BUTTER, MELTED AND CLARIFIED, OR MARGARINE, MELTED

1 POUND FILO SHEETS (ABOUT 18 SHEETS), THAWED IN THE REFRIGERATOR IF FROZEN

For the syrup:

2 CUPS WATER

2 CUPS SUGAR

2 LEMON ZEST STRIPS, EACH 3 INCHES LONG

2 TABLESPOONS FRESH LEMON JUICE

In a bowl, combine the nuts, sugar, cinnamon, and cardamom. Brush a 9-by-14-by-2-inch baking pan or baking dish with the melted butter or margarine. Have ready the filo sheets, keeping them covered with plastic wrap to prevent them from drying out. Lay a filo sheet in the bottom of the pan or dish and brush it with the butter or margarine. Repeat, brushing each layer, until you have built up 9 or 10 layers. Spread the nut mixture evenly over the stack of but-tered filo, then layer 9 or 10 more filo sheets on top, again brushing each sheet. Cover the pan and refrigerate for about 30 minutes until the butter firms up.

Preheat the oven to 350 degrees F.

With a sharp knife, cut the filo stack all the way through into about 36 diamonds. Bake until golden brown, 35 to 40 minutes. Remove from the oven and place on a rack.

While the baklava is baking, make the syrup: In a saucepan, combine the water, sugar, and lemon zest and bring to a simmer over medium heat, stirring until the sugar dissolves. Cook until the syrup thickens, 10 to 15 minutes. Remove and discard the lemon zest strips and stir in the lemon juice. You can let the syrup cool before pouring it over the hot pastry, or you can pour the hot syrup over the hot pastry. Serve the pastry warm or at room temperature.

Variation: A cream filling can be used in place of the nut filling. In a saucepan, combine 3 cups milk and 1/2 cup sugar and bring to a boil over medium heat, stirring to dissolve the sugar. Place 2/3 cup fine semolina or Cream of Wheat in a small bowl and add a bit of the hot milk, stirring to make a smooth paste. Stir this paste back into the hot milk. In a small bowl, whisk 3 eggs until blended. Whisk in a little of the hot milk mixture and then stir the eggs into the pan. Cook over low heat, stirring constantly, until the mixture thickens, about 10 minutes. Remove from the heat and stir in 2 teaspoons vanilla extract or 1 table-spoon rose or orange-flower water, if desired. Let cool completely, then use in place of the nut filling. Cut and bake as directed.

: : : : : :

BOUGATSA

CHEESE–FILLED FILO PASTRY

One of my happiest memories of being in Salonika was eating my first piece of *bougatsa*. Although not this Jewish version, it was incredibly rich and delicious. Here is Nicholas Stavroulakis's Sephardic recipe for *bougatsa* from the town of Ioannina. In earlier times it was prepared with *staka,* a very thick cream made from the milk of water buffalo or sheep and sometimes called *kaymak* in Turkey. While we cannot get such a creamy and rich product, we can make this dessert with mascarpone or cream cheese. Some versions of the recipe pour a sugar syrup over the cake, but I think it is rich enough that a simple sprinkling of confectioners' sugar and maybe a pinch of cinnamon suffice. While the cake is usually served cold, I prefer to serve it warm. That's easy to do if you assemble it up to 8 hours in advance and keep it in the refrigerator until 1 hour before serving time. Then bake and serve warm.

Serves 10 TO 12

1 POUND MASCARPONE OR OTHER RICH CREAM
    CHEESE, AT ROOM TEMPERATURE
1$^{1}/_{2}$ CUPS SUGAR
6 EGGS
1 TEASPOON VANILLA EXTRACT
$^{1}/_{2}$ CUP UNSALTED BUTTER, MELTED AND CLARIFIED
10 FILO SHEETS, THAWED IN THE REFRIGERATOR IF
    FROZEN
CONFECTIONERS' SUGAR

In a large bowl, combine the cheese, sugar, eggs, and vanilla and beat with an electric mixer or by hand until creamy. Brush the bottom of a 10-by-14-by-2-inch baking pan or baking dish with butter. Have ready the filo sheets, keeping them covered with plastic wrap to prevent them from drying out. Lay a filo sheet in the bottom of the pan or dish and brush it with the butter. Repeat, brushing each layer, until you have built up 5 layers. Pour the cheese filling over the stack of buttered filo. Drizzle the filling with a little melted butter, then layer 5 more filo sheets on top, again brushing each sheet. Cover the pan and refrigerate until the butter firms up. (Chilling makes it easier to cut.)

Preheat the oven to 375 degrees F.

With a sharp knife, score the surface of the pastry through the top 5 sheets into 10 diamonds or rectangles. Bake until golden brown, 35 to 40 minutes. Transfer the pastry to a rack and let cool for several minutes, then cut along the score marks. Let cool until warm or at room temperature, dust with confectioners' sugar, and serve.

Note: Claudia Roden's inspiring *The Book of Jewish Food* has a savory version of this pie called *boghatcha,* which she says means "drunkard" in Ladino. The cheese filling is rolled into coils, the coils are joined to form one giant coil or snake, and then a milk custard is poured over the top, and the pastry is baked until the milk is absorbed.

: : : : : :

TRAVADOS

NUT-FILLED PASTRIES

Every Sephardic cookbook and probably every
Sephardic cook has a version of these nut-filled
cookielike pastries. The Turks prefer walnuts for
the filling, but the Greeks lean toward almonds. I
prefer the filling that uses currants along with the
nuts, as I love their chewy texture after the pastry
is baked. In Rhodes, *travados* were traditionally
served at Purim, while in Turkey they were on the
table at Rosh Hashanah to celebrate the sweet new
year, and a variation called *borekas de muez* was
served at Purim. The pastries are sometimes dipped
in syrup, although the Greeks use a sweeter outer
pastry and omit the syrup, instead just sprinkling
the baked pastries with confectioners' sugar while
they are still warm. If you are not going to use the
syrup, increase the sugar in the dough, although in
this case I think the syrup adds a delicate texture to
the dough. *Travados* store well in a tightly closed
tin or plastic container for up to a week.

Makes 32 TO 36 *pastries*

For the pastry:
3 CUPS ALL-PURPOSE FLOUR
1 CUP CONFECTIONERS' SUGAR
2 TABLESPOONS GRANULATED SUGAR
$^1/_2$ CUP UNSALTED BUTTER, MELTED AND COOLED
$^3/_4$ CUP SWEET WINE SUCH AS LATE-HARVEST RIESLING
  OR MARSALA
$^1/_2$ TEASPOON ALMOND EXTRACT
1 EGG WHITE, FOR SEALING DOUGH (OPTIONAL)
1 EGG YOLK, DILUTED WITH A BIT OF WATER, FOR GLAZE

For the Greek almond-and-currant filling:
1 CUP CONFECTIONERS' SUGAR
1$^1/_2$ CUPS GROUND BLANCHED ALMONDS
$^1/_2$ CUP DRIED CURRANTS

3 TABLESPOONS COGNAC
2 TO 3 TABLESPOONS WATER
1 TEASPOON GROUND CINNAMON

For the Greek almond-and-orange filling:
2 CUPS GROUND BLANCHED ALMONDS
2 CUPS CONFECTIONERS' SUGAR
$^1/_4$ CUP FRESH ORANGE JUICE
3 TABLESPOONS GRATED ORANGE ZEST

For the Turkish walnut filling:
2 CUPS WALNUTS, FINELY CHOPPED
$^1/_2$ CUP ORANGE MARMALADE
$^1/_2$ TEASPOON GROUND CINNAMON
SUGAR TO TASTE (OPTIONAL)

For the optional syrup:
1 CUP WATER
2 CUPS GRANULATED SUGAR
3 TABLESPOONS FRESH LEMON JUICE
1 ORANGE ZEST STRIP, 3 INCHES LONG (OPTIONAL)
1 TABLESPOON ORANGE-FLOWER OR ROSE WATER
  (OPTIONAL)

CONFECTIONERS' SUGAR, IF NOT USING SYRUP

To make the pastry, in a bowl, stir together the flour
and sugar. Slowly add the butter, wine, and almond
extract, stirring until a smooth, soft dough forms. Let
rest in the bowl for 15 to 20 minutes.

Meanwhile, preheat the oven to 350 degrees F. Lightly
butter 2 baking sheets with sides or line them with
parchment paper. Select one of the fillings, place the
ingredients for it in a bowl, and stir to mix.

Pull off a walnut-sized piece of the dough and roll it into a ball between your palms. Flatten the ball and place it on a lightly floured work surface. Roll it out into a 3-inch round about $1/8$ inch thick. Moisten a fingertip with egg white or water and dampen the edge of the round. Place 2 teaspoons of the filling in the center of the round and fold the round in half to form a half-moon. Pinch the edges of the dough together. Place on a prepared baking sheet. Repeat until all the dough and filling are used. Brush the half-moons with the egg-yolk glaze.

Bake the pastries until lightly browned, 20 to 25 minutes. Remove from the oven and let cool on the baking sheets on a rack.

If you are using the syrup, prepare it while the pastries are baking: In a saucepan, combine the water, sugar, lemon juice, and the orange zest, if using, and bring to a boil over medium heat, stirring until the sugar dissolves. Boil until the syrup coats a spoon, about 10 minutes, then remove from the heat. Add the orange-flower or rose water, if using, and remove from the heat. Let stand for a few minutes, then dip the cooled pastries in the warm syrup and place on racks to drain for a few hours.

If you are not using the syrup, sprinkle the pastries with confectioners' sugar while they are still warm.

Variations: The same fillings can be enclosed in filo. Preheat the oven to 375 degrees F. Brush a baking sheet with melted butter. Cut filo sheets into 3-inch-wide strips, and stack 2 or 3 strips, brushing each one with melted butter. (Place a sheet of plastic wrap over any filo sheets you are not working with at the moment to prevent them from drying out.) Place

a rounded tablespoonful of filling near the upper corner of the stack and fold over the end on the diagonal to cover the filling, creating a triangular shape. Then fold again, maintaining the triangular shape. Continue folding in this manner, as if folding a flag, until you have a triangular pastry. Place on the prepared baking sheet. Repeat until all the filling has been used, then, just before baking, brush the triangles with melted butter. Bake until golden brown, 20 to 25 minutes. Let cool, then dip in the warm syrup, if desired.

Alternatively, make cigars: Cut filo sheets into 6-inch squares. Brush a square with melted butter and top with another square, again brushing with butter. Arrange a strip of filling along one end, fold the sides in, and then roll up the square to form a cigar shape. Seal the edge with a little water or beaten egg. Bake as for the triangles, let cool, and dip in the syrup, if desired.

: : : : : :

FRITTELLE *de* HANUKKAH

HANUKKAH FRITTERS

If you love fried foods, Hanukkah gives you a guilt-free reason to serve many of your favorites. While potato fritters are much appreciated, how can one resist a fritter for dessert? The Italian honey topping is wonderful, but, as a change of pace, you could dip these briefly in a classic Middle Eastern sugar-and-water syrup seasoned with cinnamon stick and orange zest. In Greece these fritters are called *loukoumades,* and in Turkey, *lokma.*

Serves 8 TO 10

2 ENVELOPES (2$^{1}/_{2}$ TEASPOONS EACH) ACTIVE
    DRY YEAST
1 TEASPOON SUGAR
1 CUP LUKEWARM WATER
3 CUPS ALL-PURPOSE FLOUR
1 TABLESPOON ANISEEDS
1 TEASPOON SALT
2 TABLESPOONS VEGETABLE OIL, PLUS OIL
    FOR DEEP-FRYING
GRATED ZEST OF 2 ORANGES
1 CUP RAISINS

For the glaze:
3 TABLESPOONS FRESH LEMON JUICE
1$^{1}/_{2}$ CUPS FRAGRANT HONEY, WARMED

In a small bowl, dissolve the yeast and sugar in the lukewarm water and let stand until foamy, about 5 minutes. In a large bowl, stir together the flour, aniseeds, and salt. Add the yeast mixture, 2 tablespoons oil, and the orange zest, and mix with a wooden spoon or a stand mixer fitted with a dough hook until the dough comes together. Transfer the dough to a floured work surface and knead until smooth and no longer sticky, 5 to 8 minutes. Knead in the raisins, shape the dough into a ball, place in an oiled bowl, and cover the bowl with a kitchen towel. Let the dough rise in a warm place until doubled in bulk, about 1 hour.

Turn the dough out onto a lightly floured work surface, punch it down, and flatten it into a square or rectangle $^{1}/_{2}$ inch thick. Let rest for 15 to 20 minutes, then cut into 36 diamonds or triangles.

Pour vegetable oil to a depth of 3 inches into a deep saucepan and heat to 350 degrees F on a deep-frying thermometer. Drop a handful of the cutouts into the hot oil and fry until golden, about 5 minutes. Using a wire skimmer or slotted spoon, transfer to paper towels to drain. Arrange on a serving platter and keep warm. Fry the remaining cutouts.

When all of the fritters are fried, make the glaze by stirring the lemon juice into the warmed honey. Drizzle the honey over the fritters and serve warm.

: : : : : :

GLACE *au* MIEL

HONEY ICE CREAM

In *La table juive,* I found two Turkish ice cream recipes and was torn as to whether or not to include them. They are not old recipes, but the Turks love ice cream, so it is not surprising that Jews in Turkey would love it, too. This one is like a frozen honey mousse or a rum-raisin ice cream. While Sephardic Jews do not make a habit of using alcoholic beverages, they occasionally use them in festive desserts and for holiday dishes.

Makes about 1^1/2 *pints*

2 CUPS MILK

1 VANILLA BEAN

^{1}/2 CUP RAISINS, CHOPPED

^{1}/4 CUP DARK RUM, WARMED, OR HOT WATER

5 EGG YOLKS

^{1}/3 CUP FRAGRANT HONEY, WARMED

^{1}/2 CUP CRÈME FRAÎCHE

In a saucepan, combine the milk and vanilla bean and bring just to a boil over medium-high heat. Remove from the heat and let steep for 1 hour. Meanwhile, in a bowl, combine the raisins and rum or hot water and let stand until the raisins are plumped, about 30 minutes.

Remove the vanilla bean from the milk, and reheat the milk just until small bubbles appear along the edges of the pan. While the milk is reheating, in a bowl, beat the egg yolks until thick and pale. Whisk a little of the hot milk into the yolks to temper them, then gradually stir the yolk mixture into the remaining hot milk. Simmer over medium-low heat, stirring constantly, until the mixture thickens enough to coat the back of a spoon, about 5 minutes. Remove from the heat. Stir the honey into the custard and let cool.

When the mixture is cool, fold in the crème fraîche and the plumped raisins and any liquid. For an ice-cream consistency, transfer to an ice-cream maker and freeze according to the manufacturer's directions. Alternatively, spoon the cooled mixture into custard cups or small molds, cover well, and freeze.

If you have frozen the ice cream in custard cups, you might try unmolding them into individual bowls, although this ice cream does not freeze rock hard because of the honey and rum. Dip the base of each mold briefly in hot water to unmold. If you have prepared it in an ice-cream maker, scoop it into bowls.

: : : : : :

FNARO, BALKABAK TATLISI, DULSE DE IGO ★ HONEY AND EGG SPOON SWEET, PUMPKIN SPOON SWEET, FIG PRESERVE

FNARO

HONEY AND EGG SPOON SWEET

In *The House by the Sea*, the story of a Jewish family in Salonika, authors Elia Aelion and Rebecca Camhi Fromer refer to a holiday ritual: "It was customary to serve orange glacé, homemade preserves. . . . A silver tray of delights was passed around, and confections were served in crystal ware and eaten with silver teaspoons." This might have been one of those delights. *Fnaro* is a rich sweet served by both Sephardic and Romaniote Jews in Greece at weddings and circumcisions and is very much like the Portuguese egg sweets known as *ovos moles* or the Italian *scodelline*. It is often served in a small silver container accompanied by spoons and glasses of water, in the manner of Greek spoon sweets. Because its flavor is so intense, it is offered only for these special ceremonial occasions and not after dinner.

Makes 10 TO 15 *spoonfuls*

10 TO 12 EGG YOLKS, OR 6 WHOLE EGGS

1 CUP FRAGRANT HONEY

$1/2$ CUP SUGAR

PINCH OF SAFFRON THREADS (OPTIONAL)

$1/2$ CUP BLANCHED ALMONDS, TOASTED AND CHOPPED

In a bowl, whisk the egg yolks or whole eggs until blended. In a large, deep saucepan, combine the honey and sugar and place over medium heat. Stir until the sugar dissolves completely. Raise the heat to medium-high and bring to a gentle boil. Cook, stirring often, until thickened, about 8 minutes. Gradually add the beaten eggs, a spoonful at a time, stirring constantly. (You can instead gradually add the hot syrup to the eggs, and then return the mixture to the pan.) Add the saffron, if you like, and stir over very low heat until the mixture is smooth and thick, about 5 minutes. Remove from the heat and nest the pan in a bowl of ice to cool.

Stir well and spoon the chilled sweet onto a plate. Sprinkle with the chopped almonds and serve.

: : : : : :

BALKABAK TATLISI

PUMPKIN SPOON SWEET

Pumpkin is used in savory and sweet dishes in the Sephardic kitchen. In Sicily and Spain, the pumpkin for this confection was cooked first in water until tender, drained, and then simmered in sugar syrup until it became a jam, at which point it was used as a cake filling. In Sicily, it might be scented with jasmine flowers, a little cinnamon, orange-flower water, or rose water. The tradition of pumpkin sweets made its way to Turkey, where chopped walnuts or pine nuts were added to the already-rich conserve.

Makes about 16 *spoonfuls*

1 PUMPKIN, ABOUT 2 POUNDS, HALVED, SEEDED, PEELED, AND CUT INTO 1-INCH CUBES

3 CUPS SUGAR

$2/3$ CUP WATER, OR AS NEEDED

2 LEMON ZEST STRIPS, EACH 3 INCHES LONG

A FEW WHOLE CLOVES, OR 1 CINNAMON STICK (OPTIONAL)

$1/2$ CUP CHOPPED TOASTED WALNUTS OR PINE NUTS (OPTIONAL)

CLOTTED CREAM (OPTIONAL)

Layer the pumpkin pieces in a shallow saucepan, sprinkling the sugar between the layers. Add the

$^2/_3$ cup water, the lemon zest strips, and the cloves or cinnamon, if using. Place over low heat, cover, and cook until the pumpkin has absorbed almost all of the water and is tender, about 30 minutes. If all the water is absorbed, and the pumpkin is not yet tender, add a little more water and continue to cook until tender. Remove from the heat and let cool.

Spoon the cooled pumpkin into a bowl and sprinkle with the walnuts or pine nuts, if using. Serve as is or with clotted cream at a dairy meal.

: : : : : :

DULSE *de* IGO
FIG PRESERVE

This spoon sweet or preserve was placed at the table at *desayuno,* or it was served after dinner with silver spoons for scooping up a bit of the preserve and glasses of ice water for sipping. I make this preserve every summer, sometimes adding a bit of grated fresh ginger along with the spices. You must stay by the stove to stir during the last half-hour of cooking, so the figs do not scorch or stick.

Makes 3 *pints*

3 POUNDS RIPE MISSION FIGS

3$^1/_2$ CUPS SUGAR

GRATED ZEST AND JUICE OF 2 LEMONS
    (ABOUT $^1/_2$ CUP JUICE)

GRATED ZEST OF 1 ORANGE

JUICE OF 2 ORANGES (ABOUT $^2/_3$ CUP)

1 TEASPOON GROUND CINNAMON, OR $^1/_2$ TEASPOON
    EACH GROUND CINNAMON AND GROUND CLOVES

Remove the stems from the figs. If the figs are large, you may want to halve them or quarter them lengthwise. Put them in a preserving kettle or enameled cast-iron pot and cover them with the sugar. Let stand overnight.

The next day, add the lemon zest, orange zest, orange juice, and water to cover barely. Add the cinnamon or the cinnamon and cloves and stir well. Bring to a boil over medium heat, stirring occasionally to prevent scorching and sticking. Reduce the heat to low and simmer uncovered, stirring occasionally, for 20 minutes. Remove from the heat and let stand for 1 hour to plump up a bit.

Return the pot to medium heat and bring to a boil, stirring often. Cook until the mixture is thick and large bubbles appear on the surface, 20 to 30 minutes. To test for thickness, drop a tablespoon of the preserves onto a chilled plate. If it holds its shape and doesn't run, it is ready. Add the lemon juice to taste during the last 10 minutes of cooking.

Ladle into hot, sterilized jars to within $^1/_4$ inch of the tops. Wipe the rims clean with a damp, hot towel. Top with lids and seal tightly with screw bands. Process in a hot-water bath for 10 minutes.

Transfer the jars to a metal rack and let cool to room temperature. Press the center of each lid to check the seal; they should remain slightly concave. Store in a cool, dry place for up to 1 year. If the seal is not good, store in the refrigerator for up to 2 months.

Note: Nicholas Stavroulakis makes this preserve with green figs, but he leaves them whole. He makes a syrup, lets the figs plump in it overnight, and then the next day poaches them in the syrup until tender. He then removes the figs and packs them into jars, reduces the syrup, and pours it over the figs.

: : : : : :

HAROSET

SWEET FRUIT CONDIMENT FOR PASSOVER

Haroset, the traditional fruit condiment on the Passover Seder table, represents the mortar that the Jews made while they were slaves in Egypt. Variations are endless. Some are cooked, such as this one, and some are just chopped and mixed together.

Makes about 4 cups

1 3/4 CUPS PITTED DATES, CHOPPED

2 APPLES (ABOUT 1/2 POUND TOTAL), CORED, PEELED, AND GRATED

1/2 CUP FINELY CHOPPED WALNUTS

1 ORANGE, BOILED IN WATER TO COVER FOR 1 HOUR, DRAINED, AND GROUND IN A BLENDER

1/2 CUP SUGAR

1 TEASPOON GROUND CINNAMON

PINCH OF GROUND CLOVES

1/2 CUP BOILING WATER

2 TABLESPOONS FRESH LEMON JUICE

In a saucepan, combine the dates, apples, nuts, ground orange, sugar, cinnamon, and cloves. Add the boiling water and bring to a boil again over high heat. Reduce the heat to low and simmer uncovered, stirring occasionally, until the mixture forms a smooth paste, 10 to 15 minutes. Stir in the lemon juice and simmer for 2 minutes longer.

Remove from the heat and let cool. Serve at room temperature.

: : : : : :

MANZAPADES

LEMON MARZIPAN

Marzipan is a favorite Passover sweet, and this recipe is from the Jewish community of Volos, in Greece. The Greeks seem to add lemon juice to nearly everything, and they also don't discard the peels, instead saving them for confections, as this recipe illustrates. The origins of marzipan have long been debated, but the most widely accepted theory is that it was brought to Spain by the Arabs. Yet, marzipan also has been associated with Saint Mark's bread, the *panis martis,* or March bread, of Roman antiquity that was a standard offering during the rites of spring and was later adopted by the Catholic church. Marzipan is still a popular confection in Spain and Portugal (a tradition kept alive today by the convents) and certainly would have been carried to Greece and Turkey by Jews from Sicily, an island where the marzipan tradition was entrenched.

Makes about 20 *pieces*

PEELS OF 10 TO 12 LEMONS
1 CUP BLANCHED ALMONDS, FINELY GROUND
2 CUPS GRANULATED SUGAR
1 CUP CONFECTIONERS' SUGAR

Put the lemon peels in a bowl with water to cover. Let soak for 2 days, changing the water every 3 to 4 hours during the day and evening. On the third day, rinse the peels and put them in a large saucepan with water to cover. Place over low heat, bring to a simmer, and cook until the peels are very soft, 45 to 60 minutes. Remove from the heat and mash to a pulp or pulse in a food processor. You should have about 1 cup pulp.

For every cup of lemon pulp, you need 1 cup ground almonds and 2 cups granulated sugar; if you have more or less, adjust these amounts. Put the lemon pulp in a large saucepan with the almonds and granulated sugar, mix well, and place over low heat. Cook, stirring often with a wooden spoon, until the mixture thickens and pulls away from the sides of the pan, 20 to 30 minutes. Remove from the heat and pour the mixture onto a marble slab or chilled platter. Let cool.

When the mixture is cool, spread the confectioners' sugar on a plate. Knead the mixture a bit, then pinch off pieces the size of hazelnuts, roll them into balls, and then roll each ball in the confectioners' sugar. Put the balls on a large platter and dust them with confectioners' sugar one more time. Let the marzipan rest in a cool place for 24 hours before serving.

: : : : : :

BIBLIOGRAPHY

Aelion, Elia, and Rebecca Camhi Fromer. *The House by the Sea: A Portrait of the Holocaust in Greece*. San Francisco: Mercury House, 1999.

Algar, Ayla. *Classical Turkish Cooking*. New York: Harper Collins, 1991.

Altabe, David Fintz. *Spanish and Portuguese Jews*. Brooklyn, New York: Sepher Hermon Press, Inc., 1993.

Anderson, Jean. *The Food of Portugal*. New York: William Morrow and Company, 1986.

Andrews, Colman. *Catalan Cuisine*. New York: Atheneum, 1988.

Angel, Gilda. *Sephardic Holiday Cooking*. Mt. Vernon, New York: Decalogue Books, 1986.

Aris, Pepita. *A Flavor of Andalusia*. New Jersey: Chartwell Books, 1996.

Badi, Méri. *250 recettes de cuisines juive espagnol*. Paris: Jacques Grancher, 1984.

Chiche-Yana, Martine. *La table juive*. Tome 1, Recettes & traditions de fêtes. Aix-en-Provence: Edisud, 1992.

———. *La table juive*. Tome 2, *Recettes & traditions du cycle de vie*. Aix-en-Provence: Edisud, 1994.

Congregation Or Ve Shalom Sisterhood. *The Sephardic Cooks*. Atlanta, 1981.

Cooper, John. *Eat and Be Satisfied: A Social History of Jewish Food*. Northvale, New Jersey: Jason Aronson, Inc., 1993.

David, Suzy. *The Sephardic Kosher Kitchen*. Middle Village, New York: Jonathan David Publishers, 1984.

de Latemendia, Ana, and Lourdes Plana. *The Different Flavours of Spain*. Madrid: Ediciones el Viso, Ministerio de Agricultura Pesca y Alimentacion, 1991.

der Haroutunian, Arto. *Middle Eastern Cookery*. London: Century Publishing, 1982.

———. *Sweets and Desserts from the Middle East*. London: Century Publishing, 1984.

Eden, Esin, and Nicholas Stavroulakis. *Salonika, A Family Cookbook*. Athens: Talos Press, 1997.

Gerber, Jane. *The Jews of Spain*. New York: The Free Press, Simon & Schuster, 1992.

Gitlitz, David, and Linda Kay Davidson. *A Drizzle of Honey: The Lives and Recipes of Spain's Secret Jews*. New York: St. Martin's Press, 1999.

Greene, Gloria Kaufer. *The Jewish Holiday Cookbook*. New York: Time Books, 1950.

Halici, Nevin. *Nevin Halici's Turkish Cookbook*. London: Dorling Kindersley, 1989.

Kochilas, Diane, *Food and Wine of Greece,* New York: St. Martin's Press, 1990.

———. *The Greek Vegetarian*. New York: St. Martin's Press, 1996.

Koronyo, Viki, and Sima Ovadyo. *Sefarad Yemekleri.* Istanbul: Subat
(Society of Assistance to Old People), 1990.

Machlin, Edda Servi. *The Classic Cuisine of the Italian Jews.* New York: Dodd Mead, 1981.

Manjón, Maite. *The Gastronomy of Spain and Portugal.* New York: Prentice Hall, 1990.

Marks, Copeland. *Sephardic Cooking.* New York: Donald I. Fine, 1992.

Marks, Gil. *The World of Jewish Cooking.* New York: Simon & Schuster, 1996.

Mendel, Janet. *Traditional Spanish Cooking.* Reading, UK: Garnet Publishing, 1996.

Ministry of Culture. *Samples from Turkish Cuisine.* Ankara: Turkish Historical Society, 1993.

Nathan, Joan. *Jewish Cooking in America.* New York: Alfred A. Knopf, 1994.

————. *The Jewish Holiday Kitchen.* New York: Schocken Books, 1988.

Passmore, Jackie. *The Complete Spanish Cookbook.* Boston and Rutland, Vermont:
Charles E. Tuttle Company, Inc. 1993.

Perera, Victor. *The Cross and the Pear Tree.* Berkeley and Los Angeles: University of
California Press, 1995.

Rios, Alicia, and Lourdes March. *The Heritage of Spanish Cooking.* New York:
Random House, 1992.

Roden, Claudia. *The Book of Jewish Food.* New York: Alfred A. Knopf, 1996.

Roth, Cecil. *Doña Gracia of the House of Nasi.* Philadelphia: The Jewish Publication
Society of America, 1977.

————. *The Spanish Inquisition.* New York: W.W. Norton Company, 1964.

Scheindlin, Raymond. *A Short History of the Jewish People.* New York: Macmillan, 1998.

Sephardic Temple Bikur Holem Ladies Auxiliary. *Sephardic Cooking.* Seattle, 1967, 1993.

Shaw, Stanford. *The Jews of the Ottoman Empire and the Turkish Republic.* New York:
New York University Press, 1991.

Stavroulakis, Nicholas. *The Cookbook of the Jews of Greece.* Port Jefferson, NY: Cadmus Press, 1986.

————. *The Jews of Greece.* Athens: Talos Press, 1990.

Sternberg, Rabbi Robert. *The Sephardic Kitchen.* New York: Harper Collins, 1996.

Vincent, Mary, and R. A. Stradling. *Cultural Atlas of Spain and Portugal.* Oxford:
Andromeda Books, 1994.

Vitali-Norsa, Giuliana Ascoli. *La cucina nella tradizione ebraica.* Milan: ADEI-Wizo, 1987.

Wolfert, Paula. *The Cooking of the Eastern Mediterranean.* New York: Harper Collins, 1994.

INDEX

TABLE OF EQUIVALENTS

LIQUID AND DRY MEASURES

U.S.	METRIC
1/4 teaspoon	1.25 milliliters
1/2 teaspoon	2.5 milliliters
1 teaspoon	5 milliliters
1 tablespoon (3 teaspoons)	15 milliliters
1 fluid ounce (2 tablespoons)	30 milliliters
1/4 cup	60 milliliters
1/3 cup	80 milliliters
1 cup	120 milliliters
1 pint (2 cups)	480 milliliters
1 quart (4 cups, 32 ounces)	960 milliliters
1 gallon (4 quarts)	3.84 liters
1 ounce (by weight)	28 grams
1 pound	454 grams
2.2 pounds	1 kilogram

OVEN TEMPERATURES

FAHRENHEIT	CELSIUS	GAS
250	120	1/2
275	140	1
300	150	2
325	160	3
350	180	4
375	190	5
400	200	6
425	220	7
450	230	8
475	240	9
500	260	10

LENGTH MEASURES

U.S.	METRIC
1/8 inch	3 millimeters
1/4 inch	6 millimeters
1/2 inch	12 millimeters
1 inch	2.5 centimeters

The exact equivalents in the above tables have been rounded for convenience.

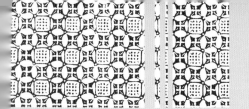

THANK YOU TO:

Bill LeBlond for being the most encouraging, gracious, and charming editor a writer could ever want.

Sharon Silva, copyeditor extraordinaire, for her demonic eye for detail, her common sense, her amazing knowledge of history, and her perseverance even while on jury duty.

Sara Schneider for her ability to meld the ancient and contemporary worlds through her sensitive use of design. Beatriz Da Costa for her lovely and evocative photographs. Alison Attenborough for making the food look delicious and appealing.

John and Michael Schwartz and the Beniroya family for sending me the cookbook from their Temple Bikur Holim in Seattle. Gabriella Isaacson for giving me her well worn copy of *The Sephardic Cooks,* recipes from the sisterhood of Or Ve Shalom congregation in Atlanta.

The San Francisco Jewish Community Federation for support and the greatly appreciated Koret Fellowship.

Oldways Preservation and Exchange Trust for sending me to Greece and Turkey for another look and another taste.

Nach Waxman of Kitchen Arts and Letters for his support and enthusiasm and for helping me track down books for my research.

Angel Stoyanof for his feedback on the recipes and personal cooking tips from his Sephardic family that has lived in Istanbul for over 200 years.

And special thank you to my family for eating everything I put before them and giving me honest (what else) critiques and feedback, even, when in a fit of over-exuberance I made them try seven desserts at one sitting! To my granddaughter Elena for her "oh-my-God" response to the custard tart. It makes me smile whenever I think of it. And to my grandson Adam, who carried bits of cake around for days, rationing the permitted sweetness so it would last longer. That is why I cook!